CW00839403

Translators on Translating

TITLES IN THE JJ DOUGLAS LIBRARY:

The story behind the book: Preserving authors'
and publishers' archives
Laura Millar

Translators on translating: Inside the invisible art
Andrew Wilson

Translators on Translating

Inside the invisible art

ANDREW WILSON

CCSP Press • *The JJ Douglas Library*
Vancouver

CANADIAN CENTRE FOR STUDIES IN PUBLISHING PRESS
515 West Hastings Street
Vancouver, British Columbia
Canada V6B 5K3
Email: ccsp-info@sfu.ca
www.ccsp.sfu.ca

LIBRARY AND ARCHIVES CANADA CATALOGUING IN PUBLICATION

Wilson, Andrew, 1956 Apr. 29–
        Translators on translating : inside the invisible art / Andrew Wilson.

(JJ Douglas Library)
Includes bibliographical references and index.
ISBN 978-0-9738727-3-6

1. Translating and interpreting. 2. Translators.
I. Title. II. Series: JJ Douglas Library

P306.W45 2009   418'.02   C2009-900935-8

Printed in Canada

Project Editor: Jim Douglas
Editor: Mary Schendlinger
Proofreader: Sarah Maitland
Text design: Mauve Pagé
Cover design: Roberto Dosil

TABLE OF CONTENTS

To Claire, who needs no translation.

ACKNOWLEDGEMENTS

I would like, first of all, to thank the many contributors for permitting their texts to be included in this book (brief biographies and full references are provided on pp. 237–53). There are some wonderful writers among them. Inevitably, many texts are much shorter than I would have liked, so if an excerpt from a larger work takes a reader's fancy I urge her or him to consult the longer originals, particularly the memoirs.

Un grand merci to Dr. Jean Delisle not only for his foreword but also for some wise counsel late in the editing process. I am immensely grateful to Scott L. Montgomery, Yael Sela-Shapiro, Tibor Várady, and Kevin Cook for the texts they wrote especially for this book. Additional thanks to Kevin, who also cast his multilingual eye over texts from several less-common languages, and made invaluable suggestions about the overall manuscript. Adriana Hunter provided expert advice with great tact, while Stuart Adams, Claire Bolderson, Anat Efron, Scott Harker, and Michael Kent read and gave useful comments on various drafts. On the publishing side, Roberto Dosil, Mauve Pagé, Mary Schendlinger, and Murray Tong, from CCSP Press at the Canadian Centre for Studies in Publishing, made the process – often a fraught one, in my experience – a pleasure. Finally, I would like to thank Jim Douglas, who conceived and guided the project, and Heather Douglas for much kindness and many years of friendship.

Thanks to all of you. Any errors are mine. (A heads-up to readers, though: don't be too quick to jump on spelling mistakes. Except for obvious typos, I have reproduced original spellings in most of the selections, so you will find a mix of American, British, Canadian, and other Englishes in the book, as well as different systems of transliteration. For example, *Koran* is also rendered as *Alcoran, Quran,* and *Qur'ān* in different texts.)

A s one of the first readers of a new book, the writer of a foreword is in a privileged position. One is sometimes pleasurably
surprised, and so it was with this book. During my first reading of *Translators on
Translating*, I found much that was new to me. Yet Andrew Wilson is by no means
the first to publish a compendium of writings in this field. In the past forty years,
traductologues (the English term is "translation studies scholars") have published a
large number of collected texts about translation: among others, Thomas R. Steiner
(1975), André Lefevere (1977 and 1992), Paul A. Horguelin (1981), Julio-César Santoyo
(1987), Lieven D'hulst (1990), Rainer Schulte and John Biguenet (1992), M.A. Vega
Cernuda (1994), Harald Kittel (1995), García D. López (1996), Douglas Robinson (1997),
Lawrence Venuti (1999), and Martha P.Y. Cheung (2006). So why publish a new selection, and how is this one different from those that came before?

First of all, it is the work of a translator, not a *traductologue*, and one who wishes
to give a voice to translators themselves rather than a theorist who presumes to
speak for them. Wilson also sets out to show that a practitioner, in reflecting on his
or her work and profession, has just as much of value to say as an academic who
extracts theory from an examination of originals and their translations. This volume
brings translators out from the shadows that most work in, whether their field of
translation is literary, technical, official, or religious. In the author's words, "One of
the most enjoyable aspects of reading translators on translating is to watch from the
sidelines as they pit creativity, experience, and tools of their trade against difficult
source and target texts (and sometimes difficult authors and publishers)."

This book offers a professional translator's view of how his past and present-day
colleagues have described their trade. His trawl through various sources has net-
ted a plenitude of challenges that translators face in attempting to render – with
elegance and precision – words said, and often well said, in a foreign language and
culture. He touches on all the classic subjects: approaches to translation, cognitive
processes, professional training, localization, translating for the theatre, literary and

technical translation, literal versus free translation, the author/translator relationship, the business of publishing, (in)visibility of the translator, film dubbing, the pleasure of translating, "improving" source texts, types of translators, ethics, contracts, and so on. There is humour too in this work, which is spiced with delicious anecdotes and punctuated with quotations. Some extracts touch us in purely human terms, notably the confidences offered by the American novelist Paul Auster and by Cathy Hirano, a Canadian translator who lives in Japan. The extracts, collected from articles, monographs, manuals, blogs, and websites, are put in context by brief introductions, giving one the impression of a dialogue between reader and translators as they talk about the trade. The sum of the book's various parts almost provides sufficient source material for a small treatise on approaches to translation.

Many of the texts take us into the translator's "workshop." We accompany translators in their tentative first passes at a text, and marvel at the inspired final draft. We look over their shoulders as they assess a difficult passage, weigh possible solutions, compare alternatives, and verbalize their reasoning, rather like the Think-Aloud Protocol sessions so beloved of psychologists (and some *traductologues*). The examples intelligently and subtly dissected for us by Robert Paquin, William Weaver, Emma Wagner, and the author himself prove that translation, although a complex art, is not an art of the impossible. Alphonse de Lamartine once said, "Of all the books one may take on, the hardest, in my opinion, is a translation." The philosopher Emil Cioran went even further: "I place a good translator above a good author." Well, that is one point of view. But what is undeniable is that a translator is a "second author," as Leonardo Bruni recognized back in the fifteenth century in his *De interpretatione recta*. "Second author" does not, however, mean "secondary author."

Even if it is true, as Eugene Eoyang says of imperfect translations, that like certain wines, language doesn't necessarily "travel well," it is also true that, yes, the miracle *is* possible. There are, doubtless, errors in translations of the Koran or the Bible, but there are also – as in any good translation – passages that truly do inspire. How else can one explain the enduring success of the King James Version? And yes, a translation can eclipse the source text. Was it not Goethe who preferred Gérard de Nerval's translation of *Faust* to his original? "I no longer care to read *Faust* in German," he said, "but in this French translation, it reads anew with freshness and vitality." A splendid compliment to a translator from an author of genius. And why should we not recognize that there are translators of genius? The occasional errors and imprecisions that mar even the best translations can be excused when one understands the fine scales and balances that are the tools of the translator's trade. The art of choosing the right word, the right tone, the right rhythm is far harder than it seems at first glance. Paradoxically – and notoriously – it is when a translation is successful that critics pay it least attention. How can one not see this as an injustice to master translators?

Paging through this volume, one is struck yet again by the extent to which the field of translation is riven by debate and contradiction. As Theodore Savory observed several decades ago, throughout history translators have "freely contradicted each other on nearly all aspects of their art." The three thousand quotes in my recently completed dictionary, *La traduction en citations* (2007), certainly testify to that. As I worked on the book, nothing struck me more clearly than the fact that translators have differing opinions on everything. Where one sees black, another sees white; opposing points of view abound. *Translators on Translating* provides yet more proof of this. Indeed, the book has barely been opened before we witness an argument, pitting the redoubtable professor Lawrence Venuti against the doyenne of British translators, Anthea Bell. The subject of their debate… Well, you'll just have to read the author's introduction and make up your mind about who is right.

The great merit of Andrew Wilson's compilation is to turn the floor over to the translators. I fully agree when he writes, "While too much of the scholarly writing about translation is turgid academic-speak, it is safe to say that the field is also well served by lively minds who express themselves very well indeed." *Translators on Translating*, engagingly written and jargon-free, is an eloquent confirmation of this point of view. I am confident that, like me, readers will find it contains unexpected delights. In publishing this book, the author performs a valuable service to translators and to our profession.

JEAN DELISLE, Gatineau, Québec, 2008

Quotations by Alphonse de Lamartine, Emil Cioran, and Johann Wolfgang Goethe are translated by Jean Delisle.

Is my invisibility showing?
A personal introduction

During the early 1980s, when I worked in Geneva, there was a legendary character – Bulgarian, I think – who worked at the World Intellectual Property Organization. This Bulgarian was known as the Phantom Photocopier. Late in the evening, he would go into certain offices (the logic of his choices was never clear), copy whatever he found on people's desks, and go back to his embassy with a large stack of paper. Copyright protocols. Position papers on patent registration. Possibly even a few memos on the rising cost of photocopying.

At the time, I often found myself imagining the translators back at the embassy, or perhaps somewhere else – Sofia? Dzerzhinsky Square in Moscow? – spending their days wading through the stuff, sorting and making précis and translating complete passages that someone else might deem useful to the prosecution of the Cold War. Poor sods. Nothing of James Bond: no derring-do, no choice of target, no nifty gadgets. Invisible professionals translating unreadable texts for anonymous readers...

If this book aims to accomplish anything, it is to make translators more visible to readers, to translation clients, and to translators themselves. It is a dipping book, with a mixture of short and long texts, serious analysis, epigrammatic zingers, and rueful reflections. The majority of the selections are about translations into or out of English, but I have tried to cover a variety of languages, subject areas, and literary genres. Although a few texts look at translation from the outside, most are by translators themselves – past and present, literary and technical, famous (usually for something other than translation) and obscure. A few of the excerpts have already appeared in anthologies aimed at the translation-studies market or other specialist fields; I hope that including them here will expose the individual texts to a different set of readers, as well as directing people to these anthologies, some of which are splendid treasure troves. Most of the extracts are just that: extracts from longer texts. Space constraints and the desire to cast my net as widely as possible forced a lot of painful editorial decisions about what to include and what to cut. If readers find their appetites whetted by the sample, I hope they will chase down the original work (the references at the end of the book should help them do so).

Until I started this project, I wasn't aware of invisibility as an issue in translation. Translation is something I do, rather than something I spend much time analyzing; like most translators I never studied translation theory. However, the moment I started reading Lawrence Venuti's influential book *The Translator's Invisibility: A History of Translation* (Venuti 1995), the term resonated strongly.

Venuti, who is one of the most prominent figures in translation studies (see his texts in chapters 1 and 9), uses the idea of invisibility in two ways. First, invisibility represents a translation approach in which translators deliberately cover their tracks. Venuti calls for translators to be more visible, and he attacks the Anglo-American assumption that a good translation is a "fluent" one "when the absence of any linguistic or stylistic peculiarities makes it seem transparent, gives the appearance that it reflects the foreign writer's personality or intention or the essential meaning of the foreign text – the appearance, in other words, that the translation is not in fact a translation, but the 'original'... "

In direct opposition to this intentional disappearing act, Venuti argues for a "foreignizing" approach that would make it clear that a second human being had a role in the relationship between writer and reader of a translated text.

Second, Venuti argues that the translator is made invisible by "the ambiguous and unfavourable legal status of translation, both in copyright law and in actual contractual arrangements." The argument, buttressed by a wealth of information from the publishing world, is convincing, and certainly jibes with the experience of most translators I know. But Venuti goes further, tying the translator's invisibility to the global domination of Anglo-American culture. In a breathtaking logical leap, he refers to "the violence that resides in the very purpose and activity of translation" and argues that "it potentially figures in ethnic discrimination, geopolitical confrontations, colonialism, terrorism, war" (Venuti 1995).

Yikes. Even in metaphorical terms (and I must admit to simplifying a complex, well-argued book), the connection of translators with violence goes against my entire experience of translators, whether working with them, listening to them at lectures and book launches, or reading their memoirs. We tend to be a reflective, gentle lot, more "jaw-jaw" than "war-war," in Churchill's terms. And yet, there is no discounting the force of Venuti's ideas, and the fact that he has been hugely influential, in academia at least. For example, a 2004 conference on translation at Oxford framed its theme as follows: "The idea that the act of translation should be visible in the finished work has come to dominate academic discussions of translated literature. This imperative arises from largely ethical considerations: the English language should not subsume the original, the reader should be made to confront the otherness of the foreign culture."

Interesting, then, that the keynote speaker at the conference, Anthea Bell, wasn't buying it. The doyenne of Britain's literary translators, with an astonishing portfolio of translations behind her (see chapter 10), she told the audience that she frankly disagreed with the conference's theme. Calling herself "an unrepentant, unreconstructed adherent of the school of invisible translation," Bell said (Bell 2004):

> The point with which I would really take issue is the idea that the reader should be made to confront the otherness of the foreign culture. The fact is, there are commercial considerations to be taken into account; many of my best friends are publishers, and I have every sympathy with a publisher's desire not to lose too much money on a book. I imagine, too, that translated authors would like their books to sell, and won't mind at all if they read naturally in English. It does not appear to me conducive to this aim to make readers confront the otherness of the foreign culture. I would hope, rather, to seduce them into enjoying and appreciating a book in translation as much as if they could read it in the original, without placing too many obstacles in the way of that enjoyment...
>
> Translation is not, by its very nature, a high-profile craft. If you have spun your illusion successfully, then you are quite rightly invisible. If reviewers don't comment on a translation, it has worked.

This is where translation theorists and translation practitioners really part company. Bell, the practitioner, wants people to *read* translations; Venuti, the academic, wants people to *see through* translations. (I hasten to add that Venuti is also a practising translator; recent works include "Melissa P.'s" erotic novel *100 Strokes of the Brush Before Bed* and Massimo Carlotto's noir thriller *The Goodbye Kiss*.)

I SUSPECT MOST TRANSLATORS HAVE MOMENTS WHEN THEY FEEL MORE INVISIBLE than they would like to be. A personal example: in November 2005, I wrote myself the following note:

Another London newspaper, another glowing review of my book,
Loving Sabotage.

That is, Amélie's book *Le Sabotage amoureux*.

That is, the British reprint of the American edition of my 1998 translation of Amélie Nothomb's bestselling 1993 novel.

And still, no call, no email from the British publisher, no "by the way, we bought the rights from the Americans, thought you'd like to know."

Typical. Who cares about the translator.

The note encapsulates several issues that relate to invisibility, in its meaning of marginalization and lack of power. First, however much one feels ownership of a translation – the product of much mental sweat and creativity – the final product is always someone else's. My *translation*, but Amélie's *book*. It doesn't bother me, since that is the deal, the job one hires on to do, but there are few other types of work that require the clarification. *I wrote every word, but it isn't mine.*

Second, the 2005 *Loving Sabotage* – part of Faber & Faber's admirable project of publishing Amélie Nothomb in English – is technically a reprint, not a new edition. Had it been a new edition, I might – might! – have been permitted to correct two or three errors that came to light after publication, or reinstate some of the British wordings that the American publisher had removed from my original. But I had no control over that. (Chapter 8 has more about translating *Sabotage*.)

Third, I received no money at all for the new book. Such was the contract I signed with the original publishers in the U.S. and Canada, and such is standard practice for all but a few star translators with tough agents. I didn't think about it at the time, and it doesn't bother me. Much. (When I made myself known to Faber & Faber, they very kindly sent me some copies of the reprint.)

A few years later, I still puzzle over some other questions. Why didn't *Loving Sabotage* become a bestseller in its American or British edition, as it did in French – Amélie is Belgian – and several other languages? The obvious and rather uncomfortable question, of course, is about the quality of the translation: was it up to scratch? It got excellent reviews, though this doesn't really tell you anything about the quality of the translation per se (few reviewers are in a position to judge that), merely that it read in a fluent, attractive way.

To ask a related question: how have translations of other books by Amélie sold in English, all by reputable translators? Referring to her track record of producing a novel each year, the *Financial Times* wrote, "How irritating she would be, if only she didn't write so well ... She could easily become an annual habit." Except she hasn't become a habit in the U.K., annual or otherwise. The editor at Faber & Faber told me, "She's been absolutely loved and supported by reviews and the trade themselves, but sales out of the shop have been disappointing..." More positively, he said he expected two of her books, *Life of Hunger* and *Fear and Trembling* (translated by Shaun Whiteside and Adriana Hunter respectively), to continue to sell well as backlist titles.

More generally, how do translations of French-language novels fare in English? Not particularly well, for the most part. Perhaps French authors just do not "click" with English readers in the way that Chinese and Spanish ones seem to at the moment – at least, that is my impression from the literary pages and bookstore shelves here in London. But unlike in the rest of the world, translations occupy only a tiny niche in English-language publishing. It is estimated that only 2 percent of books sold in the U.K. and the United States are translations, compared to 13 percent in Germany, 27 percent in France, 28 percent in Spain, and 40 percent in Turkey (Lea 2007).

Is Lawrence Venuti right about cultural imperialism, and are translators invisibly aiding and abetting a cabal of English-language publishers bent on domination of global culture? If it's true, I don't know what we can or should do about it. Certainly it is sad that English speakers are so reluctant to learn other languages (although that, of course, is what provides translators with work) and so little interested in what is being written beyond our linguistic borders (which ensures that our work is undervalued). It leaves me with a feeling expressed nicely by P.G. Wodehouse in *The Code of Woosters:* "He spoke with a certain what-is-it in his voice, and I could see that, if not actually disgruntled, he was far from being gruntled." Most translators probably know the feeling (though God help them if they had to translate Wodehouse's wordplay).

TRANSLATORS ARE MOST VISIBLE WHEN A TRANSLATION TEXT DOESN'T work – see the verse quoted by John D. Graham in chapter 6: "When they 'hit' no-one remembers / When they 'miss' no-one forgets." Interestingly, the words that translators use when something goes wrong are aural: an out-and-out error is a "howler," while an awkward turn of phrase "clangs" or "clunks."

The toughest translation job I ever had was a graphic book by the Spanish writer and actor Zoe Berriatúa. Aside from a brief introduction by the author, the source text consisted entirely of captions for sixty-eight paintings depicting, as the book's title put it, *Monstruos del Subconsciente Colectivo* – Monsters from the Collective Subconscious (Berriatúa 2006). The paintings are beautiful, unsettling, witty and psychologically insightful: a psychoanalyst friend of mine actually finds the monsters useful in her practice. This is how Zoe explains them in his introduction: "As I see it, the real monsters in life have nothing to do with the bogeyman, or our fascination with gratuitous terror. Monsters are those sick behaviours we'd rather not admit, that we banish to our mental labyrinths where they lurk like stowaways, never protesting their loveless existence for fear of further beatings... In a twisted sort of way, monsters ask for our help."

Although the deadline was ridiculously short, I accepted the job because I had already translated another book of Zoe's, *El Perro Existencialista* (The Existentialist Dog), and felt I understood him as an author. But *Monstruos* was very different from the brief, whimsical stories of *El Perro Existencialista*: the captions were often cryptic, the wordplay subtle, the cultural references obscure; and some had clever rhyming schemes. Some came relatively easily, but others were serious challenges.

Here is the first of two examples (you'll have to imagine the vibrant colours):

This one's caption read

> Monstruo que vive pendiente de lo que piensen
> de él, no sea que lo hagan sin que él se dé cuenta,
> y sabiendo ellos que él no lo sepa, puedan pensar
> cualquier cosa.

It is convoluted, but that's part of this monster's tortuous pathology, as illustrated by the graphic. So it was acceptable to produce a convoluted translation:

> The monster who obsesses about what other people think of him,
> and about their doing so without his knowing about it, and, since
> they know he doesn't know, about what awful things they might
> be thinking.

But the second example caused me a lot of grief because of the idiomatic content of the caption. The original is

> Monstruo que se cambia de acera porque la suya no le hace caso.

Literally, that means

> The monster who changes sidewalks because the one he is on pays
> no attention to him.

Eh? I understood from the graphic that the subject was sexuality, but the sidewalk business was confusing. My first attempt was:

> The monster who walks on the wild side because he can't find love
> on the hetero side of the street.

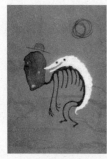

"Walking on the wild side," of course, refers to the Lou Reed gender-bending song from the 1970s, but the original wasn't a song reference: it was euphemism for switching sexual preferences, and I really needed to find an equivalent. Unfortunately, that forced a collision with my own multi-idiomatic background, which provided me with a British metaphor for the idea of switching sexualities ("batting for the other team" comes from the game of cricket) and an American metaphor for not getting sexual satisfaction ("getting to first base" comes from baseball). I knew that by mixing the two idioms, I risked creating a sentence that neither a Brit nor an American would instantly understand. In the end, I both ran out of time and lost my nerve: I put the first expression in quotation marks, and constructed a singularly graceless sentence in order to ensure that the reader "got" what Zoe meant:

> The monster who "bats for the other team" because, with his own,
> he can't even get to first base.

Clunk! The substance is accurate, the style a failure – and adding quotation marks a mortal translatorial sin. What got published is a draft, not a finished product. I'm confident that with a few more iterations I would have found something that got closer to both the sense and Zoe's eloquent brevity, but we were under a tight (and, as it so often turns out, fictional) deadline, so that is what got printed. For the most part I am very happy with the book, but that particular monster howls every time I look at it, and I wish both it and I could just disappear.

TRANSLATION IS LARGELY A SOLITARY ACTIVITY AS WELL AS AN INVISIBLE ONE, and I get the sense many translators have little idea how other people practise their craft. Certainly one of the pleasures of compiling this volume was seeing how different translators approach the job, how they feel about texts and authors, and how they have dealt with various problems – technical, professional, political, and even philosophical – that the work has thrown at them. Fortunately, translators are not at all like magicians, coyly guarding their trade secrets from their audience: they generally enjoy talking or writing about what they do, and, as I hope this book shows, they often do the latter with grace and eloquence.

The other great pleasure was looking back at the history of the profession, and finding it full of heroes, martyrs, and passionate debate. The past couple of centuries have clearly changed translation greatly; it is no longer the preserve of a small group of clerics, scholars, and wealthy amateurs. More recently, the Internet and computerization have expanded the market for translation hugely, introduced a vast array of new tools, and imposed time pressures that could not be imagined even fifty years ago. Yet I like to think that St. Jerome would easily understand the job I was doing if he suddenly appeared in my home office today. In fact, if he is like most translators I've met, he'd generously offer a few suggestions. (I'm less sure whose side he would take in the visibility debate between Lawrence Venuti and Anthea Bell!)

Art or profession? Open window, as St. James Bible translator Miles Smith saw it, or reverse side of the tapestry, as Don Quixote described it rather less positively (see chapter 1)? Conduit for the Word of God, or for the products of Mammon? As I hope this book amply shows, translation is all of these things and more. I hope it will encourage new translators in their chosen profession, give a pat on the back to experienced ones, and help readers "see" more clearly the people who move words and ideas across barriers of language and culture.

CHAPTER ONE

Open windows and reversed tapestries: The work

A great age of literature is perhaps always a great age of translations, or follows it.
— EZRA POUND in his 1917 essay "Notes on Elizabethan Classicists"
   (Pound 1954)

T he briefest and most famous aphorism about translation is the Italian wordplay *Traduttore, traditore* – literally "translator, traitor," or more accurately (but less pleasing to the ear) "translation is betrayal." Though sometimes taken as an insult to translators, to my mind it is a useful warning to readers. Many readers feel they establish a kind of relationship with an author when they read a book; in the case of a translated work, it can be salutary to remember that the cozy company of two is actually a crowd (however harmonious) of three. Etymologically, *traditore* is a remarkably apt metaphor. It is rooted in the Latin *tradere*, "handing over" – one can visualize the text being passed from author to translator to reader, even if one misses what happens during the passage.

My sense is that the phrase is so overquoted that it has become an annoyance to many in the profession. I suspect that the majority agree with the opinion cited by the literary translator Edmund Keeley, that "translation, far from being a betrayal, is in fact a salvation, bringing to the translated text the kind of long life it could not possibly have in the original alone, especially when the original is in an obscure language" (Keeley 1989).

LET THERE BE LIGHT

Over the years, many notable translators have employed metaphor to explain or describe the work they do, or the profession they belong to. They range from passages of great beauty to deliciously rude diatribes. Many descriptions of translation employ the metaphor of shedding light on darkness. A fine example comes from the theologian and scholar Miles Smith (1554–1624), a lead translator of the King James Version of the Bible. In his preface to the King James Version, Smith followed the statement "Happy is the man that delighteth in the Scripture" with the question "But how shall men meditate in that which they cannot understand?" (Presumably women couldn't be expected to meditate, much less understand…) His answer provides one of the most inspiring descriptions of translation ever written (Smith 1611):

> Translation it is that openeth the window, to let in the light; that breaketh the shell, that we may eat the kernel; that putteth aside the curtain, that we may look into the most holy place; that removeth the cover of the well, that we may come by the water, even as Jacob rolled away the stone from the mouth of the well, by which means the flocks of Laban were watered. Indeed, without translation into the vulgar tongue the unlearned are but like children at Jacob's well (which was deep) without a bucket or some thing to draw with: or as that person mentioned by Isaiah, to whom when a sealed book was delivered with this motion, Read this, I pray thee, he was fain to make this answer, I cannot, for it is sealed.

Stirring words, as befits the subject matter, yet professional translators today will not be surprised that the Authorized translation project got extremely messy once the actual translation had been handed in. Rival editions, litigation, debtors' prison for some of the publishers… It is also salutary to remember the political motivations behind the project: the agenda of King James I of England – who was also King James VI of Scotland and son of the beheaded Mary Stuart – included reasserting the Divine Right of Kings and discouraging the civil disobedience apparently permitted by earlier translations. Still, this translation-by-committee contains some of the most beautiful, resonant sentences in the English language, and it is hard to describe the King James Version without using, literally or otherwise, the word "inspired."

BABEL'S AFTERMATH

In the West, translation has always had a close association with the Bible, both as subject matter and as inspiration. The story of the Tower of Babel (Genesis 11:1–9) provides a vivid explanation of why we need translators at all. It's worth revisiting the story of Babel… but that immediately raises the question: which translation to consult? Below are three translations of the Babel story: the King James Version in all its poetic majesty, the flatter Contemporary English Version (American Bible Society 1995), and the determinedly informal rendering of *The Message* (Peterson 2001).

KING JAMES VERSION	CONTEMPORARY ENGLISH VERSION (CEV)	THE MESSAGE
1 And the whole earth was of one language, and of one speech.	1 At first everyone spoke the same language,	1–2 At one time, the whole Earth spoke the same language. It so happened that as they moved out of the east, they came upon a plain in the land of Shinar and settled down.
2 And it came to pass, as they journeyed from the east, that they found a plain in the land of Shinar; and they dwelt there.	2 but after some of them moved from the east and settled in Babylonia,	
3 And they said one to another, Go to, let us make brick, and burn them throughly. And they had brick for stone, and slime had they for morter.	3–4 they said: Let's build a city with a tower that reaches to the sky! We'll use hard bricks and tar instead of stone and mortar. We'll become famous, and we won't be scattered all over the world.	3 They said to one another, "Come, let's make bricks and fire them well." They used brick for stone and tar for mortar.
4 And they said, Go to, let us build us a city and a tower, whose top may reach unto heaven; and let us make us a name, lest we be scattered abroad upon the face of the whole earth.		4 Then they said, "Come, let's build ourselves a city and a tower that reaches Heaven. Let's make ourselves famous so we won't be scattered here and there across the Earth."
5 And the LORD came down to see the city and the tower, which the children of men builded.	5 But when the LORD came down to look at the city and the tower,	5 God came down to look over the city and the tower those people had built.
6 And the LORD said, Behold, the people is one, and they have all one language; and this they begin to do: and now nothing will be restrained from them, which they have imagined to do.	6 he said: These people are working together because they all speak the same language. This is just the beginning. Soon they will be able to do anything they want.	6–9 God took one look and said, "One people, one language; why, this is only a first step. No telling what they'll come up with next – they'll stop at nothing! Come, we'll go down and garble their speech so they won't understand each other." Then God scattered them from there all over the world. And they had to quit building the city. That's how it came to be called Babel, because there God turned their language into "babble." From there God scattered them all over the world.
7 Go to, let us go down, and there confound their language, that they may not understand one another's speech.	7 Come on! Let's go down and confuse them by making them speak different languages – then they won't be able to understand each other.	
8 So the LORD scattered them abroad from thence upon the face of all the earth: and they left off to build the city.	8–9 So the people had to stop building the city, because the LORD confused their language and scattered them all over the earth. That's how the city of Babel got its name.	

KING JAMES VERSION	CONTEMPORARY ENGLISH VERSION (CEV)	THE MESSAGE
9 Therefore is the name of it called Babel; because the LORD did there confound the language of all the earth: and from thence did the LORD scatter them abroad upon the face of all the earth.		

The literary critic George Steiner invoked the Tower story in his celebrated *After Babel*, one of the Big Books of translation theory. Implicitly, he gives translators a heroic role – that of mitigating the great catastrophe visited on mankind by God Him/Herself (Steiner 1976). Again, the metaphor of light is central:

> The tongue of Eden was like a flawless glass; a light of total understanding streamed through it. Thus Babel was a second Fall, in some regards as desolate as the first. Adam had been driven from the garden; now men were harried, like yelping dogs, out of the single family of man. And they were exiled from the assurance of being able to grasp and communicate reality.

In other words, if Babel is the problem, translation is the solution. Baroness Moura Budberg wrote this explicitly in an essay a few years before Steiner's book was published (Budberg 1971). Budberg, who died in 1974, was one of the most exotic figures in recent translation history, having also been a novelist, screenwriter, lover of both Maxim Gorky and H.G. Wells, and in all probability a spy.

> This was God's punishment on the people of Babel. And what a punishment! The curse God put on Adam in the Garden of Eden was nothing compared to that.
>
> We, the translators, came along much later, in an ever-expanding world, to reverse the trend, to make good the damage, to "un-confound" the language. We became the links, the liaison officers, the treasure sharers, the reconcilers of the often irreconcilable, the tearers-down of barriers. Fancifully, I see us as a vast army scribbling away all over the globe and over all the years, a network of industrious, often underpaid, much maligned working men and women, holding the world together often against the will of the world, fending off the ever-increasing confusion.

DEFACING MONUMENTS

Others have been less impressed. Vladimir Nabokov – brilliant novelist, literary critic, translator and butterfly expert – tended to be scathing about other translators and about the activity itself. The following masterpiece of vituperation was published in *The New Yorker* in 1955, after Nabokov had translated the libretto of Tchaikovsky's opera *Eugene Onegin*, which was based on Pushkin's verse novel. An inveterate but virtuosic showoff, Nabokov used the sonnet form from Pushkin's original to defend his own free verse rendering of the libretto, and to damn previous translators who kept to Pushkin's original rhyme scheme (Nabokov 1955).

What is translation? On a platter
A poet's pale and glaring head,
A parrot's screech, a monkey's chatter,
And profanation of the dead.
The parasites you were so hard on
Are pardoned if I have your pardon,
O, Pushkin, for my stratagem:
I travelled down your secret stem,
And reached the root, and fed upon it;
Then, in a language newly learned,
I grew another stalk and turned
Your stanza patterned on a sonnet,
Into my honest roadside prose –
All thorn, but cousin to your rose.

Reflected words can only shiver
Like elongated lights that twist
In the black mirror of a river
Between the city and the mist.
Elusive Pushkin! Persevering,
I still pick up Tatiana's earring,
Still travel with your sullen rake.
I find another man's mistake,
I analyze alliterations
That grace your feasts and haunt the great
Fourth stanza of your Canto Eight.

This is my task – a poet's patience
And scholastic passion blent:
Dove-droppings on your monument.

When Nabokov's *Onegin* translation was produced on stage ten years later, it touched off a literary fistfight with the critic Edmund Wilson, who began his elegantly double-edged review in the *New York Review of Books* as follows (Wilson 1965):

> This production, though in certain ways valuable, is something of a disappointment; and the reviewer, though a personal friend of Mr. Nabokov – for whom he feels a warm affection sometimes chilled by exasperation – and an admirer of much of his work, does not propose to mask his disappointment. Since Mr. Nabokov is in the habit of introducing any job of this kind which he undertakes by an announcement that he is unique and incomparable and that everybody else who has attempted it is an oaf and an ignoramus, incompetent as a linguist and scholar, usually with the implication that he is also a low-class person and a ridiculous personality, Nabokov ought not to complain if the reviewer, though trying not to imitate his bad literary manners, does not hesitate to underline his weaknesses.
>
> Mr. Nabokov, before the publication of his own translation of *Evgeni Onegin*, took up a good deal of space in these pages to denounce a previous translation by Professor Walter Arndt. This article – which sounded like nothing so much as one of Marx's niggling and nagging attacks on someone who had had the temerity to write about economics and to hold different views from Marx's – dwelt especially on what he regarded as Professor Arndt's Germanisms and other infelicities of phrasing, without, apparently, being aware of how vulnerable he himself was. Professor Arndt had attempted the tour de force of translating the whole of *Onegin* into the original iambic tetrameter and rather intricate stanza form. Mr. Nabokov decided that this could not be done with any real fidelity to the meaning and undertook to make a "literal" translation which maintains an iambic base but quite often simply jolts into prose. The results of this have been more disastrous than those of Arndt's heroic effort. It has produced a bald and awkward language which has nothing in common with Pushkin or with the usual writing of Nabokov. One knows Mr. Nabokov's

virtuosity in juggling with the English language, the prettiness and wit of his verbal inventions. One knows also the perversity of his tricks to startle or stick pins in the reader; and one suspects that his perversity here has been exercised in curbing his brilliance; that – with his sado-masochistic Dostoevskian tendencies so acutely noted by Sartre – he seeks to torture both the reader and himself by flattening Pushkin out and denying to his own powers the scope for their full play.

A GREAT PEST

Two centuries earlier, in the preface to his *Dictionary of the English Language*, Dr. Samuel Johnson also damned translators, but for different reasons. In his mind, the English language was endangered by the larger number of translated texts being published in the United Kingdom, particularly from the French (Johnson 1755). Today, with English the dominant international language, it is interesting to read his pessimism about his native language's future – and to note that his great project, the dictionary, is one of the essential tools in any translator's work.

> The great pest of speech is frequency of translation. No book was ever turned from one language into another, without imparting something of its native idiom; this is the most mischievous and comprehensive innovation; single words may enter by thousands, and the fabric of the tongue continue the same; but new phraseology changes much at once; it alters not the single stones of the building, but the order of the columns. If an academy should be established for the cultivation of our style – which I, who can never wish to see dependence multiplied, hope the spirit of English liberty will hinder or destroy – let them, instead of compiling grammars and dictionaries, endeavour, with all their influence, to stop the license of translators, whose idleness and ignorance, if it be suffered to proceed, will reduce us to babble a dialect of France.

> If the changes that we fear be thus irresistible, what remains but to acquiesce with silence, as in the other insurmountable distresses of humanity? It remains that we retard what we cannot repel, that we palliate what we cannot cure. Life may be lengthened by care, though death cannot be ultimately defeated: tongues, like governments, have a natural tendency to degeneration; we have long preserved our constitution, let us make some struggles for our language.

In hope of giving longevity to that which its own nature forbids to be immortal, I have devoted this book, the labour of years, to the honour of my country, that we may no longer yield the palm of philology without a contest, to the nations of the continent. The chief glory of every people arises from its authors: whether I shall add any thing by my own writings to the reputation of English literature, must be left to time: much of my life has been lost under the pressures of disease; much has been trifled away; and much has always been spent in provision for the day that was passing over me; but I shall not think my employment useless or ignoble, if by my assistance foreign nations, and distant ages, gain access to the propagators of knowledge, and understand the teachers of truth; if my labours afford light to the repositories of science, and add celebrity to Bacon, to Hooker, to Milton, and to Boyle.

. . . .

When transferring Sanskrit into Chinese, the flavor of the original style is lost, even though the main ideas can be more or less conveyed. It is like feeding a person with chewed food, which not only has lost its taste, but might cause nausea.
— KUMARAJIVA, monk and translator of Buddhist Sutras (344–413)

A MAN MAY BE FAR WORSE EMPLOYED...

Somewhere in the middle is the Knight of the Sorrowful Countenance, Don Quixote, who compared reading a translation to looking at the wrong side of a tapestry ("es como quien mira los tapices flamencos por el revés"). But the famous quote is rarely put in context. It occurs in Don Quixote, Part II, Chapter LXII, when the old nobleman visits a print shop and meets a man who is overseeing the typesetting of a book he has translated from Italian (Cervantes Saavedra 1780). Don Quixote compliments the translator on his erudition, but voices some reservations about translation itself. The first translation of Don Quixote into English (and indeed into any language) was by Robert Shelton, with Part I published in 1612 and Part II in 1620 (Cervantes Saavedra 1620). It is interesting to see the difference between that first translation, with its Shakespearean flavour, and the recent one by John Rutherford (Cervantes Saavedra and Rutherford 2003).

CERVANTES, 1780	SHELTON, 1620	RUTHERFORD, 2003
Pero, con todo esto, me parece que el traducir de una lengua en otra, como no sea de las reinas de las lenguas, griega y latina, es como quien mira los tapices flamencos por el revés, que aunque se veen las figuras, son llenas de hilos que las escurecen y no se veen con la lisura y tez de la haz; y el traducir de lenguas fáciles ni arguye ingenio ni elocución, como no le arguye el que traslada ni el que copia un papel de otro papel. Y no por esto quiero inferir que no sea loable este ejercicio del traducir, porque en otras cosas peores se podría ocupar el hombre y que menos provecho le trujesen.	...[M]ee thinks this translating from one language to the other (except it be out of the Queenes of Tongues, Greeke and Latine) is just like looking upon the wrong side of Arras-Hangings that although the pictures are seen, yet they are full of thread ends, that darken them, & they are not seene with the plainenesse and smoothnesse, as on the other side; and the translating out of easie languages, argues neither wit, nor elocution, not more than doth the copying from out of one paper into another; yet I inferred not that from this, that translating is not a laudable exercise: for a man may be far worse employed, and in things lesse profitable.	And yet it seems to me that translating from one language into another, except from those queens of languages, Greek and Latin, is like viewing Flemish tapestries from the wrong side, when, although one can make out the figures, they are covered by threads that obscure them, and one cannot appreciate the smooth finish of the right side; and translating from easy languages is no indication of talent or literary ability, any more than transcribing or copying a document onto another piece of paper is. By this I do not mean to say that the exercise of translation is not to be given any credit, because there are worse and less profitable things that a man can do.

"SHALL I APOLOGIZE TRANSLATION?"
THE RESOLUTE MR. FLORIO

Louis Kelly's judgement that "Western Europe owes its civilization to translators" may sound grandiose, but few specialists in intellectual history would disagree with it (Kelly 1979). Imagine, for example, how impoverished the rest of Renaissance Europe would have been if Michel de Montaigne's *Essais* had remained only in French. Whatever generations of schoolchildren might have to say about the matter, Montaigne's invention of the essay form provided Europe with one of its most enduring tools of intellectual discourse. His first English translator, John Florio (1553–1625) was a fascinating character: scholar, lexicographer, spy, and teacher of Italian and French at the Court of James I. A great defender of translation, his pugnacious "Preface to the Essays" begins with an attack on scholarly types who felt that the Classics should be left in their original languages (Montaigne 1910):

> Shall I apologize translation? Why but some holde (as for their free-hold)
> that such conversion is the subversion of Universities. God holde with

them, and withholde them from impeach or empaire. It were an ill turne, the turning of Bookes should be the overturning of Libraries.

Florio mentions many of the problems familiar to scholarly translators today – errors in the originals he worked from, his own publisher's inadequacies, the pressure of other work – and ends on a defiant note. (N.B., the original is one long paragraph, and I have taken the liberty of inserting some line breaks but have left the original spelling.)

Yet are there herein errors. If of matter, the Authours; if of omission, the printers: him I would not amend, but send him to you as I found him: this I could not attend, but where I now finde faults, let me pray and entreate you for your owne sake to correct as you reade; to amend as you list.

But some errors are mine, and mine by more then translation. Are they in Grammer, or Ortographie? as easie for you to right, as me to be wrong; or in construction, as mis-attributing him, her, or it, to things alive, or dead, or newter; you may soone know my meaning, and eftsoones use your mending: or are they in some uncouth termes; as entraine, conscientious, endeare, tarnish, comporte, efface, facilitate, ammusing, debauching, regret, effort, emotion, and such like; if you like them not, take others most commonly set by them to expound them, since there they were set to make such likely French words familiar with our English, which well may beare them.

If any be capitall in sense mistaking, be I admonished, and they shall be recanted: Howsoever, the falsenesse of the French prints, the diversities of copies, editions and volumes (some whereof have more or lesse then others), and I in London having followed some, and in the countrie others; now those in folio, now those in octavo, yet in this last survay reconciled all; therefore or blame not rashly, or condemne not fondly the multitude of them set for your further ease in a Table (at the end of the booke) which ere you beginne to reade, I entreate you to peruse: this Printers wanting a diligent Corrector, my many employments, and the distance betweene me, and my friends I should conferre-with, may extenuate, if not excuse, even more errors.

In summe, if any thinke he could do better, let him trie; then will he better thinke of what is done. Seven or eight of great wit and worth have assayed, but found these Essayes no attempt for French apprentises or Littletonians. If this doone it may please you, as I wish it may, and I hope it shall, I with you shall be Pleased: though not, yet still I am the same resolute — JOHN FLORIO.

Truth be told, Florio was a terrible translator for this particular job, at least by modern standards. His biographer, Dame Frances Yates, wrote (Yates 1934):

> It is somewhat ironical that Montaigne, who was one of the first great writers in a modern tongue to write in a modern manner, using words simply as the exact clothing of his thought, and relying for beauty of style solely upon the aptness of the word to the thought and upon emotional rhythm, should have had as his translator one to whom elaborate rhetorical word-pattern was an instinctive necessity and a habit deeply ingrained by long training... For the Italian applied his own methods to Montaigne's matter. He stopped over nearly every statement, embroidering it with repetition, decorating it with sound-pattern, so that the periods should advance in the balanced, musically adorned manner that he knew and loved. He made, in fact, such a bad translation that it is nearly an original work, not Montaigne but Florio's Montaigne.

Yet it is also true that Florio's translation featured some very beautiful and inventive language, and there is considerable evidence that William Shakespeare borrowed from both Florio's words and Montaigne's thoughts. If Florio's intention was to spread Montaigne's ideas beyond the French language, he certainly had nothing to apologize for.

FROM GREY MICE TO E-WORKERS

Idle thought: if John Florio were working today, would he favour a Mac or a PC...?

Florio would doubtless have recognized the tools of translators who lived several centuries before and after he did – pen, paper, a few reference books – and the tasks they worked on. But today's translator works in a vastly different technological and commercial environment than even twenty years ago. Mary Snell-Hornby describes some of the major changes that have affected the profession in recent years (Snell-Hornby 2006).

> In general, we can say that during the 1990s new developments in technology brought radical changes in the "language material" (formerly understood globally as "text") with which the translator works. These can be summarized as follows:

1. Due to the vast amount of material transmitted by telecommunication, the speech with which it is processed, the increasing use of colloquial forms and the tolerance of what were traditionally viewed as language mistakes or typing errors, some communication relies simply on basic mutual intelligibility, and here translation has to some extent been made obsolete (much communication is carried out in lingua franca English). Formal business correspondence has partly been replaced by informal e-mail correspondence, much is dealt with by fax and mobile phone.

2. The same necessity for speedy processing and the tolerance of less than impeccable language forms, along with the levelling of culture-specific differences within the technological "lingua franca," mean a potentially greater role for machine translation (e.g. as "gisting," or rough versions of insider information for internal use within a concern).

3. Multimedia communication creates new text types (the audio museum guide is one example), some of them multisemiotic, with the verbal signs interacting with icons, layout tricks, pictorial images and sounds (as can increasingly be seen in advertising techniques).

4. In the area of intercultural communication, requiring not only language mediation but heightened cultural expertise, the (human) translator (and interpreter) plays an increasingly important role, whereby he/she will take the full responsibility for the "final product".

Meanwhile the dominance of technology in our lives has meant that technical texts have come to occupy over 75% of professional translators, and new areas of work, such as technical writing, content management, multilingual documentation and software localization have been created. The basic work profile of the translator has also radically changed: this has been vividly described, for example, by [Karl-Heinz] Stoll, who contrasts the "grey mice in the back room functioning as walking dictionaries" of former times, with the successful translators of today, "die mit allen verfügbaren Computer-Tools die Verarbeitung riesiger Textmengen Software-Lokalisierung und E-Commerce managen" (who, with all the available computer tools, manage the processing of vast amounts of text as software localization and e-commerce).

SUBVERSIVE, OPPRESSED, AND A TOOL OF DOMINATION

Technology has moved on, but have the fundamentals of power and position in society really changed so much over the centuries? Few people have written so incisively about the role played by translation in today's globalized, politicized, and commercialized world as Lawrence Venuti. In this extract from his *Scandals of Translation,* he suggests that it will take more than a change of operating system to improve the position of translators in the real world (Venuti 1998).

> Translation is stigmatized as a form of writing, discouraged by copyright law, depreciated by the academy, exploited by publishers and corporations, governments and religious organizations. Translation is treated so disadvantageously, I want to suggest, partly because it occasions revelations that question the authority of dominant cultural values and institutions. And like every challenge to established reputations, it provokes their efforts at damage control, their various policing functions, all designed to shore up the questioned values and institutions by mystifying their uses of translation...
>
> By far the greatest hindrances to translation, however, exist outside the discipline itself. Translation is degraded by prevalent concepts of authorship, especially in literature and in literary scholarship, and these concepts underwrite its unfavourable definition in copyright law, not only the codes of specific national jurisdictions, but the major international treaties. Translation lies deeply repressed in the cultural identities that are constructed by academic, religious, and political institutions; in the pedagogy of foreign literatures, notably the "Great Books," the canonical texts of Western culture; and in the discipline of philosophy, the academic study of philosophical concepts and traditions. Translation figures hugely in the corporate world, in the international publishing of bestsellers and the unequal patterns of cross-cultural commerce between the hegemonic Northern and Western countries and their others in Africa, Asia, and South America. Translation powers the global cultural economy, enabling transnational corporations to dominate the print and electronic media in the so-called developing countries by capitalizing on the marketability of translations from the major languages, pre-eminently English.

....

*I'm not a translator so much as a tightrope walker between two
unreliable dictionaries.*

— LINH DINH on tinfishpress.com (Dinh 2007)

A SELF-EFFACING SERVANT

The public image of translators today is more grey mouse than subversive pawn.
Certainly, things are safer that way. It is rare for translators to hit the newspaper
headlines, and when they do it is likely to be for the saddest of reasons: the 1991
killing of Hitoshi Igarashi, Japanese translator of Salman Rushdie's *The Satanic Verses*,
was an untimely reminder that fanatics prefer to shoot (or in this case stab, repeatedly) the messenger than to argue with the message.

Among translators themselves, the prevailing self-image seems to be an ambivalent one, as proud of their work as any professional, but less than happy with their
trade's invisibility. A good example can be seen in the musings of Peter France, editor of *The Oxford Guide to Literature in English Translation* (France 2000).

> Translation is, or can be, both absorbing and rewarding. As a translator
> I know that there is a fascination in living at such close quarters with a
> writer, engaging with every word they wrote, trying to make another text
> which is worthy of the original. But there is also a melancholy of transla-
> tion. Compared with other writers, translators feel undervalued. It is not so
> much that they are badly paid (this is a problem they often share with those
> they translate) as that they are downgraded, damned with faint praise, criti-
> cized in passing and, unkindest of all, ignored. All are aware, and if they
> weren't critics would remind them, of the inadequacy of their efforts – "the
> translator is a betrayer" goes the old refrain, unthinkingly.
>
> Translation, seen by Florio, the great Montaigne translator, as a second-
> ary and "female" activity, has little status compared with "original" cre-
> ation. It often seems that the translator's best role is that of self-effacing
> servant, a transparent glass through which the original is viewed. But if
> the translator as traitor is uncomfortably visible, the translator as servant
> suffers from invisibility. His or her work is taken for granted, as if it were
> simply mechanical, the translator's name is often barely acknowledged in
> title pages, reviews and the like, translators struggle to achieve the recogni-
> tion implied by royalties.

Translation problems are like wild animals: the answers tend to lurk in the under-growth of your brain, and only come out when they think no-one is looking.
— ANDREW FENNER in the *Translator's Handbook* (Fenner 1989)

SEPARATING THE PEACOCKS FROM THE PIDGINS

In a mixture of wit, whimsy, and scholarly erudition, professor Eugene Eoyang describes different types of translators in his essay "Peacock, Parakeet, Partridge, 'Pidgin': An 'Ornithology' of Translators" (Eoyang 2003).

I choose as a specimen of the translator "peacock" the redoubtable Edward Fitzgerald. His memorable quatrains [from the fifth edition of his *Rubaiyat of Omar Khayyam*, 1889], not so much translations as embroideries and a patchwork of different texts, are not always easy to trace to their originals, but their gaudy, spectacular display is undeniable:

> A Book of Verses underneath the Bough,
> A Jug of Wine, a Loaf of Bread – and Thou
> Beside me singing in the Wilderness –
> Oh, Wilderness were Paradise enow!

A less flamboyant version would read as follows [from Avery and Heath-Stubbs' 1979 translation]:

> I need a jug of wine and a book of poetry,
> Half a loaf for a bite to eat,
> Then you and I, seated in a desert spot,
> Will have more than a Sultan's realm.

Notice that in the more faithful version there is no singing, and there is no subtle, unspoken inference – as there is in the Fitzgerald – that the companion is a woman, so ardently invoked by the phrase "… and Thou." Fitzgerald erases the Sultan and all his wealth and universalizes the earthly pleasures in the deliberate archaism of "Paradise enow!" What is striking is that the original appears not to involve a wilderness at all: it is a "desert spot" in one version, a "desert place" in another. What, indeed, would a wilderness be doing in Arabia Deserta? Fitzgerald has so completely transformed the poem into a northern setting, forested it with wilderness, Christianized it with the notion of "Paradise," archaicized it with obsolete diction, and sexualized it with an implied female companion. But the most subtle trans-mogrification in Fitzgerald is his manipulation of case, changing the specu-latively conditional to the wilfully subjunctive, from "I need... then you and I... will have more than..." to the very presently indicative enumeration of the first three lines: "... Wine... Bread... singing... wilderness" concluding with the wish-fulfilment of the "were" in "were Paradise," which is neither past nor present, but ideally and contingently indicative. The final touch, archaic though it may seem at the outset, but necessarily paranomasic, is the use of the word "enow," in "... Wilderness were Paradise enow!" – mean-ing not only "enough" but carrying with it phonetically more than a hint of "now," meaning present. Where the original is a plain statement of what one hopes for, Fitzgerald presents not only the ardent prospect of paradise, but, subjunctively and indicatively, a present "Paradise enow!"

Consider the following literal rendition of another quatrain from Omar Khayyam [by Avery and Heath-Stubbs]:

> The characters of all creatures are on the Tablet,
> The Pen always worn with writing "Good," "Bad":
> Our grieving and striving are in vain,
> Before time began all that was necessary was given.

These are certainly thoughtful, even philosophical ruminations, but they are, for the most part, an abstract delineation of a familiar predeterminism. These drab formulations flash into colour under Fitzgerald's dramatic eye:

> The Moving Finger writes; and, having writ,
> Moves on: not all your Piety nor Wit
> Shall lure it back to cancel half a Line,
> Nor all your Tears wash out a Word of it.

Never has allusion been used more effectively or more ironically, for with the simple phrase "the Moving Finger," Fitzgerald transports us to Belshazzar's feast, as recorded in the Book of Daniel (5:5), when "Immediately the fin-gers of a man's hand appeared and wrote on the plaster of the wall of the king's palace... and they saw the hand as it wrote."

... Fitzgerald's liberties can be faulted as inaccurate interpretations of the text, yet he never fails to realize the full potential of the poetry. What we read in him is more Fitzgerald than Omar Khayyam, and it is clear from his own comments that he suffered from no lack of vanity with regard to his sources. Like a peacock, he preened about his own dazzling display: "It is an amusement for me to take what liberties I like with the Persians, who (as I think) are not Poets enough to frighten one from such excursions, and who really do want a little Art to shape them" [from a letter written to E.B. Cowell in 1857].

Eoyang's essay covers the parakeet (a mimic) and the partridge (more of a grouse, always criticizing other people's translations and insisting on narrow renderings of text – Nabokov being the most famous example) before coming to the last of his translatorial birds:

Finally, we come to "pidgin," which, as you may have already guessed, is not even a bird, but merely sounds like one. According to the OED, "pidgin" is a "Chinese corruption of Eng. business, used widely for any action, occupation, or affair. Hence, pidgin-English, the jargon, consisting chiefly of English words, often corrupted in pronunciation, and arranged according to Chinese idiom, orig. used for intercommunication between the Chinese and Europeans at seaports, etc., in China, the Straits Settlements, etc."

"Pidgin-English" is a jargon familiar enough, but I should like to sample a bit of "Pidgin-Chinese" to illustrate the disastrous consequences of following Nabokov's advice, of rendering with "absolute exactitude" the original text. Here are a few examples, some rather surprising to natives, most amusing to bilinguals:

小心	"small-heart" / Take care
马上	"horse-on" / right away
生意	"grow-meaning" / business
点心	"dot-heart" / dim sum (dumplings)
天花	"heaven-flower" / smallpox
客气	"guest-air" / polite(ness)
赤足	"red-foot" / barefoot
虚字	"empty-word" / grammatical particle
那里	"that place" / where?
哪里哪里	"where? where?" / (modestly deflecting compliment)
人山人海	"people mountain people sea" / a big crowd
马马虎虎	"horse horse tiger tiger" / sloppily

Clearly, absolute word-for-word translation (or even compound-for-compound – see "where? where?" example) cannot capture the sheer idiomaticity of language, its gestalt structures of meaning, which refuse to be disassembled, like a machine, into its constituent parts, to be conveniently reassembled on foreign soil. That's why the import-export model for translation is so faulty, because the commodities that can be shipped from a source to a destination, carefully handled, usually arrives intact. Language, however, is no commodity, and is inchoate material: with a life and a personality of its own, it can scarcely be shipped without some loss in meaning or nuance. Like some wines, language does not "travel well": it carries the original soil of its provenance.

Our aviary of translators permits us the perspective of taxonomic clarity. We can differentiate between species of translators, and will not need to muddy the waters by venturing apples-and-oranges comparisons. We can ask, more precisely, which peacock is the more colourful; which partridge the grousier, which parakeet the more skilful, which "pidgin" the more ridiculous. Tellingly, each of the four avian counterparts emphasises a different sense: the peacock is clearly visual, and graphic; the parakeet is definitely aural, and phonetic; the grouse is, by instinct, olfactory: he knows when something smells; the "pidgin" is a groper and has only a clumsy tactile sense of words as objects, not as abstractions.

Having strained my original premise, perhaps I should escape by way of conclusion. When asked which bird I aspire to when I translate, my response is: none.

I try to emulate the chameleon.

TRANSLATION ON THE ROCKS

Margaret Sayers Peden is one of the most distinguished translators of Spanish-language literature into English. In this extract from her essay "Building a Translation, The Reconstruction Business: Poem 145 of Sor Juana Ines De La Cruz," she provides a charming metaphor for the work of the translator (Peden 1989).

For Walter Benjamin a translation had to fit itself into its own language "with loving particularity... just as the broken pieces of a vase, to be joined again, must fit at every point, though none may be exactly like the other." One can understand why a translator would not be thrilled with this figure

– the marks of the patching are all too readily observable, the translator's work distressingly exposed. I like to think of the original work as an ice cube. During the process of translation the cube is melted. While in its liquid state, every molecule changes place; none remains in its original relationship to the others. Then begins the process of forming the work in a second language. Molecules escape, new molecules are poured in to fill the spaces, but the lines of molding and mending are virtually invisible. The work exists in the second language as a new ice cube – different, but to all appearances the same.

REBUILDING THE *ARGO*: TRANSLATION AND SCIENCE

As in so many other fields, translation has been essential to the development of science. Yet the historiography of scientific translation is a relative latecomer in translation studies, at least in comparison to literary and religious translation. This has begun to be remedied in recent years, notably with Scott L. Montgomery's magisterial yet pacily written *Science in Translation: Movements of Knowledge Through Cultures and Time* (Montgomery 2000). The book is an engrossing wander through the scientific past, taking the reader into all sorts of interesting historical nooks and crannies. One of my favourites – unfortunately, too long to include in this anthology – is his discussion of how the concept of evolution was translated into Japanese and was adopted by Japanese scientists. For several decades in the twentieth century, evolution as a scientific theory was hijacked in ways that served the ambitions of Japan's imperialist factions. Darwin's "survival of the fittest" somehow became *yūshō repai* – "victory of the superior and defeat of the inferior" – and, as with social Darwinism in the West, was applied not just to the natural world but to human beings and nations. Today, fortunately, the accepted term is the more temperate *tekisha seizon*, or "survival of the most suitable."

Here, Montgomery provides our final translatorial metaphor, which he draws from classical mythology.

Translation, as a human activity, has attracted many metaphors. It has been called a process of decanting and conversion, a method for erasing or displacing authorship, even for appropriating or stealing the work of another writer, nation, culture. Literary critics sometimes talk of writing itself as a process of translation, whether from thought to word or symbol to text. No doubt, all of these imaginative uses have their place. Recently, I was struck by a different kind of image, a metaphor of more historical proportions. It came to me as I was reviewing abstracts in French, German, and English for an article I had written on the introduction of the periodic table to Japan. Along with the editor's changes, these different voices, or ingredients, had gone into the making of the final piece, which had my name on it, but was really the work of many hands.

Who, then, were the Argonauts? They were a group of warriors, athletes, and sailors, men of the world in other words, who accompanied Jason on his journey to the ends of the known Earth, the land of Colchis, at the eastern shore of the Black Sea. Their mission was to reclaim the Golden Fleece, a gift of the gods that brought prosperity to any land that held and protected it. But their real aim was adventure, loss of the familiar. They were something else, too – builders, or re-builders I should say. The Argo, designed and assembled by the famous shipbuilder Argos, is the first vessel that we know of with a name. It reaches back to that period when culture was crossing the borderline between the oral and the written. The ship was longer than any that had come before it, and at its prow Athena (goddess of wisdom) had placed a "speaking timber" from the oak of Dodona, an oracle of Zeus, that would guide the Argonauts and urge them on.

But the ship, in its original form, as a kind of text of adventure, did not last. The voyage to Colchis was so extended, so full of adversity and storm, that it required those aboard to continually replace portions of it. The "speaking timber" itself was lost, and this was irreplaceable. But the rest of the ship was not: bit by bit, plank by plank, using wood that they could find along the way, whether oak, pine, beech, or olive, the Argonauts remade the Argo over entirely – not once but several times. Its precise shape changed; its materials altered; its size grew. The living wood of each locale was transformed into a vessel whose motion never ceased.

It is this ship, then, that I would call "science" and the process of rebuilding it over distance, translation. We say, after all, that science advances, progresses, accumulates. But in a very real sense it also moves – from one people to another, across boundaries of place, time, and, not least, language. And at each "stop" – whether ancient Greece, Tang Dynasty China, medieval Islam, Renaissance Italy, or 17th Century England – what had existed before was transformed and enlarged.

Can we find a small but meaningful example – a sliver from the mast, so to speak? Here is one. We know that the study of alchemy formed an important precursor to modern chemistry. Indeed, the two words "alchemy" and "chemistry" share an obvious covalent linguistic bond. Where did this come from? "Alchemy" is a 12th century Latin rendition of "Alkimiya," which is Arabic – like al-cohol, al-gebra – and means "the study of Khemeia." Khemeia, meanwhile, is ancient Greek for the art of physical conversion – creating something of value out of something worthless or of lesser value. The Greeks specifically applied this to metals, but it really came from Egypt – whose ancient name, in fact, is "Khmi," signifying "black land." Black, of course, because of the rich organic silts and muds that the floods of the Nile would spread over the spring land each year, converting the valueless desert into a precious paradise of agricultural bounty. But what of the "al" in "alchemical"? This, it appears, was stripped off sometime in the 15th–16th centuries, when much of the obvious debt to Islamic science was being replaced by a preference for things Greek: it was certainly finalized by the time of Robert Boyle's *Skeptical Chymist* in 1665. By simply stating the word "chemistry," therefore, we are invoking a complex, even somewhat troubled journey that spans more than 2000 years.

I realize this might sound a bit dramatic or exaggerated. But consider: the Greeks borrowed and reformed much scientific knowledge from Egypt and Babylonia, then the Nestorian Christians, Syrians, and Persians adopted this knowledge from the Greeks (only a small part of Greek science went to Rome). This knowledge, and much from India as well, was next taken up by Islamic thinkers, in the 9th and 10th centuries especially, and, after being much rebuilt in the Arabic tongue, passed to Latin Europe, in the great 12th Century Renaissance. By that time, the age of the great cathedrals and flowering of vernacular tongues and literatures, the ship of "science" had been re-made many times and could hardly be called "Greek" or "Arabic" or "Western."

What we call the Scientific Revolution was founded upon this enormously rich legacy, with ingredients from all these varied ports of call. And consider, too: the journey hardly stopped there. In just the past two centuries, modern science has made its way into all the world's major languages – from Turkish to Japanese. The odyssey of even a single term, "chem," is therefore no small thing. We snatch it from a vast and magnificent flow of transfer.

All of this might seem a bit grandiose. It is especially out of proportion to the small amount of credit (and other remunerations) normally given to translators of scientific material today, many of whom are scientists themselves. These workers, as far as their translations are concerned, are the most "invisible" of all authors, I wager. How often do they even get to see their names in print, on any translation they've produced? No "Argo," it would seem, for them. Yet science moves throughout the world today because of their work. Yes, because of a global language (English) too, without doubt. But a lingua franca, whether English or Latin or Arabic or Greek, does not eliminate translation but can actually increase the need for it – due to the simple fact that a majority of its users may hold it as a second or third language and are thus constantly engaged in "decanting" and "converting" material into it. Translators, though so often unseen to others, remain the Argonauts of science.

CHAPTER TWO

Art, profession, or vocation? The trade

As with a seashell, the translator can listen strenuously but mistake the rumour
of his own pulse for the beat of the alien sea.

— GEORGE STEINER in *After Babel* (Steiner 1976)

T ranslation is a profession, and therefore something one does for
money. But of course, it's never that simple with any profession.
People do it for many reasons, and love seems to come into it as often as money.

Occasionally the motivations are darker. The author and translator Jorge Luis
Borges (see also chapter 7) once wrote a long, literally and figuratively fabulous essay
about the translation history of *The Thousand and One Nights*, which describes the
competition between successive translators. The essay begins in novelistic fashion,
peering over the shoulder of the adventurer-diplomat-translator Richard Burton
(see also chapter 2) as he sits in a musty palace in Trieste, preparing his translation
of the Arabic classic, which, he hopes, will "annihilate" the translation by Richard
Lane, a noted Orientalist scholar. Lane's translation had done much to correct the
Nights' first Western translation, by the Frenchman Jean Antoine Galland. As Borges
sets the scene, "Lane translated against Galland, Burton against Lane; to understand
Burton we must understand this hostile dynasty." The essay, translated by Esther
Allen, appears in at least two anthologies, so I have not included it here, but I highly
recommend it for anyone with an interest in translation, literature, cultural history,
and, dare I say, damn good reads (Borges 1999; Venuti 2000).

Some of the selections in this chapter deal with how people started their careers,
others with why they stayed in it. I am always struck by the enjoyment that so many
translators seem to get from their work.

STARTING OUT: HOW DID WE EVER ACQUIRE AN EMPIRE?

Denys Johnson-Davies has been a champion of modern Arabic literature for over sixty years. In this passage from his *Memories in Translation: A Life Between the Lines of Arabic Literature*, he describes his first job as a translator. After several years at Cambridge studying Arabic ("dogged by the feeling that I was being taught a dead language, another Latin," by teachers who "had never, to the best of my knowledge, visited anywhere in the Arab world and their interest in it was confined to the past"), he found himself at the BBC's Arabic section in the rural town of Evesham (Johnson-Davies 2006).

My duties at Evesham included what was known as switch censorship, especially of the main evening transmission, which included not only a news bulletin but cultural talks and music. Switch censorship meant being in the studio with the broadcaster and cutting him off the air if he were suddenly to begin spouting anti-British sentiments. The task of switch censorship having been assigned to me, the rest of the English staff were free to go home at a reasonable hour and be with their families. My other duties included the checking of translations made into Arabic of talks to be broadcast, and reading through scripts from other services and choosing those I considered suitable for being broadcast in Arabic; these I was then required to shorten and adapt. Additionally, together with my boss, I would read and comment on any scripts that were submitted for broadcast.

What surprised me greatly was that, apart from some twenty Arabs, not a soul in the Arabic section of the BBC could be said to have more than a superficial command of the language. How was it that Britain had acquired this great empire, which included a large number of people whose native language was Arabic, and yet appeared to boast virtually no one who knew the language? I remember, later on, David Cowan telling me that, given the job of testing the ex-members of the Sudan Political Service (of which at one time my father had been a member), he had found not a single person who knew anything better than kitchen Arabic, although all of them had been required to pass examinations in the language. And how was it that the BBC was successful in its special application to have me – a reasonably healthy young man of eighteen, with virtually no experience of the Arab world – exempted from military service on the basis of my knowledge of Arabic? Were there no old dodderers who had served their time in the Arab world and were capable of performing such duties? The fact that for most of the time I was at Cambridge I was the only person studying Arabic hardly shows – as suggested for example in Edward Said's bestseller *Orientalism* – that Britain was busy training people to study Arabic so that they could become spies and so forth. At that time no attempt was made to teach Arabic other than as a dead classical language. It took the war itself to show that Britain possessed virtually no Arabists, or people with any knowledge of other oriental languages, and it was only then that the government arranged for special scholarships to be given to those willing to take up such languages...

For me my five years with the Arabic section of the BBC amounted to a period of attendance, as it were, at a third university – a university where my studies were more concentrated than they had so far been, in that for most of my waking hours I practiced Arabic, at the hands of Arabs, in both its written and spoken forms.

For a time I shared an office with my boss. Then came the time when I bought myself a large cherrywood pipe and began smoking a herbal mixture, which was much cheaper than tobacco. The choking bush fire that resulted meant that I was soon found an office to myself, complete with an attractive young secretary, who turned up daily with a large black cat in a basket. I have never been known for my tidiness, but the black cat further increased the chaotic state of the office, with its saucers of milk and toilet tray.

The Arabs, mostly Egyptian, employed as broadcasters, translators, and typists, had chosen for the most part to be housed in one of the Nissen huts set up in the same area as the offices and studios. This saved them from making the daily trip by special bus into the somewhat dull town of Evesham, where one could be billeted. I myself had initially been automatically billeted in the town. I found myself in the same house as a Moroccan Jew named Leon Abulafia; he was the person nearest to me in age in the department, and we became good friends. He had been born in the seaside town of Mogador in Morocco, a town with a large community of Jews, and had spent most of his life there; his father had been in the tea trade. I heard a lot about his early life in Mogador, little knowing that more than fifty years on I would come to know Mogador well under the new name it had been given of Essaouira. While Leon spoke Moroccan Arabic fluently, he could neither read nor write the language. The BBC, realizing that many Moroccans were unable at that time to follow a news bulletin in the classical language, had decided to have several newscasts in the colloquial Moroccan dialect. For this purpose they hired three Moroccans from the Free French forces. None of these, however, spoke any English, and so Leon had been employed to translate and dictate the news bulletins to them – also, as best he could, to see that they didn't get into any trouble, for they were a rough trio. One day I remember walking with Leon all the way from Evesham to the offices and studios: it was a Saturday and, being an Orthodox Jew, he refused to take the bus, and I accompanied him on the walk. This I soon regretted as it came on to rain, and on we trudged; the bus came by and the driver stopped for us, looking in disbelief as we both turned down the offer of a lift!

The advantages of transferring to the Nissen hut were only too obvious. My English bosses showed their disapproval, but it turned out to be one of the best decisions I have ever made. Not only was I in walking distance of work and the 24-hour canteen, but I found myself housed with some twenty Arabs who naturally didn't stop conversing among themselves in Arabic just because a young Englishman was now living among them. Intrigued by my seeming determination to learn Arabic, several of them went out of their way to help me. I was persuaded to keep one notebook in which I wrote down words that were new to me; another notebook contained lines of poetry and of *zagal* (poetry in the colloquial language); while a third notebook was devoted to recording proverbs in the Egyptian dialect. In the evenings I would sit around, following as best I could their conversation and asking for the meaning of words or phrases I didn't know. Gradually I found myself understanding more and more, and after a time I ventured to utter the odd sentence. Evenings were generally spent playing poker, often into the early hours of the morning so that the session would break up and everyone would go off for an early breakfast before snatching a few hours of sleep. I would sit up with them and follow the game being played, with large sums of money being won and lost. I then began playing and became addicted, playing each night to win or lose more than my meager monthly salary. All of them, of course, earned considerably more than I did, and I understood why gambling is forbidden in Islam and saw how it affected several of my colleagues...

As Arabic gradually became less of a closed book, I tried to find out whether there was any sort of literary renaissance in the Arab world. Were novels and short stories being written? I learned that the short story was being practiced by a small number of writers, the best known of whom was Mahmoud Teymour. As it happened, my father, while in Cairo, had somehow met Mahmoud Teymour, who sent me several volumes of his short stories. I also became aware of the writings of Tewfik al-Hakim through my colleague Nevill Barbour. During this time I translated one or two of Teymour's short stories and was able to have them published in some of the "little" magazines, such as *International Short Story* and *The Wind and the Rain,* that were being produced at that time.

STARTING OUT: "THAT'S *NOT* WHAT A DENTIST WOULD SAY!"

Per Dohler is from a more recent generation of translators, and works with a very different set of source texts. His "How Not to Become a Translator," published in the web-based *Translation Journal*, provides a witty introduction to the field of technical translation (Dohler 2003).

My native language is German. My extraction is German, Romanian, Hungarian, Polish-Jewish, and other things I will never know about. My country is Germany, but if I hadn't adopted the U.S. and Sweden on the side I could never stand being here. I translate from English and the Scandinavian languages into German. My fields are dental, medical, financial, marketing, PR, IT, localization. I live and work in Barendorf, a small community in the center of Northern Germany, together with said Thea, who is an independent consultant, my best editor, and a lot of other things that don't belong here. And in case I have forgotten something, you can always look it up at www.triacom.com.

Unfortunately, on top of all that, I am also probably one of the world's most eminent experts on how not to become a translator.

I know what I am talking about. In my first years as a translator I did almost everything wrong, and I certainly made plenty of the most elementary mistakes.

I'd say I wasn't even a translator initially; I was just posing as one. True, I had an academic background in U.S. literature and English linguistics, painfully acquired after meandering through the academic system for too many years (easy enough to do at those unstructured German universities). And, having spent a couple of years in California, I felt that my English was adequate and that I knew a little about the U.S. But that, of course, is nowhere near good enough to hang out one's shingle as a translator.

My first paid translations were done, somewhat accidentally, in 1982, for a professor of history. I had to translate source documents from U.S. history into German for inclusion in an annotated textbook. The volume in question did eventually appear; my contribution was hardly recognizable. But no one told me what I had done wrong, or how.

The next step in that dubious career of mine came over a year later, when my father – a dentist and director of the state dental association – referred Germany's largest dental publisher to me (just like that, he had no idea whether I would perform OK or not). So I started doing dental translations, all of which were edited by my father. ("That may sound good, Per, but it's not what a dentist would ever say!") (HINDSIGHT: What I gained from this cooperation over the next few years was the best practical education in the field I could have had, short of actually becoming a dentist myself.) But from a business angle, the whole setup was a disaster because I simply swallowed what I was fed. I would receive two or three dental articles a month to translate from English into German. I was getting paid by the printed page, a few months after the article appeared in print (if it appeared), at a rate set by the publisher. It was not until over a year later that a new editorial coordinator took pity on me and suggested that I submit an invoice for what I had not heretofore thought of as accounts receivable.

Meanwhile, my M.A. thesis was finally completed, even well received – but there were no jobs for linguists. I'd had an invitation to work toward a Ph.D. at the University of California at Berkeley, but the family finances did not stretch that far. To turn a dead end into something useful, I started out to get a second degree, this time in computer science (there were, and still are, no tuition charges at German universities, so that was no problem). Something with language and computers – that could be hot, or so we thought, even though it was not quite clear how. (HINDSIGHT: This was going to give me an enormous advantage in the 1990s, when localization became a big hit.) To put bread on the table, I continued working for my dental publisher, even acquired a second one and a pharmaceutical company somehow (word of mouth, probably), and audited assorted university-level classes in medicine and dentistry. I managed to muddle through in this manner for some time more.

Finally, one morning in 1988 – six years after my first translation! – I looked at myself in the mirror and said, almost a bit surprised, "You, Per, are actually a translator." (HINDSIGHT: I was not, yet.) I dropped out of school, bought a new computer and more dictionaries, sent out some makeshift mailings – I didn't know anything about marketing either – and actually landed one or two new clients.

But I still hadn't ever spoken to a "real" translator, had never had a translation of mine critiqued, had been denied membership by the regional translators' association, had never participated in any kind of professional exchange, had never even read a book on the art or the craft of translation – nothing. Despite all that, I was doing relatively well financially, and I even became accredited by the Chamber of Commerce in my home state. I was translating more and more, but I still wasn't a translator. Not until 1991 – nine years after my first translation. (HINDSIGHT: Most of the little odds and ends picked up along the way will ultimately come in handy in some translation. There may be no more "renaissance men" in this world, but a broad range of interests does not hurt.)

So what happened in 1991? CompuServe, the U.S.-based online service, started doing serious business in Germany. I signed up and soon found the legendary FLEFO community of translators – then just about the only such online community, with the possible exceptions of sci.lang.translation on Usenet and LANTRA-L, if I remember correctly. A new world opened up for me – the world of actual translation. And actual translators. (And virtual translation. And virtual translators.)

Translators must be one of the most interesting breeds of people. Many are probably a little weird, myself quite possibly not excluded; but most of those I met in the ensuing years – and I met plenty of colleagues at home and abroad over the years, enjoyed their company, enjoyed their hospitality, tried to lure them to Barendorf ("Hotbed of North German Translation"), almost as if to make up for lost time – are really interesting people with strong opinions, which they are eager to try on others. We come from an incredible wealth of backgrounds and bring this diversity to the incredible wealth of worlds that we translate from and into.

I don't know who said it, I may even have made this up myself:

"Everything I ever learned I learned from someone else." In my case, when it comes to the art, the craft, and the business of translation, the "someone else" would usually have been someone I originally met on FLEFO, and the time would have been the early 1990s.

So in this manner, I became a translator after all. Things have been largely uphill ever since.

STARTING OUT: I WAS READING THIS BOOK ON COSMOLOGY...

Some translators are literally amateurs – people with other jobs who are seduced by a particular book and wish to share it with friends who can't read the source language. One such translator is the Oscar-winning film editor and sound designer Walter Murch, known for his work on films such as *The Godfather* and *The Godfather* II), *American Graffiti*, *Apocalypse Now*, and *The English Patient*. Writing in the journal *Zoetrope: All-Story*, Murch describes how he came to translate short stories by the German-Italian author Curzio Malaparte (Murch 1998):

> As fascinating as Malaparte's life was, it was not this that attracted me to his writing, but a chance encounter twelve years ago in a French book about cosmology, where one of Malaparte's stories was retold to illustrate a point about conditions shortly after creation of the universe. The imagery was so strange and captivating, and managed so carefully to tread the tightrope between the real and the surreal, that I was compelled to find the book from which the story was taken: it turned out to be *Kaputt*, Malaparte's first-person novel about his experiences in and around the eastern and northern fronts of World War II.
>
> It is impossible to overestimate the effect *Kaputt* had on me. I became (and remain) a little unbalanced on the subject: reading it resembled falling into a waking dream. I could not understand why I hadn't heard of Malaparte before, nor why *Kaputt* was not required reading for every citizen of the Twentieth Century... I bought dozens of copies to give to my friends, anticipating an explosion of interest. The result: a little smoke – perhaps a flame or two – and lots of raised shoulders and eyebrows. I read the two other books of Malaparte's that have been translated into English: *The Skin* (1949) and *The Volga Rises in Europe* (1943). I resumed my

study of Italian, which I had left off in 1964, and asked friends in Italy to send me books of his that were unobtainable in the States: *Mamma Marcia* (from which "Partisans, 1944" is taken), *Fughe in Prigione, Maledetti Toscani,* and others.

But my interest never extended to translation. At least not until about a year and a half ago, after I had been interviewed by *Parnassus* [the poetry journal] on the subject of film adaptation. In the course of my conversation with the interviewer, Joy Katz, I offered an analogy: that filmmakers adapting a short story or a novel are performing a kind of multiple translation from the language of text to the languages of image, movement, and sound; and that the old Italian adage *traduttore, traditore,* (translator, traitor) particularly applies: an attempt to be overly faithful to the text often results in a damming up of the deeper currents of the project, so that an artful betrayal of the original work seems to serve an adaptation best, something along the lines of Picasso's famous statement that "art is a lie that tells the truth."

After finishing the interview, though, I was suddenly shaken by the knowledge that I didn't really know what I was talking about, at least as far as my personal experience of language translation was concerned. Under the circumstances, I decided to try my hand at it – and what better subject than Malaparte?

I was relieved to find that everything went smoothly, and although I had not done translation before, the process felt familiar and comforting. What was a surprise, however, was to find that, even though Malaparte wrote in prose, my English translations seemed to want to be arranged on the page in blank verse... Giving more space on the page seemed to aerate the density of Malaparte's text, allowing it to breathe and permitting his startling images to be savored in a different, more measured way. And since Italian – particularly Malaparte's Italian – is a more musical language than English, the poetic form helped to restore some of the musicality rhythms lost in a prose translation.

In the process, I also rediscovered the obvious, which is that the ragged structure of free verse emphasizes the internal rhythms and tensions of each line and puts an added, if subliminal, emphasis on the line's last word, an emphasis that is independent of the grammatical construction of the sentence. It was this last realization that led me to the source of the familiarity I had felt earlier: translating from prose to poetry turned out to be similar to film editing and sound design, which are my central occupations. I found that although I was doing different things physically, the state of mind I entered as I translated these poems was identical to my state of mind when I am putting a film together.

Rhythm – both internal to the shot (or line) and in the overall sequence of shots (or lines) – is, of course, as central to film editing as it is to poetry. Once a shot is selected, the crucial decision becomes at what precise moment to bring it to an end, even though this decision is perceived only subliminally by the audience. Just as the end of a line in poetry is usually independent of the grammatical structure of the sentence, the end of a shot in a film is usually independent of the overt dramatic structure of a scene. But in both cases, the ending of a line (or shot) is a seemingly arbitrary but secretly architectural way for the creators to shape the arc of the poem or story, largely by drawing subtle comparisons and contrasts between the final image of the outgoing shot and the first image of the next.

There are also the larger questions common to translation and film editing: when to follow the text or the script literally; when to eliminate; when to augment or repeat; when to transpose; when to invent. Once the technical issues have been mastered, these become the dominant questions in the postproduction of film.

And then there was an added bonus: I found that the directness and immediacy of language translation helped to solve – for me, anyway – a persistent practical dilemma in the life of every film editor, which is that there is usually no way to edit, in a fully creative sense, without actually working on a film. It is as if a musician found he could only perform in official full-dress concerts, without the ability to practice on his own or in smaller groups; or a writer found he could only write when he was being paid to write. The resonances between film editing and translation provided me with an alternate, inexpensive, immediate, and relatively risk-free "cross-training," which is so important to the lives of artists and athletes but which is generally denied to most filmmakers because of the technical and expensive nature of our particular crafts.

KEEPING FAMILY MEMORIES ALIVE

Translators' baby steps in the profession are often small jobs for friends and acquaintances. Common ones seem to be correcting "bilingual" restaurant menus and translating visa requests while sojourning in foreign lands. In my case, my first substantial translation tasks were family memoirs.

My mother's people came from several countries in Central Europe, and since the 1930s have been scattered across the globe. Two generations ago the shared language was German. But the relatives in their late seventies and eighties live in other languages now, to which they bring a particular accent and diction (my great-aunt Dora liked to say that she spoke "fluent immigranto"). At our family reunion held in Prague in 1996, a total of twelve countries were represented. Since many of us speak English as our native tongue and many more read it fairly comfortably, I and others have encouraged our elders to write their memoirs, and have translated the ones written in other languages. The following was written as part of a larger discussion about translating memoirs, using examples from my own family.

The voices that come through in these translations are, I hope, as different as the women – almost always women, the "glue" that kept our far-flung family connected – who wrote the originals. One of these was my late great-aunt Gaby, who fled in 1940 to Ecuador, the last place that was offering visas. Her memoir *From Innsbruck to Ecuador*, written in Spanish, is very much as I remember her: straightforward, unadorned, and unsentimental. The narrative is full of plot and action: her comfortable middle-class life comes to an end in 1939; she struggles to reinvent herself and make a living in a different language and culture; takes in washing, runs an isolated farm which is destroyed in an earthquake, starts a dry-cleaning business, eventually owns a successful hotel. And always, however painful the subject or dramatic the event, the same matter-of-fact tone and simple diction that made translation easy. This is how she describes the aftermath of the earthquake, when all the family members had been found:

> Now. What were we going to do, and where were we going to cook and sleep? We were all exhausted, and it was drizzling – and every few minutes the hills would move again. As night approached we were still without a roof, so the four of us got under a mandarin tree with dense foliage. The maid and her child came there as well. The leaves kept us dry but I don't think anyone could sleep. The earth

continued to shake. We were like a herd of sheep seeking shelter close to each other, anxiously awaiting the dawn.

The next morning we could see the destruction around us...

Can you see her? Stern, phlegmatic, a tough cookie even as an octogenarian grandmother. A stocky, plainly dressed figure, she had little time for reflection or self-pity, despite the desperately hard times she had lived through. Her Spanish, which she began to speak in her late 30s, was simple and grammatically correct, though with a marked Germanic accent. We had some good editorial sessions over strong coffee and European pastries in the flat she eventually retired to in Guatemala City. In translating her, I didn't have to think hard about her voice: it seemed to come out naturally in simple, straightforward English.

Much less straightforward was the translation from Italian of *Four Lives of Adrienne F.*, the memoir of my great-aunt-once-or-twice-removed Adrienne. In contrast to Gaby's down-to-earth simplicity, Adrienne is a tall, elegantly dressed Roman, quick to smile and laugh, but with an aura of sadness held in check by her exquisite manners. She too lived through dramatic times – her four lives included a wealthy "middle European" childhood, teenage years as a refugee hiding from the Nazis, a virtual "kidnapping" by a husband who took her back to his native Sicily, and her creation of a successful business in Rome. However, as her memoir's title alone attests, Adrienne is an imaginative writer, with a command of literary technique and the ability not only to distance herself from her story but to manipulate language – not, please note, her native language – in order to tell it vividly.

Since Italian is not one of my working languages, I did the translation in two stages, the first of which was to run her Italian original through a commercial translation software called Systran. That took her vivid, swirling first paragraphs:

Gli ultimi abbracci, gli ultimi baci, e tante raccomandazioni e
finalmente il treno si mosse.
Con un grande sospiro mi appoggio allo schienale e mi abbandono
ai miei pensieri. Finalmente! Il viaggio lungamente sognato,
accuratamente preparato ebbe il suo inizio. Eccomi qua: un sogno
che stava per diventare realtà.

and turned them into a fine example of "machinetranslation-ese":

> the last ones it embraces, the last kisses, and many recommendations
> and finally the train movements.
> With a great sigh me support to the back and abandons to me to
> my thoughts. Finally! The long dreammed travel, accurately pre-
> pared had its beginning. Eccomi here: a dream that was in order to
> become truth.

Not yet English, but very helpful. This is the final result:

> Last hugs, last kisses, so many best wishes and bits of advice,
> and the train is on its way, at last.
> With a deep sigh, I settle into my seat and abandon myself to my
> thoughts. Finally! This trip, long hoped for, painstakingly prepared,
> is at last beginning. A dream becoming real.

The finished translation is very close to the original; by leaving it so, and not smoothing it out into more standard English as I did with Gaby, I tried to retain more of Adrienne's unique voice. To me (and according to relatives who are native Italian speakers), that voice is both very Italian and distinctly foreign. This is a matter of content as well as style. In contrast to Gaby's matter-of-fact style and bare-bones reporting of content, Adrienne's storytelling is both emotional and artful, and her memoir shared some of the most intimate and painful details of her life:

> My water breaks, everyone panics, the doctor arrives – the first
> woman from this province to qualify in medicine. She examines me:
> "The baby will be born dead, and it's better if you are prepared for
> it," she says. Over and over I say NO: you will be born alive!
> They make me lie down on a kitchen table, with my legs settled
> on two chairs. Four women dressed in black hold my arms and legs,
> my uterus won't open, it needs forceps to dilate it. Will I ever forget
> that pain?
> Suddenly a scream. The baby is coming out feet-first, with the umbili-
> cal cord around its neck. No hope is left: the women pray, invoking
> the saints in an unknown language, and every now and then

screaming in Sicilian dialect that I can barely understand,
Sta morendo, sta morendo!
Who is dying? Me? The baby? I feel nothing but pain and fear,
so much fear.

I hope that doesn't sound like a native English speaker, but like someone from somewhere else who speaks English confidently and well; not incorrectly but with an "accent." The foreignizing had its limits, though. In some places, the original seemed almost operatic when translated closely, and I toned it down in order to avoid sounding overwrought and false. But in others, it seemed right to emulate the way Adrienne speaks English – a more-than-fluent immigranto.

The differences between Gaby and Adrienne's voices brought up another issue. Translators often have to decide whether to "help" a text in places where the intended readers may not have sufficient background information to fully understand a text. The young people who read my great-aunts' memoirs today are well educated, but they cannot be expected to know a great deal about European politics in the first half of the 20th century, or the cultural landscape in the different countries where Gaby and Adrienne alighted. In Gaby's case, it didn't hurt the text at all for me to insert – with her permission – a few words or even sentences of historical background here and there. My doing so remains invisible to the reader. With Adrienne, I had to resort to footnotes in order not to impede her narrative flow or break up carefully written sentences, and thus made myself visible as someone at work between the writer and the reader.

WHY WE CONTINUE TRANSLATING

Some translators sound almost apologetic for their work, yet simultaneously feel it is an important and positive part of who they are. This example comes from Howard Goldblatt, Research Professor of Chinese at the University of Notre Dame in the United States, who has translated novels and short stories by a wide range of writers from China, Taiwan, and Hong Kong (Goldblatt 2002).

Translators may well agree with George Steiner's observation that "Ninety percent of all translation is inadequate," but only as an acknowledgment that, once threshed into a different language, a piece of writing is transformed, changed, not as a measure of the quality of our work. Translation is inadequate, but it's all we have if good writing is to have its life extended, spatially and temporally.

Translation is, of course, an unfinished project, while an original work is frozen in time at the moment of publication. Unlike musical compositions or dramas, however, novels and poems are not written to be re-performed or re-created; they are, in a sense, irreplaceable. That we must nonetheless replace them, if the works are to have wider readership, is a given. How translators go about the task, how we deal with the intricacies of cross-cultural communication – these are the things at issue.

Some languages can resist adequate translation – the words are simply unavailable or inefficient – while other languages may provide richer choices. In a novel I recently co-translated with Sylvia Li-chun Lin – *Red Poppies*, by the ethnic Tibetan Alai – a mild oath used by all characters is "Tian na!" The closest literal (and obviously inadequate) English rendering is "Heavens!" After wrestling with several possibilities, we decided to have each character say something different, in languages that – for each context – worked better than English. We used "Ay caramba!" "Ach du Lieber!" "Mamma mia!" "Oy gevalt!" and, even, "Merde!" Alas, we couldn't get them past the editor. Damn!

... I am sometimes asked why I translate, since to many it seems a thankless vocation. Why, they ask, don't I write my own novels, since I have lived (they assume) an interesting life and must by now have an idea of what a novel should be? I can only say that not all translators are closet novelists, and that I do not consider translation to be a lesser art – one that ought to lead to something better. The short, and very personal, answer to the question is: Because I love it. I love to read Chinese; I love to write in English. I love the challenge, the ambiguity, the uncertainty of the enterprise. I love the tension between creativity and fidelity, even the inevitable compromises. And, every once in a while, I find a work so exciting that I'm possessed by the urge to put it into English. In other words, I translate to stay alive. The satisfaction of knowing I've faithfully served two constituencies keeps me happily turning good, bad, and indifferent Chinese prose into readable, accessible, and – yes – even marketable English books. Tian na!

A LOVE AFFAIR

Great literary translators are necessarily people who love language, and often write beautifully in their "own" voice. Take Barbara Reynolds, probably best known as a translator of Dante and of Ludovico Ariosto's epic poem *Orlando Furioso*. In her contribution to *The Translator's Art*, a book to commemorate the longtime Penguin Classics editor Betty Radice, Reynolds displays not only grace and erudition but also a keen awareness of modern fashion – how many scholars born in 1914 would comment favourably on punk fashion (Reynolds 1987)?

Sometimes I had to spend several days on a stanza before I could get it right. But the solution was there all the time, in among the resources of English, which is so much vaster than any one individual's command of it. It is awe-inspiring to experience a sudden disclosure of its possibilities. My most exciting moment occurred in canto XIV, stanzas 83–4. Ariosto here introduces one of his few allegorical figures, Discord. In stanza 83 she is described as being a rag-bag of tatters and conflicting colours:

> *La conobbe al vestir di color cento,*
> *fatto a liste inequali et infinite,*
> *ch'or la coprono or no; che i passi e 'l vento*
> *le gíano aprendo, ch'erano sdrucite.*
> *I crini avea qual d'oro equal d'argento,*
> *e neri e bigi, e aver pareano lite;*
> *altri in treccia, altri in nastro eran raccolti,*
> *molti alle spalle, alcuni al petto sciolti.*

> He knew her by her multicoloured dress,
> Made of unequal lengths, one up, one down,
> Which sometimes covered her, now more, now less,
> As the wind blew her tattered, unstitched gown.
> Her hair, one tress of which was gold, one tress
> Was silver, and another black, or brown,
> Was looped in ribbons, or else tightly plaited,
> Or hung about her shoulders, loose and matted.

After this startlingly prophetic picture of punk comes the idea of legal disputation. Discord is hung about with documents, like a personification of the Circumlocution Office or the Court of Chancery. A key word caught

my eye in the original: *chiose* – glosses. Feeling bold, I put it in the rhyme
position. What would rhyme with it that was relevant to the context? The
documents were stuck all over with seals: very well – "seals and bosses":

> Her hands were full of legal documents,
> Bundles of charters, hung with seals and bosses,
> Counsels' opinions, summonses for rents, Verbatim records,
> affidavits, glosses,
> Powers of attorney, deeds and instruments,
> ?   ?   ?
> Ready at hand, to illustrate the code,
> A group of notaries about her strode.

The sixth line eluded me. The meaning to be provided was that poor men
were the victims of all this. For hours I twisted the idea round and round,
juggling the Italian words against the English. I thought I might have to give
up the rhyme in -osses and begin again. Suddenly, without conscious effort
on my part, a line dropped into place, like a string of beads into a groove:

> Which lawyers' pockets line with poor men's losses.

I could hardly believe my luck. The meaning was right, the rhyme was relevant, the stresses were perfect, there was even a touch of alliteration and
the whole line had a proverbial ring. If I hadn't persevered I should never
have found it. The exhilaration was so great I was obliged to go out into the
garden and run and leap about. I could do no more work for hours. I was
rejoicing, not in my own cleverness, but in the English language.

THE HUNTING OF THE SMIRK

Peter Newmark, who is both a translator and teacher of translation, describes the
pleasure that the activity can give (Newmark 1987):

> There is an exceptional attraction in the search for the right word, just out
> of reach, the semantic gap between two languages that one scours Roget
> to fill. The relief of finding it, the "smirk" after hitting on the right word
> when others are still floundering, is an acute reward, out of proportion
> and out of perspective to the satisfaction of filling in the whole picture,
> but more concrete. The quality of pleasure reflects the constant tension
> between sentence and word.

Newmark gives an example of a smirk-in-the-making when he comes across an obscure word in a text he is translating (Newmark 1993):

> *Acribie* in a French text? (*Pourquoi le critiquer avec la même acribie?*) I knew the word, I had seen it before, I knew it meant "meticulousness," "finicky detail," "overscrupulous accuracy." I failed to find it in French, English, Italian, Spanish dictionaries, not even the Webster. I considered various spellings and misspellings. Then I found it, there it was in the German dictionaries, as *Akribie, akribisch*, even in the new good Penguin. What a relief.
>
> The word derives from Greek *akribeia* – acro = tip, top, a point, cf. acronym, acropolis. (Etymology or other associations are the best way to remember (internalise) the form or meaning of any word.)
>
> And it's a lovely expressive word: the *kr* is relentless (scrupulous, critical, cribbing), the repeated *i* is sharp, spitting (*sang craché* – "spat out blood" – see Rimbaud's *Les Voyelles*), finicky, acrimonious.

· ·

I very much hope that Chekhov is an even greater writer in Russian than he is in French or English...

— MICHEL TREMBLAY in an interview with Alexander Craig (Craig 1993)

THE COMPOSING OF THE SNARK

Sir Richard Burton, so used to exploring the wilder shores of geography and culture, didn't feel he had to limit himself to English already "on the map." In the preface to his version of *The Thousand and One Nights*, he vaunts his lexicographic fearlessness and denigrates the less adventurous translations of his predecessors (Burton 1885).

> Moreover, holding that the translator's glory is to add something to his native tongue, while avoiding the hideous hag-like nakedness of Torrens and the bald literalism of Lane, I have carefully Englished the picturesque turns and novel expressions of the original in all their outlandishness; for instance, when the dust-cloud raised by a tramping host is described as "walling the horizon." Hence peculiar attention has been paid to the tropes and figures which the Arabic language often packs into a single term; and

I have never hesitated to coin a word when wanted, such as "she snorted
and snarked," fully to represent the original.

MANUSCRIPT LOST

As well as its pleasures, translation has its stories of pain and frustration. The novelist Paul Auster made his living as a translator for many years. In 1998, his translation of Pierre Clastres's *Chronique des indiens Guayaki* was published as *Chronicle of the
Guayaki Indians* – almost twenty years after he had completed the translation. The
following is the Translator's Note from the beginning of the book (Clastres and
Auster 1998).

This is one of the saddest stories I know. If not for a minor miracle that
occurred twenty years after the fact, I doubt that I would have been able to
summon the courage to tell it.

It begins in 1972, I was living in Paris at the time, and because of my
friendship with the poet Jacques Dupin (whose work I had translated), I was
a faithful reader of *L'Ephémère,* a literary magazine financed by the Galerie
Maeght. Jacques was a member of the editorial board – along with Yves
Bonnefoy, Andre du Bouchet, Michel Leiris, and, until his death in 1970,
Paul Celan. The magazine came out four times a year, and with a group
like that responsible for its contents, the work published in *L'Ephémère* was
always of the highest quality.

The twentieth and final issue appeared in the spring, and among the
usual contributions from well-known poets and writers, there was an essay
by an anthropologist named Pierre Clastres entitled "De l'Un sans le multiple" (Of the one without the many). Just seven pages long, it made an
immediate and lasting impression on me. Not only was the piece intelligent, provocative, and tightly argued, it was beautifully written. Clastres's
prose seemed to combine a poet's temperament with a philosopher's depth
of mind, and I was moved by its directness and humanity, its utter lack of
pretension. On the strength of those seven pages, I realized that I had discovered a writer whose work I would be following for a long time to come.

When I asked Jacques who this person was, he explained that Clastres
had studied with Claude Lévi-Strauss, was still under forty, and was considered to be the most promising member of the new generation of anthro-
pologists in France. He had done his fieldwork in the jungles of South

America, living among the most primitive Stone Age tribes in Paraguay and Venezuela, and a book about those experiences was about to be published. When *Chronique des indiens Guayaki* appeared a short time later, I went out and bought myself a copy.

It is, I believe, nearly impossible not to love this book. The care and patience with which it is written, the incisiveness of its observations, its humor, its intellectual rigor, its compassion – all these qualities reinforce one another to make it an important, memorable work. The *Chronicle* is not some dry academic study of "life among the savages," not some report from an alien world in which the reporter neglects to take his own presence into account. It is the true story of a man's experiences, and it asks nothing but the most essential questions: how is information communicated to an anthropologist, what kinds of transactions take place between one culture and another, under what circumstances might secrets be kept? In delineating this unknown civilization for us, Clastres writes with the cunning of a good novelist. His attention to detail is scrupulous and exacting; his ability to synthesize his thoughts into bold, coherent statements is often breathtaking. He is that rare scholar who does not hesitate to write in the first person, and the result is not just a portrait of the people he is studying, but a portrait of himself.

I moved back to New York in the summer of 1974, and for several years after that I tried to earn my living as a translator. It was a difficult struggle, and most of the time I was barely able to keep my head above water. Because I had to take whatever I could get, I often found myself accepting assignments to work on books that had little or no value. I wanted to translate good books, to be involved in projects that felt worthy, that would do more than just put bread on the table. *Chronicle of the Guayaki Indians* was at the top of my list, and again and again I proposed it to the various American publishers I worked for. After countless rejections, I finally found someone who was interested. I can't remember exactly when this was. Late 1975 or early 1976, I think, but I could be off by half a year or so. In any case, the publishing company was new, just getting off the ground, and all the preliminary indications looked good. Excellent editors, contracts for a number of outstanding books, a willingness to take risks. Not long before that, Clastres and I had begun exchanging letters, and when I wrote to tell him the news, he was just as thrilled as I was.

Translating the *Chronicle* was a thoroughly enjoyable experience for me, and after my labors were done, my attachment to the book was just as ardent as ever. I turned in the manuscript to the publisher, the translation was approved, and then, just when everything seemed to have been brought to a successful conclusion, the troubles started.

It seems that the publishing company was not as solvent as the world had been led to believe. Even worse, the publisher himself was a good deal less honest in his handling of money than he should have been. I know this for a fact because the money that was supposed to pay for my translation had been covered by a grant to the company by the CNRS (the French National Scientific Research Center), but when I asked for my money, the publisher hemmed and hawed and promised that I would have it in due course. The only explanation was that he had already spent the funds on something else.

I was desperately poor in those days, and waiting to be paid simply wasn't an option for me. It was the difference between eating and not eating, between paying the rent and not paying the rent. I called the publisher every day for the next several weeks, but he kept putting me off, kept coming up with different excuses. At last, unable to hold out any longer, I went to the office in person and demanded that he pay me on the spot. He started in with another excuse, but this time I held my ground and declared that I wouldn't leave until he had written out a check to me for the full amount. I don't think I went so far as to threaten him, but I might have. I was boiling with anger, and I can remember thinking that if all else failed, I was prepared to punch him in the face. It never came to that, but what I did do was back him into a corner, and at that moment I could see that he was beginning to grow scared. He finally understood that I meant business. And right then and there, he opened the drawer of his desk, pulled out his checkbook, and gave me my money.

In retrospect, I consider this to be one of my lowest moments, a dismal chapter in my career as a human being, and I am not at all proud of how I acted. But I was broke, and I had done the work, and I deserved to be paid. To prove how hard up I was during those years, I will mention just one appalling fact. I never made a copy of the manuscript. I couldn't afford to xerox the translation, and since I assumed it was in safe hands, the only copy in the world was the original typescript sitting in the publisher's office. This fact, this stupid oversight, this poverty-stricken way of doing business would come back to haunt me. It was entirely my fault, and it turned a small misfortune into a full-blown disaster.

For the time being, however, we seemed to be back on track.

Once the unpleasantness about my fee was settled, the publisher behaved as if he had every intention of bringing out the book. The manuscript was sent to a typesetter, I corrected the proofs and returned them to the publisher – again neglecting to make a copy. It hardly seemed important, after all, since production was well under way by now. The book had been announced in the catalogue, and publication was set for the winter of 1977–78.

Then, just months before *Chronicle of the Guayaki Indians* was supposed to appear, news came that Pierre Clastres had been killed in a car accident. According to the story I was told, he had been driving somewhere in France when he lost control of the wheel and skidded over the edge of a mountain. We had never met. Given that he was only forty-three when he died, I had assumed there would be ample opportunities for that in the future. We had written a number of letters to each other, had become friends through our correspondence, and were looking forward to the time when we would at last be able to sit down together and talk. The strangeness and unpredictability of the world prevented that conversation from taking place. Even now, all these years later, I still feel it as a great loss.

Nineteen seventy-eight came and went, and *Chronicle of the Guayaki Indians* did not appear. Another year slipped by, and then another year, and still there was no book.

By 1981, the publishing company was on its last legs. The editor I had originally worked with was long gone, and it was difficult for me to find out any information. That year, or perhaps the year after that, or perhaps even the year after that (it all blurs in my mind now), the company finally went under. Someone called to tell me that the rights to the book had been sold to another publisher. I called that publisher, and they told me, yes, they were planning to bring out the book. Another year went by, and nothing happened. I called again, and the person I had talked to the previous year no longer worked for the company. I talked to someone else, and that person told me that the company had no plans to publish *Chronicle of the Guayaki Indians.* I asked for the manuscript back, but no one could find it. No one had even heard of it. For all intents and purposes, it was as if the translation had never existed.

For the next dozen years, that was where the matter stood.

Pierre Clastres was dead, my translation had disappeared, and the entire project had collapsed into a black hole of oblivion. This past summer (1996), I finished writing a book entitled *Hand to Mouth,* an autobiographical essay about money. I was planning to include this story in the narrative (because of my failure to make a copy of the manuscript, because of the scene with the publisher in his office), but when the moment came to tell it, I lost heart and couldn't bring myself to put the words down on paper. It was all too sad, I felt, and I couldn't see any purpose in recounting such a bleak, miserable saga.

Then, two or three months after I finished my book, something extraordinary happened. About a year before, I had accepted an invitation to go to San Francisco to appear in the City Arts and Lectures Series at the Herbst Theatre. The event was scheduled for October 1996, and when the moment came, I climbed onto a plane and flew to San Francisco as promised. After my business onstage was finished, I was supposed to sit in the lobby and sign copies of my books. The Herbst is a large theater with many seats, and the line in the lobby was therefore quite long. Among all those people waiting for the dubious privilege of having me write my name in one of my novels, there was someone I recognized – a young man I had met once before, the friend of a friend. This young man happens to be a passionate collector of books, a bloodhound for first editions and rare, out-of-the-way items, the kind of bibliographic detective who will think nothing of spending an afternoon in a dusty cellar sifting through boxes of discarded books in the hope of finding one small treasure. He smiled, shook my hand, and then thrust a set of bound galleys at me. It had a red paper cover, and until that moment, I had never seen a copy of it before. "What's this?" he said. "I never heard of it." And there it was, suddenly sitting in my hands: the uncorrected proofs of my long-lost translation. In the big scheme of things, this probably wasn't such an astonishing event. For me, however, in my own little scheme of things, it was overwhelming. My hands started to tremble as I held the book. I was so stunned, so confused, that I was scarcely able to speak. The proofs had been found in a remainder bin at a secondhand bookstore, and the young man had paid five dollars for them.

As I look at them now, I note with a certain grim fascination that the pub date announced on the cover is April 1981. For a translation completed in 1976 or 1977, it was, truly, an agonizingly slow ordeal.

If Pierre Clastres were alive today, the discovery of this lost book would be a perfect happy ending. But he isn't alive, and the brief surge of joy and incredulity I experienced in the atrium of the Herbst Theatre has by now dissipated into a deep, mournful ache. How rotten that the world should pull such tricks on us. How rotten that a person with so much to offer the world should die so young.

Here, then, is my translation of Pierre Clastres's book, *Chronicle of the Guayaki Indians.* No matter that the world described in it has long since vanished, that the tiny group of people the author lived with in 1963 and 1964 has disappeared from the face of the earth. No matter that the author has vanished as well. The book he wrote is still with us, and the fact that you are holding that book in your hands now, dear reader, is nothing less than a victory, a small triumph against the crushing odds of fate. At least there is that to be thankful for. At least there is consolation in the thought that Pierre Clastres's book has survived.

THE GIFT OF LANGUAGE

And when a translator finally shuffles off Hamlet's mortal coil, what does she or he leave behind? The impact of some translators goes well beyond their own individual translations; some have enabled new areas of scientific discovery, or opened up entire literary traditions to new audiences. Translators who are teachers as well as practitioners leave a special kind of legacy, not just to individual students but to the profession itself – and on both sides of the language barrier they have worked to cross.

The following passage shows that rendering homage across cultures can have its own translation challenges, as Paula Richman and the late Norman Cutler showed in "Gift of Tamil: On Compiling an Anthology of Translations from Tamil Literature" (Richman and Cutler 1995). The object of their homage, K. Paramasivam, was professor of Tamil literature at Madurai, Southern India, and a mentor to a generation of Western students and scholars who studied and translated from Tamil. He was also a translator himself, having published Tamil versions of Western novels by authors such as Jane Austen, Emily Brontë, Charles Dickens, and Sir Walter Scott. The efforts by his admirers to celebrate his work appropriately seem remarkably similar to the process of translation.

Late in 1990 we learned that Professor K. Paramasivam was dying of cancer. K.P., as we all knew him, had been our teacher during the early rears of our study of Tamil, a language spoken by more than fifty million people, primarily in South India. Over the years, K.P. had been a tremendous source of advice and knowledge about Tamil literature. We and his many other former students and colleagues realized the enormous impact he had had upon two generations of American scholars of Tamil. We decided that, in his honor, we would compile and present to him an anthology of translations from Tamil literature into English. In the course of compiling the volume, we encountered a number of seemingly intractable problems. Although some of these problems were technical in nature, it became apparent over time that many of them were political in origin, insofar as they involved delicate negotiations between and across cultures, negotiations concerning definitions of bodies of knowledge, and the appropriateness of various modes of translation. The process of creating this book involved "cultural commuting" of several different kinds.

Whenever one compiles an anthology of translations, difficult decisions must be made. In retrospect, we see that our decisions involved three kinds of negotiations. First, because the project originated in response to a specific situation in the life of K.P., the selection of our contributors and our timetable for the project were shaped by contingent factors. We were determined that K.P. receive this volume before he left us; the contributors were all students or colleagues of K.P. Second, we were maneuvering within a complex literary tradition that had been self-critical about its own verbal art for hundreds of years. One of the oldest regional literatures from the Indian subcontinent, Tamil literature is known for the beauty of its classical love poetry and heroic poetry, the variety of its religious texts, and the existence of a sophisticated and self-commentarial tradition. Certain decisions regarding selection of and categorization of translations involved negotiations between competing notions of what comprises "Tamil literature." Third, certain decisions involved the particular and dual-faceted nature of our intended readership. We were compiling an anthology of literature from the "Third World" for readers located *both* in India and in the United States...

The conception for the volume emerged in response to two different cultural models for honoring a teacher or scholar. Initially we sought to create a volume in the form of a European-style festschrift, a compilation of scholarly essays by contributors who have all studied with a particular teacher. We also considered another model, the Indian felicitation volume presented to celebrate the sixtieth birthday of a prominent professor by students and admirers. Yet neither model was entirely satisfactory... The idea of creating an anthology of translations from Tamil literature into English occurred to us. It struck us as an appropriate way to honour K.P. Paramasivam because it would create a volume symbolic of his extensive involvement with projects of translation...

In light of this transformative process our anthology can be described as an innovation; however, the book was received in a very traditional fashion – on the occasion of a book-releasing ceremony. Initially, we assumed that our goal of honoring K.P. would be met when we completed the volume. But our conversations with Tamil friends and colleagues indicated that, according to the norms of traditional Tamil "book" culture, the volume, once complete, should be "released" in an appropriately coded ritual. Although we both had editorial experience which assisted us in compiling the anthology of translations, neither of us had the specialized knowledge needed to plan this particular event. In attempting to construct the symbolism and structure of the book-releasing ceremony, we once again found ourselves trying to bridge two cultural worlds while trying to be sensitive to the constraints of each.

Essentially, the book-releasing ceremony is one among a series of celebratory events, often referred to as "functions" in contemporary South Asian culture. There are marriage functions, betrothal functions, first haircut functions, sacred thread investiture functions, retirement functions, opening of a new concert hall functions, first classical dance recital functions. The list is long. A function generally includes a core of fairly standard key ceremonies that can be condensed or elongated, ceremonies geared to the symbolic significance of the event.

In a book-releasing function, a prominent person presents the first copy of the book to another prominent person while an audience of well-wishers observes. Although our project did not exactly fit into the pattern of a function for a teacher's sixtieth birthday (as mentioned earlier), some nuances of that kind of function seemed to color the celebration as well. In addition, there was an award for distinguished service presented by a representative of the International Studies Office at the University of Wisconsin-Madison. Such an addition also gave the ceremony something of the tenor of an American academic honors or award assembly. Because the final ceremony contained elements of all three kinds of events, it possessed a hybrid cultural content and tone.

Initially we envisioned a simple ceremony for a few people held in the building where K.P. taught Tamil, followed by some tea and snacks, but Tamil friends insisted that proper procedure called for a far more elaborate and formal event than we had planned. The ceremony that finally occurred was structured according to elaborate social and ritual practices. The event took place in a high status hotel, multicolored invitations were sent, more than one hundred and thirty guests attended, and a company that specializes in weddings videotaped the entire affair...

We had assumed that the ceremony would focus upon honoring a single individual, but it ended up celebrating the achievements of K.P.'s employer as well as his place of residence, Madurai... Just as the ceremony was less exclusively oriented to K.P. than we had expected, it was also more hierarchical. The determination of who received honour focused to a large extent on the group of people permitted to sit on the dais, a raised platform at the front of the hall. Those qualified to sit on the dais were restricted to the presider, the book releaser, the chief guest who receives the first copy (the president of AIIS [American Institute of Indian Studies, the academic institution that employed K.P. as a Tamil teacher for the last fourteen years]), the master of ceremonies, K.P., his wife, and the editors of the book. Other people – a colleague from the college where K.P. had taught who gave a speech about K.P. as a teacher, the student who presented a velvet purse of money, and the person who proposed a vote of thanks – all sat in the audience and mounted the dais when it was time to perform their prescribed role. The people on the dais received brightly colored garlands made of high-quality silk and a greater share of the honor than those who merely sat in the audience.

The core of the event was two ritual sequences. First the book needed to be officially "released," that is, unwrapped and presented to the chief guest. At first this ritual seemed puzzling to us because it directed attention away from K.P., for whom the ceremony was being held, and toward the book-releaser and chief guest. Eventually it became clear that the prominence of each of these two people was critical: the status of the person to be honored was enhanced by the status of the chief guest and book-releaser. Second came the felicitation. K.P., his wife, the presider, and the editors each received a shawl, a gift traditionally given to indicate respect for the wearer and to bestow prestige upon him or her. The culminating vote of thanks expressed gratitude toward everyone who had anything to do with the project, including the proofreader, the person who typed the manuscript, the publisher, the manager of the hotel, and all the guests who attended. Clearly a link between the book and this wider community had been established by the ceremony...

In comparison to the book-releasing ceremony in Madurai, the introduction of the book to the U.S. market was rather dull. It appeared first at a book exhibit at the Association of Asian Studies meeting in Washington, D.C., three months after its appearance in India, having survived the long trip by sea mail. But there it was just one among a number of books on Indian literature, politics, religion, art, economics, and other topics, lying on a table while convention-goers perused the books in the booths.

During the several months when we were busy with the time-consuming arrangements for the book-releasing ceremony, we viewed the ceremony at times as a weighty and burdensome addition to the task of completing the anthology of translations, an addition loaded with excessive ceremony and sentimentality. To our surprise, however, we found the event to be a deeply moving tribute to a Tamil scholar about whom all involved cared a great deal, as well as a meaningful way to send the anthology of translations out into the world. The ceremony showered K.P. with honor, and when, a few days later, he was released from this world and his physical pain, he died an appreciated man. In the end the final product, the anthology compiled in his honor, seemed to justify the delicate and complex cultural negotiations involved.

CHAPTER THREE

Betray, domesticate, or negotiate? The process

Writing is to translation what being a father is to being a grandfather.
— PRIMO LEVI to interviewer Giovanni Tesio in *Nuova Società* (Tesio 1983)

Even without getting deep into translation theory (see chapter 9), every translator soon bumps up against contradictions that are built into the business of transferring meaning between languages. Take for example the contradiction visible in paragraphs 4 and 5 of the Translator's Charter (International Federation of Translators 1994):

4. Every translation shall be faithful and render exactly the idea and form of the original – this fidelity constituting both a moral and legal obligation for the translator.

5. A faithful translation, however, should not be confused with a literal translation, the fidelity of a translation not excluding an adaptation to make the form, the atmosphere and deeper meaning of the work felt in another language and country.

So. On the one hand you have to "render exactly" and on the other hand you have to avoid literal translation in order to communicate "form, the atmosphere and deeper meaning." How to begin?

FIRST, YOU READ THE SOURCE TEXT...
Andrew Fenner gives some basic advice for tackling any translation job (Fenner 1989). Written barely two decades ago, the piece is irretrievably dated by the words "If you have a word processor." It is hard to imagine a working translator who hasn't.

Let's assume that you have now got to the point where you have the source language text in front of you and are ready to start translating. If you have a word processor, you can type onto the screen right from the start; if not, you will first need to make a rough draft and then type it up when you have the final corrected version. Remember that nothing is right first time.

The first stage, if you have the time, is to read the document right through to get an overall idea of what it is about, the key words and concepts involved and the overall tone. (You should also be considering the audience for whom it is intended: this will affect the register, i.e. the style, which may be formal, colloquial, bureaucratic, legalistic, etc.)

On the first reading of a text, you will almost inevitably come across places where you are either unsure of the exact meaning or a number of possibilities suggest themselves and you do not yet know which one to select. There are two ways of dealing with this: either leave a gap and let your subconscious mull over the problem or put down anything you can think of, even if it sounds nonsensical at the time. It is surprising how something that sounds absolutely meaningless the first time round will make sense when you come back to it after studying the rest of the text. I put anything I am not sure about in square brackets so that I will know that there is a query at that point the next time around.

Once you have finished the raw draft, leave it alone for as long as possible, preferably at least a day. If there is not plenty of time, take a break or do anything which will clear your brain. Translation problems are like wild animals: the answers tend to lurk in the undergrowth of your brain, and only come out when they think no-one is looking. When you feel ready, or when time is up, go back for the first edit.

When doing the first edit, read through the original text in parallel with the translation and make a small tick in pencil against each paragraph or item to ensure that you have actually translated it. It is all too easy to miss small items out, or even tack the end of one paragraph onto the end of another, especially if time is short. The less time you have, the more you should assume that things are likely to go wrong. Check that the translation is at least reasonably close to the original; check that your spelling is correct (especially if using a word processor!); and if there is anything in the original which has no exact equivalent in the target language, think of some possible alternatives, but do not commit yourself finally as yet. Make a note of any inaccuracies or inconsistencies you find (or believe you have found) in the original, e.g. *"No section 1.4.1.1," "contradicts statement on page xx,"* etc. These must be pointed out to the client if you are to avoid liability for any results of misreading the text.

Make a note, too, of anything that seems ambiguous or difficult to understand. It is possible to write any amount of rubbish in one language (the phrase that will always stick in my mind is one from a document from an automotive engineering consultancy which read, "We have optimised procedures to an acceptable level..."); the real acid test of a document is when you try to translate it.

After another suitable lapse of time, you can then proceed to the second check. The process is repeated as many times as it takes until you are happy that you cannot improve the translation any further. (I usually try and make three checks.) Never make the final check on the same day as the second-to-last check (if time allows, of course). Especially with large documents, it may also be a good idea to have the final text read through by someone who only knows English (or whatever the target language is). It is very difficult to proof-read your own work, as it is difficult to be objective and decide where any problems exist.

SL TO TL: TEXTS PULLED IN TEN DIRECTIONS

Sounds simple enough. But even this basic advice brings up a few problems the translator will have to take into account, notably the appropriate register to adopt for a given readership. In his *Textbook of Translation*, Peter Newmark explains the factors that "pull" a text in different directions on its way to the target language (Newmark 1987).

In many types of text (legal, administrative, dialect, local, cultural) the temptation is to transfer as many SL (Source Language) words to the TL (Target Language) as possible. The pity is that the translation cannot simply reproduce, or be, the original. And since this is so, the first business of the translator is to translate. A text may therefore be pulled in ten different directions, as follows:

(1) The individual style or idiolect of the SL author. When should it be (a) preserved, (b) normalised?

(2) The conventional grammatical and lexical usage for this type of text, depending on the topic and the situation.

(3) Content items referring specifically to the SL, or third language (i.e. not SL or TL) cultures.

(4) The typical format of a text in a book, periodical, newspaper, etc., as influenced by tradition at the time.

(5) The expectations of the putative readership, bearing in mind their estimated knowledge of the topic and the style of language they use, expressed in terms of the largest common factor, since one should not translate down (or up) to the readership.

(6), (7), (8) As for 2, 3 and 4 respectively, but related to the TL.

(9) What is being described or reported, ascertained or verified (the referential truth), where possible independently of the SL text and the expectations of the readership.

(10) The views and prejudices of the translator, which may be personal and subjective, or may be social and cultural, involving the translator's "group loyalty factor," which may reflect the national, political, ethnic, religious, social class, sex, etc. assumptions of the translator.

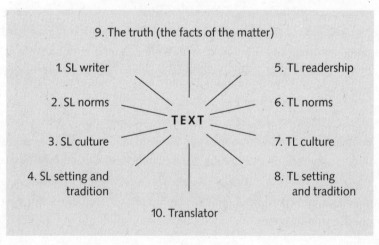

Figure 1: The dynamics of translation

"MAYBE" ON THURSDAY, "PERHAPS" ON FRIDAY

That's the schematic from the user manual – how does the job look in practice? The answer is: messy, though sometimes gloriously so. Here the literary translator William Weaver provides a close-up look at what he actually does when he tackles a new text (Weaver 1989). The text was originally published in Biguenet and Schulte's *The Craft of Translation*, which presents nine essays by some of the most famous literary translators working into English.

In the pages that follow I have tried to fix on paper the stages of an elusive process: the translation of an Italian text into English. For the operation I have chosen also an elusive author, Carlo Emilio Gadda, partly because his work is not well known to English-language readers, but mostly because he is an author I am particularly fond of and enjoy translating. I have settled on the first paragraph of "Notte di luna," the opening chapter (or story, as Gadda would have us believe) in the volume *L'Adalgisa*, originally published in 1944. I have used the Einaudi edition of 1963.

I need hardly say that the description that follows is partial, perhaps even somewhat misleading, because I have tried to make conscious and logical something that is, most of the time, unconconscious, instinctive. Faced with a choice between "perhaps" and "maybe," the translator does not put the words on trial and engage attorneys to defend and accuse. Most probably, he hears the words in some corner of his mind, and likes the sound of one better than the other. Of course, his decision is only apparently instinctive. His instinct will be guided by his knowledge of the author's work, by his reading in the period. It will almost certainly not be guided by any rules, even self-made ones. On Thursday, translating Moravia, he may write "maybe," and on Friday, translating Manzoni, he may write "perhaps."

Because there are no rules, no laws, there cannot be an absolute right or an absolute wrong. There can be errors (and even the most experienced translator has an occasional mishap); there can be lapses in tone. The worst mistake a translator can commit is to reassure himself by saying, "that's what it says in the original," and renouncing the struggle to do his best. The words of the original are only the starting point; a translator must do more than convey information (a literary translator, that is).

If someone asks me how I translate, I am hard put to find an answer. I can describe the physical process: I make a very rapid first draft, put it aside for a while, then go over it at a painfully slow pace, pencil – and eraser – in hand. But that is all outside. Inside, the job is infinitely complex, and what's more, it varies from one author to another. I wish I could describe the thrilling tingle I feel when something seems, finally, to have come right. I prefer not to dwell on the sinking sensation felt when it is obvious that something is dreadfully wrong.

Here, in Italian, is the Gadda paragraph:

> Un'idea, un'idea non sovviene, alla fatica de' cantieri, mentre i sibilanti congegni degli atti trasformano in cose le cose e il lavoro è pieno di sudore e di polvere. Poi ori lontanissimi e uno zaffiro, nel cielo: come cigli, a tremare sopra misericorde sguardo. Quello che, se poseremo, ancora vigilerà. I battiti della vita sembra che uno sgomento li travolga come in una corsa precípite. Ci ha detersi la carità della sera: e dove alcuno aspetta moviamo: perché nostra ventura abbia corso, e nessuno la impedirà. Perché poi avremo a riposare.

And here (without any subsequent cosmesis) is the absolutely first draft of the translation, complete with doubts, alternative solutions, puzzlements. This is the raw material:

> An idea, an idea does not (recall/sustain/aid/repair, in the labor of the building sites, as the hissing devices/machinery of actions transform things into things and the labor/toil is full of sweat and dust. Then distant gold(s) and a sapphire, in the sky: like lashes, trembling above compassionate/merciful/charitable gaze. Which, if we cast it, will still keep watch/be wakeful/alert. The pulses/throbbing of life, it seems, can be overwhelmed/swept away by an alarm, as if in a (precipitous race/dash. The charity of the evening has cleansed us (We are cleansed by the... : and where someone is waiting, we move: so that our fate/lot may proceed, and no one will block/impede/hinder it. Because then/afterwards/later we will rest/be able to rest/have our rest.

First thoughts: the passage contains several words I hate. *Cantiere* has to be translated "work site," I suppose, but the Italian word is simpler and more commonplace. Sometimes I translate *cantiere* simply as "job" (cf. *al cantiere* or *in cantiere* can be rendered "on the job"). But I don't think that will work in this case, also because I may have to use "job" immediately afterwards for *il lavoro*. *Sguardo*. Again, the almost obligatory translation is "gaze." But "gaze" is much more highfalutin than *sguardo*, which could also be "look." But "look" in English is too vague, can mean too many things. *Dacci uno sguardo*, can be "take a look," but when it is more isolated – as here – probably has to be "gaze." Another word that always seem to cause me problems is *sgomento*. As an adjective, it can sometimes be "aghast." But here it is a noun. "Alarm" does not satisfy me.

Gadda has appended two notes to this first paragraph. As usual, they do not explain much, but rather extend the sentence he is annotating. Here he is concerned that the *alcuno* remain sexually ambiguous. "Someone" will probably do perfectly well. Similarly, he glosses the *nessuno* in the same sentence: it refers to fathers, police, firemen – those who can enforce prohibitions. And he lists, among these, the governor of Maracaibo and tells of a youth who, flouting a veto, tore up his sheets, tied them to make a rope, and escaped from his room, to go off and join Garibaldi.

Notes to myself: avoid ironing out the rhythm, making the sentence structure more normal or conventional; do not try to clarify the meaning when Gadda has deliberately made it murky (translation is not exegesis); try to maintain Gadda's balance between ordinary words (*sudore, lavoro*, etc.) and more exotic words (*zaffiro, detersi*). Find a suitably poetic and cadenced solution to the final, short sentence of the paragraph.

Now a second draft: In the opening sentence, how to capture the force and poetry of the initial repetition? Literally translated ("An idea, an idea...", it sounds wrong to me. How about shifting the negative from the verb to the subject? "No idea, no idea..." Here the repetition sounds even worse. But perhaps, instead of repeating, I should simply enforce the noun. "No idea at all..." "Not the least idea..." "No, no idea..."

I like this last solution best, because it allows a repetition, even if not the same repetition as Gadda's. It is not the perfect solution, but in translating – and especially in translating Gadda – there are no perfect solutions. You simply do your best.

Sovviene means something like "come to the aid of." In my rapid first draft I even put down "recall" because it can also have the meaning, and, when reflexive, can mean "remember." But here it is the verb related to "subvention," not to "souvenir."

Fatica: "effort," but also "toil, labor." There must be a sense of expenditure of strength, a physical effort. *Atti* is more "deeds" than "actions." One of Gadda's quirkish choices (rather than *azioni*).

Now try the first sentence. "No, no idea brings relief to the labor of the work sites, as the sibilant instruments of action transforms things into other things, and the job is full of sweat and dust."

Sibilanti means "hissing," but I have rejected this in favor of "sibilant" as more Gaddian. It almost suggests speech. And after first translating *congegni* as "machinery," avoiding the dictionary translation ("devices," "apparatuses") I settle on "instruments," which seems to have more resonance. But then I omit the plural of *atti*. Why? It is hard to explain, but partly because I dislike two plurals in a row, and "instruments" has to remain plural. I have also added the word "other." Is this exegesis? I hope not. The more literal first translation sounds gibberish-y.

Next sentence. Another problem of plural. *Ori*. This is common Italian usage, often meaning something like "jewelry" or "treasure." The successful show of Scythian gold was called in Italy, *Gli ori degli sciti*, I believe. A husband will jokingly refer to his wife's jewelry as her *ori*. But this will not work in English, will it? We use the plural only in discussing painting ("The reds and golds in Beato [Fra] Angelico"), if then.

Other solution: add something like "streaks." "Streaks of gold" retains the plural; but no, too banal. But perhaps the *uno* before "sapphire" could be translated as "one," instead of being an indefinite article. *Uno/a* is often a problem in this sense. I'll try it: it may give the sentence a boost.

> Then distant gold and one sapphire, in the sky: like lashes quivering
> above a compassionate glance.

I discard the more literal "trembling," in favor of the less violent "quivering." And I decide on "compassionate" rather than "merciful," which, for me, is somehow too physical (perhaps I am influenced by my memory of the Corporal Works of Mercy, which I had to learn by heart in the second grade). "Charitable" will not do, because we have "charity" two sentences later.

Quello, beginning the next sentence, can be troublesome. In English, we don't like to begin sentences with a relative pronoun. Here the *poseremo* (of which *sguardo* is the object, and to which *quello* refers) is a pre-echo of the final word of the paragraph, *riposare*. This assonance will almost surely be lost in English.

Third sentence, then: "The one which, if we cast it, will still remain vigilant."

In the end I decided that *Quello che* has to be "The one which" or "That one which." I hate "cast" for *posare*, but what can I do? In English we cast a glance; the Italians "set" a glance. I decided, too, that the verb *vigilare* was best turned into a predicate and adjective. But, in a further revision, I may change my mind.

Battiti is tough. Heartbeats are called *battiti* in Italian, but Gadda obviously wants the word also to suggest the banging and pounding of the work site. "Pounding" will not do, because the "poundings of life" sounds like grievous bodily harm. "Throbbing" and "pulse" or "pulsation" rob the sentence of the work-site echo. The *sembra* is also awkward, coming in the middle of the sentence and rerouting its meaning. In a normal English sentence, the "It seems" would come at the beginning, and the sentence would flow smoothly, if boringly, thereafter.

Here's a stab at the sentence: "The beating of life, it seems, can be swept away by a sudden alarm as if in a headlong dash."

I know, "beating" could raise the same objection as "pounding," but – with luck – it may still suggest heartbeat to the reader, and it retains the sense of work at the site. The "it seems" separated necessarily by commas is a somewhat stronger interruption than the *sembra* in Italian, but I think it can stay. And I had to add "sudden" to "alarm" for *sgomento*, partly because the word "alarm" by itself is weak, and also because it could be mistaken for "alarm signal" or even for the work site's siren. I like "headlong," which gives the sense of speed and confusion. In the Italian, *corsa* ("race" or, here, "dash") pre-echoes *corso* in the next sentence. I cannot think of any way to avoid the loss here.

Next sentence: "The charity of the evening has cleansed us: and we move toward someone waiting, that our future may take its course, and no one shall hinder it."

In the first part of the sentence, I reject, of course, the passive. After the colon, I have to shift the Italian word order. "Toward someone waiting we move" sounds poetical in the bad sense. *Ventura* is another word I prefer not to encounter. It means "fortune," in the sense of "soldier of fortune" (*soldato di ventura*), or good luck (*sventura* is "bad luck"). But "fortune" seems too ambiguous in English, and "destiny" or "fate" or even "lot" would be too pretentious and perhaps also too specific.

The meaning of the final sentence is easy enough to understand. It is, more or less: "Because we will later be able to rest." But in the Italian it has an almost biblical ring, and the trick is to exalt the sentence without losing its simplicity, without making it pompous.

I will use the conjunction "for" instead of "because." It has, I believe, a King James version sound. I am tempted to use "shall find rest" or something of the sort, but then I decide it is too risky, too obvious a reference to the Beatitudes. In the end, perhaps simplicity is the best course, as it so often is.

I would say then: "For afterwards we can rest."

One bad loss here: the future tense of *avremo*. But "we shall rest" has a tinge of pompousness.

Now let's put all the sentences together:

> No, no idea brings relief to the labor of the work sites, as the sibilant
> instruments of action transform things into other things, and the
> toil is full of sweat and dirt. Then distant gold and a sapphire, in the
> sky: like lashes quivering above a compassionate glance. The glance
> which, if we cast it, will remain watchful. The beat of life, it seems,
> can be swept away by a shock, as if in a headlong dash. The charity
> of the evening has cleansed us: and we move toward the place where
> someone is waiting, that our future may unfold, and no one shall
> hinder it. For afterwards we can rest.

In copying out the separate sentences and combining them, I make some little changes. I decide that "toil" is better than "job," which can suggest more "task." I decide against "one" sapphire, after all; and prefer "watchful" to "vigilant" (too close to the Italian, a *faux ami?*). As I write out "beating," I realize that "beat" conveys the same meaning(s), and I can avoid the -ing, of which there are probably too many in this passage. "Shock" seems to do the work of "sudden alarm" and spares me the adjective. I amplify the *dove alcuno aspetta* clause: a little swell is permissible here, before the almost curt conclusion. Anyway, I have also condensed the clause by using "unfold" for "take its course."

Is that it? Is the translation finished? No. For most of my translating life, I have worked with living authors, and, at this stage, I would probably take my problems to their source, for further discussion, enlightenment, and – afterwards – revision. When I translated Gadda's novels *That Awful Mess on via Merulana* and *Acquainted with Grief* I would submit queries to him. Often, in his shy, but imposing manner, he would dismiss the problem, saying simply "cut that." Instead of obeying him, I would approach the tricky passage by another route, taking it up with Gadda's younger friend, the scholar Gian Carlo Roscioni, who could almost always either offer the solution himself and, frequently, overcome Gadda's prickly reluctance to reveal his meanings.

Gadda died some years ago; but, happily, I can consult Roscioni. I send him my paragraph, with the pages above; he answers by return mail and, as usual, comes to my aid. First he informs me – what I should have known – that "*Notte di luna*" was originally a fragment of an unpublished novel written in 1924 and published posthumously in 1983. Roscioni supplies me with a photocopy of the first version of the difficult paragraph. And it is immediately clear that, in the first sentence, *sovviene* does not have the "subvention" meaning, but is closer to the Latin *subvenit* ("comes up," "appears," "materializes"). Gadda, in Roscioni's opinion – and in mine, now – is saying that no exceptional thought materializes to relieve the labor of the work site.

More important, the pesky verb *posare* ("to cast" as "cast a glance") is, in the original version, *riposare*, and so Gadda is saying that when we rest (or are dead) a gaze keeps watch – the eye of God – from the starred heavens.

Roscioni has some doubt about "shock" which is, he thinks, less subjective than *sgomento*. I will think about that, as I write out yet another "final" version of the paragraph:

> No, no Idea appears, in the labor of the work sites, as the sibilant
> instruments of action transform things into things, and the toil is full
> of sweat and dirt. Then a distant gold and sapphire in the sky, like
> lashes quivering above a compassionate gaze. That, if we are at rest,
> will remain vigilant. The beat of life, it seems, can be swept away
> by fright, as if in a headlong race. The charity of the evening has
> cleansed us: and we have moved toward the place where someone

is waiting, so that our future may unfold, and no one shall hinder our lot. For afterwards we can rest.

In the end, I decided against "shock" though I am not entirely happy with "fright." "Sudden fear" would be closer, but wasn't it the title of a Joan Crawford movie? It sounds like one. Roscioni disliked "future" for *ventura* but again "destiny," "fate," have a pompous ring to me. I have stuck with "future" but added "lot" later, less conspicuously at the end of the sentence. If I were translating all of *L'Adalgisa* (and how I wish a publisher would give me the job/task/toil/blessing), I would have several further opportunities to study and revise this paragraph. My "fair" copies are never completely free of x'd-out words and pencilled-in emendations; and even on the proofs – braving the publisher's reproaches – I make a few, last-minute changes. Once a translation of mine is published, I never re-read it. I know that, if I did, I would soon be reaching for a pencil, to make further additions and subtractions, in the futile pursuit of a nonexistent perfection.

....

Translations are a partial and precious documentation of the changes the text suffers... The concept of the "definitive text" corresponds only to religion or exhaustion.
— JORGE LUIS BORGES in *Selected Non-Fictions* (Borges 1999)

LIGHTS, CAMERA, TRANSLATION!

Weaver was working with materials (words on paper) that St. Jerome would have recognized and understood, though he might have thought it frivolous. But what would Jerome have made of film translation, in which the script is only the starting point and both sound and image must be taken into account? I suspect the good saint might have got his subtle mind around the demands of the job itself, but what of the business environment? Anathema! Or "Ἀνάθεμα!," as Jerome would have put it.

Robert Paquin's essay "In the Footsteps of Giants: Translating Shakespeare for Dubbing" is an entertaining introduction to both the craft and business of screen translation. But it is also a vivid reminder that Shakespeare's plays, which too many of us only see on the printed page, were written for actors to speak out loud. Paquin

– who sometimes performs his own poetry accompanied by blues musicians in Montreal nightclubs – explains how this informed his translation of *Titus Andronicus* into French (Paquin 2001).

A translator is a tracker, stepping in the tracks of the writer who came before, careful not to step on anybody's toes, alert to the direction the tracks are pointing, attentive to the scenery, the context, trying not to disturb anything. What happens when a translator attempts to walk in the tracks of a giant?

Just before Christmas, I got a call from a Montreal dubbing studio. The speaker wanted to know if I was free to write the French script of a film for dubbing. I said, "Sure, what is it?" "Oh," the woman said, "it's called *Titus*." An alarm bell went off in my head. I said, "*Titus*? The only *Titus* I know is *Titus Andronicus*, by Shakespeare." She said, "Well, I don't know about that. All I know is it's out as a video already, but it's not been shown in theatres in Montreal and there is no French version, and we want to make a French version to be distributed as a video."

So I went to my neighbourhood video store, where I'd seen the box on the shelf, though I'd not yet rented it. And there it was! The blue face on the blue cover which said, in large Roman capitals, "TITUS, with Anthony Hopkins, Jessica Lange, and Harry Lennix, directed by Julie Taymor." Sure enough, on the back of the box, in the writing credits, I saw, "Screenplay by Julie Taymor and William Shakespeare." I had read the play *Titus Andronicus* as an undergraduate, but had never studied it and had never seen it performed. I rented the video so I could watch it before getting back to my client, Covitec, the big Montreal dubbing studio. I wanted to see how much Julie Taymor had adapted the play.

A film is a translation; written words are interpreted in images and sound. All films are a cinematic translation of a written script. But sometimes the script itself is the translation of a novel. In this case, a play. But what about this film? Were they going to be Shakespeare's lines, in verse, or was it a prose adaptation?

During the first six minutes of this 162-minute film, there is no dialogue, but such powerful images! Stylized violence with a sound track of TV cartoon lines, air raid sirens, the roar of bomber airplanes, explosions, a boy sobbing, then silence, then the cheer of a crowd, then drums accompanying the jerky ballet movements of Roman soldiers covered in blue dust. After six minutes, a camera-shot from below shows Anthony Hopkins slowly taking off his helmet and shouting: "Hail Rome, victorious, in thy mourning weeds!" I knew I was in the presence of giants.

I watched the film, riveted. Then I called the dubbing studio again to discuss this. How long were they going to give me to write this? The person I spoke to had not seen the film. I explained that it was a play by Shakespeare and that it was all in verse, and therefore must also be in verse in French. And I couldn't do that in a week. Luckily, the material I needed wasn't ready yet, and I had a few days to get ready. So while somebody was making a time-coded VHS version of the film, someone else was preparing a typed copy of the entire script, and another person was "detecting" the film, that is to say, observing all the mouth sounds, words, inspirations, expirations, yells, smacking of lips, and so forth produced by the screen actors and noting them with a lead pencil on a strip of white 35 mm film, indicating, synchronously with the image, precisely when the lips of the actors were closed to pronounce bilabial consonants like *m*, *b*, or *p*, or half-closed to pronounce semi-labials like *f*, *v*, *w*, or *r*. While this was being done, I read the original play by Shakespeare and all the critical material I could find, both on the play and on Julie Taymor's adaptation of it. I rushed to Montreal's largest public library and borrowed two translations of *Titus Andronicus*. One, in prose, by François-Victor Hugo, son of the great 19th-century French poet, and the other in verse, by J. B. Fort. The latter is a bilingual edition, with English on one page and French on the opposite page.

The Giants

First, I had to read about the play. *Titus Andronicus* is Shakespeare's first tragedy, and there are doubts about his authorship of the play. Indeed, for many critics, the patent barbarity of theme, the apparent crudity of workmanship, and the bloody succession of unrelieved horror place the tragedy among Shakespeare's doubtful plays, despite the fact that *Titus Andronicus* was published under his name and is attributed to him by his contemporaries... But internal evidence strongly suggests that Shakespeare did have a hand in *Titus*. There are too many parallels and correspondences between it and such classics as *Macbeth* and *King Lear* for it to have been written by anyone else.

I can imagine the actors of "the Right Honourable the Earle of Darbie,

Earle of Pembrooke, and Earle of Sussex" going to the young Shakespeare one day and saying, "Hey, Bill, listen. We've got a play here we'd like to perform, but first we want you to read it over and make it a little more presentable and poetic. We'll give you a couple of weeks to do this, okay?" Something like the phone call from the woman at the dubbing studio who gave me a week to translate/adapt the film *Titus* for dubbing in French, without even being aware that the dialogue was in blank verse.

Julie Taymor is a stage director whose stature as film director became firmly established with *Titus*, her first feature film. She had directed the off-Broadway stage production of the play, which had been a success and was well reviewed, and she thought "it would make a great movie." Julie Taymor had also directed the stage production of *The Lion King*, which was a tremendous success on Broadway. She is presently shooting a film on the Mexican artist Frida Kahlo, wife of the renowned mural painter, Diego Rivera.

Julie Taymor showed her script of *Titus* to Sir Anthony Hopkins, whose film career covers 95 feature films over a period of 40 years (who could forget the sinister Dr. Hannibal Lecter in *The Silence of the Lambs?*). He "liked the screen adaptation," liked her concepts, and agreed to play the leading role. Jessica Lange was chosen to play Tamora, Queen of the Goths; Alan Cumming was Saturninus; and Harry Lennix personified Aaron the Moor, as he'd already done in Taymor's stage production...

Titus Andronicus is a fictitious story that comes from the Middle Ages, is set in Ancient Rome, and contains references to issues that were contemporary to Shakespeare in the 16th century. No wonder Julie Taymor chose to underline this confusion in chronology by showing motorcycles and cars along with horse-drawn chariots, and soldiers in Roman costumes along with emperors in tuxedos. Shakespeare's 16th-century English, on the other hand, is consistently slightly archaic to the contemporary audience. In my translation I was careful to use only French words that existed in the late 16th and early 17th centuries. Strangely enough, though, French has not undergone as many changes as English has since that time, and the French version sounds more contemporary than the English.

The Language

Titus Andronicus is in blank verse, with an occasional rhyming couplet, and no prose. I felt it was necessary to render it in verse in French as well. And it seemed to me that the equivalent of the iambic pentameter was the classical Alexandrine line. Unlike English, all syllables count in French scanned poetry. So, whereas iambic pentameter is the alternating succession of five unstressed and five stressed syllables, for a total of ten syllables, the French Alexandrine is usually composed of 12 syllables in two segments with a caesura, or pause, at the hemistich, that is, after six syllables; sometimes it consists of three segments of four syllables each. But since in French only the last syllable of the last word of the utterance is stressed, the Alexandrine line has either two or three stressed syllables where the vowel is longer. In other words, the French line can be said more quickly than the English line. It is therefore possible to cram more syllables into a line in French than in English. This is a major issue when translating for the cinema, since the translated dialogue must be synchronous with the lip movements of the screen actors. Not only must the screen translator/adapter follow the original text stylistically and semantically, he or she is also subject to the additional constraint of its rendition. The lines have already been said, and the studio actor must follow the rhythm of the screen actor.

Synchronicity

This is one of the major differences between translating for a book and translating for the screen. And it is illustrated perfectly with the first lines in the film *Titus*. Julie Taymor did a serious editing job on Shakespeare's play, deleting, re-ordering, and re-assigning speeches. Thus, the film begins at line 70 of the original play with Titus's opening speech:

> Hail, Rome, victorious in thy mourning weeds!
> Lo, as the bark that hath discharg'd her freight,
> Returns with precious lading to the bay
> From whence at first she weigh'd her anchorage,
> Cometh Andronicus, bound with laurel boughs,
> To re-salute his country with his tears. (i, i, 70–75)

François-Victor Hugo translates this as:

> Salut, Rome, victorieuse dans tes vêtements de deuil! Ainsi que la barque, qui a porté au loin sa cargaison, retourne avec une précieuse charge à la baie d'où elle a naguère levé l'ancre, ainsi Andronicus, couronné de lauriers, revient pour saluer sa patrie avec ses larmes. (Hugo, 384)

J.B. Fort writes:

Rome, salut à toi, victorieuse en deuil!
Tel qu'un navire au loin a déchargé son fret,
Puis revient, les flancs lourds d'un précieux fardeau,
Au port même où naguère il avait levé l'ancre,
Voici qu'Andronicus, couronné de lauriers,
T'offre, Rome, à nouveau le salut de ses larmes. (Fort, 11)

This is where it gets complicated. I could not simply put either Hugo's or Fort's French words in Anthony Hopkins's mouth, because neither translation would fit. Indeed, Hopkins begins with a long open diphthong, *Hail*. So, the studio actor can neither begin with *Salut*, where the French vowel *u* is a closed vowel, nor with *Rome*, since the mouth would close on the *m*.

I chose to begin with:

Ave, Rome, victorieuse en vêtements de deuil.
Telle une barque qui a déchargé son fret
Et revient rapportant des trésors à la baie,
Là même où elle avait naguère levé l'ancre,
Ainsi Andronicus, ployant sous les lauriers,
Revient saluer sa patrie avec ses larmes.

The word *Ave*, readily recognizable as a Roman greeting, sets the tone. The vowel sounds are open and the word *Rome* falls in the right place. I wanted to keep Hugo's *vêtements de deuil*, because it is closer to *mourning weeds* than simply the *en deuil* in Fort's translation.

A close comparison of the English with the three translations – Hugo's, Fort's, and mine – will show that my choices were dictated by the need to fit either the screen actor's rhythm of elocution, or the position of labial consonants, where the screen actor's lips close and the studio actor needs to pronounce either a *b*, a *p*, or an *m*, or a semi-labial such as *v*, or *f*, and so forth. Thus, the second line in my translation closely matches the English:

"Telle une barque qui a déchargé son fret"

"Lo, as the bark that hath discharg'd her freight"

in contrast to:

"Ainsi que la barque, qui a porté au loin sa cargaison" (Hugo, 384) or

"Tel qu'un navire au loin a déchargé son fret" (Fort, 11)

The guiding principle, therefore, is to match the text to the screen. There must be a close correspondence between the actor's interpretation and the translation. Indeed, while recording in the studio, dubbing actors always carefully listen to and watch the screen actors, trying to imitate them, and following them as closely as possible, just as the translator attempts to walk in the author's tracks. Likewise, the screen translator must watch attentively and take his or her cues from the actors on the screen. There were a few cases in the writing of the French script for *Titus* where the actor's interpretation of the lines helped me understand the true meaning of the text, which had eluded the two previous French translators.

The Actors Rule

In Act IV, scene 2, Aaron the Moor confronts the racist nurse who wants him to kill his newborn son because she finds him "loathsome as a toad." Aaron replies:

Zounds, ye whore! Is black so base a hue?
Sweet blowse, you are a beauteous blossom sure. (IV, ii, 71–72)

This Hugo translates as:

Fi donc! Fi donc, putain! Le noir est-il une si ignoble couleur?... Cher joufflu, vous êtes un beau rejeton, assurément. (Hugo, 419)

And Fort:

Morbleu, garce! Le noir est-il couleur si vile?
Pour sûr, mon doux poupon est une belle fleur. (Fort, 119)

Obviously both Hugo and Fort, translating from the text, misunderstood the second line, thinking it was addressed to the baby. But watching Harry Lennix in the role of Aaron, I could easily see he was speaking to the nurse, and not to the baby. And the venom in his voice made it clear that his calling her a "beauteous blossom" was meant as irony. The same with "sweet blowse," which both Hugo and Fort interpreted as a term of endearment addressed by Aaron to his son, when in fact the word "sweet" is meant to contrast with "blowse," which the *Oxford English Dictionary* defines as "a ruddy fat-faced wench" – hardly a compliment.

Therefore my screen translation was:

> Chienne éhontée! Le blanc est moins vil que le noir?
> Tu te prends toi, souillon, pour une fleur, bien sûr.

Note how the labial consonant *p* of *prends* matches the *b* of *blowse*, and how *pour une fleur, bien sûr* corresponds to *beauteous blossom, sure*, where the *p* of *pour* covers the initial *b* of *beauteous*, the *f* of *fleur* falls on the *b* of *blossom*, and the *b* of *bien* masks the final *m* of *blossom*. Note also how, in the first line, I managed to put *blanc* (white) in the place of *black*, by phrasing the question differently.

Translation for the screen is dictated by the image and by the playing of the actors, which in the end must reign supreme, since it is the image and the acting on the screen that the translator-tracker must follow...

TRANSLATOR AS NEGOTIATOR

Umberto Eco, bestselling author of *The Name of the Rose* and much (much!) else, gave a series of lectures on translation in 1998, which was published a few years later as *Mouse or Rat? Translation as Negotiation* (Eco 2003). As the title suggests, Eco sees a finished text as a kind of "deal" arrived at through a form of trading.

> Negotiation is a process by virtue of which, in order to get something, each party renounces something else, and at the end everybody feels satisfied since one cannot have everything.
>
> In this kind of negotiation there may be many parties: on one side, there is the original text, with its own rights, sometimes an author who claims right over the whole process, along with the cultural framework in which the original text is born; on the other side, there is the destination text, the cultural milieu in which it is expected to be read, and even the publishing industry, which can recommend different translation criteria, according to whether the translated text is to be put in an academic context or in a popular one. An English publisher of detective novels may even ask a Russian translator not to transliterate the names of the characters by using diacritic marks, in order to make them more recognisable to the supposed readers.

A translator is the negotiator between those parties, whose explicit assent is not mandatory. There is an implicit assent even in the reading of a novel or of a newspaper article, as in the former case the reader implicitly subscribes a *suspension of disbelief,* and in the latter relies on the silent convention that what is said is guaranteed to be true...

....

TRANSLATION IN DARK-STAINED OAK VENEER

For those with slightly smaller budgets, there are still plenty of pieces to choose from among a new crop of shape-shifting furniture... Best of all is the coffee table called Translation, designed by Cinna and the Ligne Roset team (€1,874). It starts as a sober little square in dark-stained oak veneer but four sections can be coaxed apart to reveal a flash of red, white or guava lacquer – like the silk lining of a business suit – and it becomes a larger rectangular table. Fully extended, Translation is double its original size, a Miro-like composition of interlocking squares.

— From a 2006 article in the House & Home section of London's *Financial Times* (Burroughs 2006)

BETRAYAL MOST FOUL: SO I GRABBED HIM
BY THE EUPHEMISM...

Since we've just been reading Italian, let's go back to *traduttore traditore* and the idea that translation is always a form of betrayal. The late André Lefevere offered a bouquet of bowdlerizations in his *Translation, Rewriting, and the Manipulation of Literary Fame* (Lefevere 1992). The examples show the extent to which most published translations are firmly rooted in the mores of the period in which they are written.

At the end of Aristophanes' *Lysistrata*, the heroine asks "Peace," an allegorical character played by a naked young lady of great beauty, to bring the Spartan peace emissaries to her, and she adds the line "En mē dido tēn cheira, tēs sathēs age." The line translates literally as: if he doesn't give you his hand, take him by the – what is in the 1968 reprint of Liddell and Scott's famous *Greek-English Lexicon* still translated by means of the Latin phrase, *membrum virile* – the penis, in other words. Since the way these and other *membra* can be referred to in literature is to no small extent indicative of the ideology dominant at a certain time in a certain society, this may be as good a point as any to enter *in medias res.*

Patric Dickinson [in 1957] translates the line quoted above as: "But if they *won't* / Give you their hands, take them and tow them, *politely*, / By their... life-lines." Sixty-eight years earlier William James Hickie, who translated Aristophanes for the Balm Classical Library, rendered the same line as: "If any do not give his hand, lead him by the nose." Hickie is fond of noses in this connection, witness his translation of "kou mē tot alle sou kuon ton orcheon labetai" [lest not any other of the dogs grab you by the testicles] as "And no other bitch shall ever lay hold of your nose." He goes on to explain in a footnote: "meaning that she would anticipate such a casualty by pulling it off." He then proceeds to shore up his interpretation of the line in a somewhat incongruous manner, by quoting Droysen's German translation of it: "doch sollte bei den Hoden dann kein Koeter mehr dich packen" [then no dog should take you by the testicles again].

Fifty-nine years after Hickie, Sutherland translated the same line as: "If he won't give his hand, then lead him by the prick." Three years later Parker translated: "If hands are refused, conduct them by the handle." Ten years earlier Fitts wrote: "Take them by the hand, women/or by anything else if they seem unwilling," and twenty years before that Way had written: "If they don't give a hand, a leg will do." We could keep going, and there is no lack of passages in Aristophanes that could keep us entertained in a similar manner as we shake our heads over so many different translations.

....

MY SMALL DETECTIVE
We use expletives which, by tradition, vary from country to country, depending on deep-rooted superstitions or religion. Words connected with the devil are much more shocking and effective in Swedish, for instance, than those associated, for example, with our reproductive organs. The Swedish for "dick" is even used as a pet name for little boys. It is perfectly natural for a mother to address her little son affectionately with: "How is my little dick today then?" Curiously enough, the female equivalent is not used in the same way. Similarly, words which were shocking a hundred years ago have naturally lost their edge by now, so we have

to push the boundaries and try to find the modern equivalent, which is always a question of personal judgment.

— EIVOR MARTINUS in "Translating Scandinavian Drama" (Martinus 1996)

BETRAYAL BENIGN: THE URGE TO "IMPROVE" A TEXT

For the most part, translators do their best to be faithful to the source text. But occasionally they feel they are serving both the author and the reader by "improving" on the source text. The New York translator Estelle Gilson warns against doing so, after noting a number of historical examples of betrayal (Gilson 1998).

> Translations of popular contemporary works sometimes read like "betrayals" as well. This is true no matter whether the author is dead or alive, though without an author looking over their shoulders, translators are by necessity or desire, freer to impose their own ideas on a text. I don't know a translator who hasn't at one time or another had to battle the urge to improve a spot here and there in the original text. There are times when this may be justified, but for the most part I've found that when I have a problem with a word, a connection, or a thought, it is because I have misread the text.

BETRAYAL MOST LAUGHABLE:
THE INCOMPETENT TRANSLATION

Bad translations may have serious consequences – wrangles stemming from the French-to-English translation of the Warsaw Convention on international air travel have enriched many lawyers over the years – but they are more often the butt of jokes. Perhaps the most famous example of bad translation – and the delight people take in criticizing it – is the book that came to be known as *English as She Is Spoke*, originally published in 1855 with the title *O Novo Guia da Conversaçao, em Portuguez e Inglez, em Duas Partes: The New Guide of the Conversation, in Portuguese and English, in Two Parts*. Advertising itself as a Portuguese-to-English phrasebook, the book was entirely constructed of howlers like the following, presented as phrases useful for those intending to hunt on horseback (da Fonseca and Carolino 2001):

Âs súas pistólas estão carregádas?	Your pistols are its loads?
Não. Esquecêu-me comprár pólvora e bála. Piquêmos, vamos máis depréssa. Núnca vi peior bésta. Não quér andár; nêm pâra diânte, nem pâra trâz.	No; i forgot to buy gun-powder and balls. Let us prick. Go us more fast never i was seen a so much bad beast; she will not nor to bring forward neither put back.

The book's preface was, if anything, even worse – or better for millions of incredulous English-speaking readers as it became an international laughingstock. The preface began:

> A choice of familiar dialogues, clean of gallicisms, and despoiled phrases, it was missing yet to studious portuguese and brazilian Youth; and also to persons of others nations that wish to know the portuguese language. We sought all we may do, to correct that want, composing and divisin the present little work into two parts. The first includes greatest vocabulary proper names by alphabetical order; and the second fourty three Dialogues adapted to the usual precisions of the life. For that reason we did put, with a scrupulous exactness, a great variety own espressions to english an portuguese idioms; without to attach us selves (as make some others) almost at a literal translation; translation what only will be for to accustom the portuguese pupils, or foreign, to speak very bad any of the mentioned idioms.
>
> We were increasing this second edition with a phraseology, in the first part, and some familiar letters anecdotes, idiotisms, proverbs, and to second a coin's index.

For almost a century and a half, the blame for *English as She Is Spoke* was attributed to the translator Pedro Carolino. He spoke little or no English, and instead had arrived at the finished product via a Portuguese-to-French phrasebook and then a French-to-English dictionary. In a 2001 edition, however, the editor Paul Collins presents a somewhat kinder explanation of the book's genesis, and one that may remind many professionals of the less-than-kosher literary enterprises that can be found in the market (da Fonseca and Carolino 2001).

> Traditionally, the book has been ascribed in tandem to José da Fonseca and Pedro Carolino. Although Fonseca (1788–1866) was memorably described by Twain as "an honest and upright idiot," he had a long and respectable list of distinguished works in poetry, linguistics, and translation behind him. How could he have been involved in such a farrago? On closer examination,

Fonseca appears to have suffered a sort of literary carjacking. After reading our reprint of the book, UCLA linguist Alex McBride determined that "coauthor" Pedro Carolino created the ill-fated *Novo Guia* by commandeering Fonseca's 1837 *Guide de la Conversation Française et Anglaise* – a perfectly competent phrasebook – and crudely translating the translations. Carolino then included Fonseca's name with his own on the new book's title page, even though it seems likely that the upstanding scholar was oblivious of Carolino's bumbling act of piracy. He may not have even been aware of his would-be collaborator's existence: little is known about Carolino, though he did previously author a manual on letter-writing. In all likelihood he was a hack who, with next month's rent due, assured a publisher that *of course* he could write an English phrasebook.

And it might have worked, except that English is a damnably illogical language. But it is easy to imagine attempts at translation between any two languages bringing about some of the same mistakes. One can only wonder whether, lurking on our library shelves, there is an equally atrocious phrasebook written for American students that will someday bring tears of helpless laughter to the eyes of Portuguese readers.

I AM NOT A CAMERA

A subtle and inventive commentator on translation and many other subjects is Douglas Hofstadter, who is probably best known for his 1979 book *Gödel, Escher, Bach: An Eternal Golden Braid.* I love his description of himself as "pi-lingual" (i.e., conversant in 3.14159... languages), which he bases on the fact that he speaks English, Italian and French fluently, along with smatterings of several other languages. The following text is from his extraordinary book *Le Ton beau de Marot: In Praise of the Music of Language* (Hofstadter 1997):

> Any good translator's ideal is to get across to a new group of readers the essence of someone else's fantasy and vision of the world, and yet, as we have repeatedly seen... the mediating agent necessarily plays a deep and critical role in doing such a job. A translator does to an original text something like what an impressionist painter does to a landscape: there is an inevitable and cherished personal touch that makes the process totally different from photography. Translators are not like cameras – they are not even like cameras with filters! They distort their input so much that they

are completely unique scramblers of the message – which does not mean that their scrambling is any less interesting or less valuable than the original "scene."

A curious aspect of this analogy between the translation of a piece of text into a new language and the rendering of a scene as a painting is that the original text... plays the role of the scene in nature, rather than that of something created by a human. The original text is thus a piece of "objective reality" that is distorted by the translator/painter. But what, one might then ask, about people who read the text in the original language? Are native-language readers able to get the message as it really is, free from all the bias and distortion inevitably introduced by a scrambling intermediary?

As the letters and words of the original text leap upwards from the page into a native reader's eyes and brain, they shimmer and shiver and then suddenly splinter into a billion intricately-correlated protoplasmic sparks scattered all over the cerebral cortex and deeper within – unique patterns in the unique mind of the unique reader that each distinct person constitutes. The idea that all native-language readers see "the same thing" falls to bits. It's true that in the case of native-language readers, there is no intermediary human scrambler, but it's not true that, because of this lack, there is no idiosyncratic perceptual distortion. How sad it would be if that were the case!

I AM NOT A TRANSLATOR

A few translators don't like the label. Herbert Kretzmer, the South African-born journalist and songwriter, is probably most famous for having written the English lyrics for *Les Misérables* and for his longtime songwriting collaboration with the French singer Charles Aznavour (Britons of a certain age will also remember the hit song he wrote for Peter Sellers in 1960, "Goodness Gracious Me"). Kretzmer has an uneasy relationship with the translation world, and even told an interviewer in 1993 that the word *translator*, for him, was "a soul-less function" (Snell-Hornby 2006).

> You do not have to bring intelligence, you do not have to bring passion to the job of translation, you only have to bring a meticulous understanding of at least another language. You do not bring yourself, you just bring knowledge and skill.

Certainly, the English version of *Les Misérables* first performed in London in 1985 cannot rightly be called a – one hesitates to say "mere" – translation of the original French "concept album" written by Alain Boublil and Claude-Michel Schönberg in 1980. Only a third of the original survived in direct translation; another third features completely new words to existing music, and the remainder consists of completely new songs Kretzmer created in collaboration with Boublil and Schönberg. Kretzmer explains more of the process in a magazine interview with Al Sheahen (Sheahen 1998).

SHEAHEN: You were the drama critic of the London *Daily Express* for 18 years and the TV critic of the London *Daily Mail* for a further eight years. On the side, you wrote lyrics for the stage and TV. How did you come to write the lyrics for *Les Misérables*?

KRETZMER: Cameron Mackintosh had liked some lyrics I had written for the Parisian singer/composer Charles Aznavour. These included "Yesterday When I Was Young," which I'm pleased to say has become something of a standard in the U.S., and "She," which topped the British charts for four weeks back in 1974. So when he was preparing *Les Misérables*, and the rehearsal dates (already delayed a year, I was told) were getting closer every day, and a final approved libretto was still a hope rather than a reality, Cameron felt that urgent action was required and recalled my collaborations with Aznavour and other French writers. He took me to lunch at the Ivy and asked me to join the *Les Misérables* team, to take responsibility, in short, for the lyrics for the forthcoming London production. That was late January '85. I devoted the next four weeks to reading Victor Hugo's novel, in English. And speaking to everyone involved in the project. Well, almost everyone. By the end of February, I had organized a six months' leave from the *Daily Mail*, whose editor, Sir David English, told me that he was "far from happy" about his senior television critic disappearing from his pages for so long a stretch. Neverthless, I was excited by Cameron's invitation and went to work on *Les Misérables* in my flat in Basil Street – less than a block away from Harrods – on March 1, 1985.

SHEAHEN: In the programme notes, you say you were given a tape of the original 1980 Paris production, as well as a word-for-word literal translation of Alain Boublil's French libretto, plus a new and detailed synopsis of the projected London production. What were you asked to do?

KRETZMER: Initially I was asked to team up, to collaborate, with James Fenton – English poet, much respected here – who had been working on an English-language libretto of *Les Misérables* for maybe a year. However, after surveying the sheer weight of work needed to get the show written and ready for rehearsal within five months, I resolved to follow a wise old rule: he travels fastest who travels alone. So I did not meet James Fenton, and still haven't. Our paths have simply not crossed. The job Cameron asked to do involved writing a significant amount of brand new material, i.e. stuff which had not figured in the original Paris show at all, plus translating and adapting exisiting lyrics, notes and ideas – wrestling it all into shape.

SHEAHEN: In the programme note you discuss the "challenge of matching singable English phrases to a decidedly Gallic score... the French language being so full of emphatic consonants, staccato tricks of rhythm and fading syllables at the end of sentences which have no ready equivalent in English." How did you do it ? How did you make it rhyme and make sense?

KRETZMER: I always felt drawn to French songs – even their happy songs had a kind of minor key plaintiveness about them. As a lyricist I have in particular enjoyed a long and fruitful connection with Charles Aznavour, undisputed grand master of the chanson... Besides Charles Aznavour I have occasionally written lyrics for other French-language stars – Gilbert Bécaud, Zizi Jeanmaire, Moustaki. I did a couple of Jacques Brel songs. Perhaps that's what Cameron Mackintosh saw. Why he asked me in. The French connection.

SHEAHEN: You were given the literal translation of Boublil's libretto. Did you stick closely to that text? Or was it like writing entirely new lyrics? Can you give examples of the various stages that took you from the original French to your final lyric?

KRETZMER: Here are two examples chosen at random. The first is the opening of Fantine's Act 1 lament "I Dreamed A Dream." Here is a precise literal translation of Alain Boublil's original French lyric.

I had dreamed of another life
In which my life would pass like a dream
I was prepared for all follies
All passions which arise.

And here is my own interpretation of those same lines:

> I Dreamed a Dream in time gone by
> When hope was high and life worth living
> I dreamed that love would never die
> I dreamed that God would be forgiving...

Another example. Into the mouths of the defiant students Alain put stirring words which literally translate into English as follows:

> At the will of the people
> And to the health of progress
> Come fill your heart with the wine of rebellion
> And tomorrow, faithful friend,
> If your heart beats as strongly
> As a drum in the distance,
> It is because hope still exists for the human race.

My own take on those lines went like this:

> Do You Hear The People Sing
> Singing the song of angry men?
> It is the music of a people
> Who will not be slaves again
> When the beating of your heart
> Echoes the beating of the drums
> There is a life about to start
> When tomorrow comes!

I offer this advice to any lyricist invited to adapt or translate foreign songs into English... Do not follow the original text slavishly. Re-invent the lyric in your own words, remembering that there may be better ways of serving a master than trotting behind him on a leash. Working on *Les Misérables* I did not see myself as a translator, but as a co-writer... an equal among equals.

SHEAHEN: Was it necessary for you to speak French to do the job?

KRETZMER: No. My French is wretched. No other word for it. I can muster a few words in an emergency but I could not long sustain a conversation with a French person. I regret this. French was not taught in my high school in South Africa. Though I lived in Paris for a spell when I was young and hungry, my friends there tended to be English-speaking self-exiles like myself, mainly American. I was able to read Victor Hugo's novel only in translation...

EVERYONE'S A TRANSLATOR (NOT!)

If globalization really takes hold and huge numbers of people use English as their functional second language, does that mean translators will be out of job? Kevin Cook, who translates from many languages into English, and lives in the famously multilingual Netherlands, doubts it (Cook 2008).

I'm struck by how often the phrase "lost in translation" is used by people who evidently have little notion of what the process involves. There seems to be an idea that any translation is bound to be an unfaithful rendering of the original, and that it's the translator's fault. The Italian phrase *traduttore traditore*, which means "a translator is a traitor," lays the blame even more explicitly at the alleged culprit's door. Chortling with glee, he leads his readers up one garden path after another, secure in the knowledge that their ignorance of the source language will prevent them from catching him out.

But in some cases his readers *aren't* ignorant of the source language. You might think this would make them more aware of what it takes to translate from one language into another. But it often only increases their contempt for the translator – for they are only too ready to believe that they could have made a better job of it themselves.

A case in point is my adopted homeland, Holland, whose inhabitants are rightly renowned for their command of foreign languages, especially English. The problem is that too many of them leave off just when they ought to carry on. They have come to believe in a myth perpetuated by the thousands of Anglophone visitors to this country who pay their hosts well-meaning but fatuous compliments such as "Your English is even better than mine!" or "People back home could learn a lot from the way you speak our language!" (to which I can only reply "You should hear the way people here speak their own language!"). The unrelenting deluge of English-language music and subtitled TV also encourages Dutch people to think that English comes as naturally to them as their mother tongue. As if to prove it, they dot their everyday speech and writing with often unidiomatic English, which then gets copied from person to unsuspecting person like an address-book virus.

From here it is only a small step to believing that they already know all they need to know about English. This is reflected in indignant complaints that the inhabitants of various popular holiday destinations "can't speak proper English" (as other languages decline in popularity, English is the only foreign language most Dutch people still have a reasonable command of) or that the Dutch prime minister's command of English is a national disgrace (a charge levelled at everyone who has held that office in the twenty-five years since I moved here). At the same time, since English is the "world language" (and hence "belongs to everybody"), those who use it are surely free to do so in whatever way they like. English is spoken differently in Ireland, Pakistan, Canada, Guyana and Australia, so why not in Holland? What's the fuss about?

The fuss, of course, is about the fact that English is more than just a "global pidgin". It is a language in its own right, with many specific features that differ substantially from those of its fellows – in fact, English is very often the odd man out, for example in its vowel system and its use of verb tenses. It has its own particular rules and boundaries between correct and incorrect usage.

Even so, it is by no means unknown for Dutch people to take the liberty of changing translations by native English-speakers into the kind of English they are familiar with (and then embarrass the translator by publishing the disfigured result under his name!). Rather than a translation, what they seem to want is a piece of English they can easily understand and could perhaps have written themselves.

Those confronted with this often protest as follows: "Languages change all the time. Don't pretend you speak the same English as Shakespeare did [I don't, and I don't]. Why shouldn't English change under the influence of other languages? After all, it's a Germanic language strongly influenced by Norman French. All we're doing in Holland is continuing that process. You can't stop it!" The implication is that translators' insistence on correct usage is some obscurantist attempt to halt natural progress – a kind of linguistic Luddism.

I'm sorry, languages don't "change all the time." They evolve over long periods, which isn't the same thing. At any given stage, there is a consensus among native speakers about what is correct and what is not. This will shift in the manner of a sand dune, incorporating grains at the front and losing them at the rear, but the bulk of the grains will remain part of the dune over a substantial period of time. So it is with languages. Without a consensus about usage, it would be difficult to communicate at any advanced level. We quite literally need to know what we're talking about.

That's why good translation matters, and why it isn't something just anyone can do. If a text is translated from Dutch to English by a native Dutch-speaker, there are those who would dismiss any errors in it as "Dutch usage." That's absurd. There is no such thing as Dutch usage in English, any more than there is such a thing as English usage in Dutch (or Inuit usage in Swahili).

....

Yet another Quixote *translation? Isn't it an act of quixotry to write the thirteenth English translation of the great Spanish novel?*

— JOHN RUTHERFORD in the introduction to his translation of *Don Quixote* (Cervantes Saavedra and Rutherford 2003)

CHAPTER FOUR
"If Swahili was good enough for Jesus Christ...":
Translating religion

He who translates a verse literally is a liar, and he who makes additions
to it is a blasphemer.

— RABBI JUDAH BEN ILAI, second century CE (Metzger 1993)

You've probably heard some variation of "If English was good enough for Jesus Christ, it's good enough for me," generally tossed off as a joke about Christian fundamentalists in the United States. According to a post by Benjamin Zimmer on the blog Language Log (April 26, 2006), something like it was quoted in the *New York Times* in 1881 and again in 1905, with the butts of the joke being, respectively, a Massachusetts farmer and two Irish New Yorkers (Zimmer 2006). The most durable version, perhaps because it is attached to a historical figure, has a governor of Texas, Miriam Amanda "Ma" Ferguson, declaring "If the King's English was good enough for Jesus Christ, it's good enough for the children of Texas!" sometime during her two terms of office in the 1920s and '30s. Zimmer notes that in his research he was unable to come up with any firm attribution of the quote to Ferguson, and observes:

> Considering how the quote in all its variants has been used primarily to ridicule the backwardness of unnamed Christians (a farmer, a pious deacon, and so forth) wary of new approaches to the Bible, I highly doubt Ma Ferguson ever said it – or if she did, she probably would have said it in self-effacing jest. My guess is that this was a free-floating bit of preacher humour that unfairly got attached to Ma Ferguson, much as Winston Churchill attracts various apocryphal witticisms.

The joke is a good illustration of how Venuti's notion of "invisibility" applies in real life. When most people read the Bible, they do so in their own language rather than ancient Hebrew or Aramaic. It can be an intensely personal activity, in which the reader feels she or he is reading the Word of God and is therefore privy to His (usually not Her) thoughts. The idea that the comforting stories and familiar cadences of either Testament are not only translations from one or more foreign tongues, but the work of one or more demonstrably fallible human beings, can be a tough one to face – and in fact has been a source of strife and stress for literally ages.

EDITING GOD

For centuries, the most influential versions of the Old Testament (read to Christian congregations in Latin) were based on Greek translations collectively called the Septuagint. These had been translated by Jewish scholars – supposedly seventy of them, hence the name – in Alexandria between the first and third centuries BCE. At the end of the fourth century CE, St. Jerome rocked the theological world by casting a rigorous eye at Latin translations based on the Septuagint, finding so many discrepancies and inconsistencies that he eventually re-translated the Old Testament into Latin directly from the Hebrew. The Bishop of Hippo, Augustine (a saint himself, eventually), was sufficiently worried by the impact of the new translations on Christian congregations that he began a series of letters with Jerome, some of them heated. Letter 112 is a corker. In it, the testy Jerome – "virtually decrepit as I am, and living in my rural monastery" – replies to a number of points made by the much younger Augustine. Jerome explains his methods, and addresses an incident recounted by Augustine in which a congregation rebelled against the "corrected" version of the Word of God (White 1990):

> As to the question in your other letter of why my earlier translations of the canonical writings had asterisks and commas marked, while my later translation omitted such critical signs – with all respect I must say that you do not appear to understand what you ask. For the former translation is from the Septuagint and wherever there are commas, like little daggers, it indicates that the Septuagint expands on the Hebrew text, while where there are asterisks, like little stars shining onto the following words, something has been added by Origen from the edition of Theodotion. The first translation was made from the Greek, while the second I made direct from the Hebrew and it translates the true meaning, as I understood it, without

necessarily preserving the word order. I am surprised that you are not reading the Septuagint in the original form as it was produced by the Seventy,
but in an edition corrected, or corrupted, by Origen using daggers and aster-
isks and that you are not following the translation, undistinguished though
it may be, of a Christian, especially when he has removed those additions
which came from the edition of a Jew and blasphemer after Christ's passion. Do you wish to be a true admirer of the Septuagint? Then you should
not read what is preceded by an asterisk – in fact you should delete such
passages from your copy, to prove yourself to be a supporter of the ancient
translators. But if you were to do this, you would be forced to condemn all
church libraries for only one or two copies are to be found which do not
contain these passages...

I have not attempted to do away with the works of my predecessors
which I emended and translated from Greek into Latin for those who
spoke my language, but rather to publish the evidence which had been
overlooked or corrupted by the Jews, so that Latin-speakers might know
what was really in the Hebrew text. If someone does not wish to read my
version, he will not be forced to do so against his will. Let him drink the old
wine with enjoyment and reject my unfermented wine which was offered
as an explanation of the commentaries of earlier writers with the intention
of clarifying what was unintelligible.

As to the question of what method one should follow in interpreting
the Holy Scriptures, this is dealt with in the book which I wrote entitled,
"The Best Method of Translation," as well as in all the short prefaces which
I wrote for each divine book and added to my edition; I think that the serious reader should be referred to these. And if, as you say, you approve of
my revision of the New Testament, the reason you give for your approval
being that there are many people with a knowledge of Greek who can
judge my work, then you ought to believe that my work on the Old
Testament is equally authentic, for in it I did not include my own ideas
but only translated the divine texts as I found them in the Hebrew. If you
do not believe me, ask the Hebrew scholars. You may perhaps say, "What
if the Hebrew scholars refuse to answer or wilfully give a wrong answer?"
Will the whole Jewish population keep silent about my translation? Will
it be impossible to find anyone who has a knowledge of Hebrew or will
they all follow the example of those Jews in some small African town who,

according to you, have conspired to misrepresent me? For this is the tale you tell in your letter:

> When one of our fellow bishops arranged for your translation to be read in the church in his diocese, they came across a word in your version of the prophet Jonah which you had rendered very differently from the translation with which they were familiar and which, having been read by so many generations, was ingrained in their memories. A great uproar ensued in the congregation, especially among the Greeks who criticised the text and passionately denounced it as wrong, and the bishop (the incident took place in the city of Oea) was forced to ask the Jews to give evidence. Whether out of ignorance or spite, they replied that this word did occur in the Hebrew manuscripts in exactly the same form as in the Greek and Latin versions. In short, the man was forced to correct the passage in your version as if it were inaccurate since he did not want to be left without a congregation as a result of this crisis. This makes even us suspect that you, too, can be mistaken occasionally.

You allege that I made a mistake in my translation of the prophet Jonah and that the bishop almost lost his congregation when the people rioted in protest because of a difference of one word. You fail to mention what it was that I mistranslated, thereby depriving me of a chance to defend myself; maybe you were afraid that my answer might make it clear that there were no grounds for an objection. Perhaps you are referring to the fact that many years ago, "gourd" cropped up, when Cornelius and Asinius Pollio insisted that I had translated "ivy" for "gourd." I have discussed this problem at greater length in my commentary on the prophet Jonah; now it is enough for me just to say that in the passage where the Septuagint gives "gourd" and Aquila and the rest translate "ivy" i.e. kitton, the Hebrew text has "ciceion" which the Syriac speakers commonly call "ciceia." There is a kind of shrub with broad leaves like a pumpkin; when it is planted it grows quickly into a bush without the support of any of the poles or props which cucumbers and ivy need, supporting itself on its own stem. If I had wanted to give a literal translation and used the word "ciceion," no one would have understood it; if I had translated it as "gourd" I would be putting something which was not in the Hebrew, so I put "ivy" to be in agreement with other translators. But if your Jews, as you claim, whether out of spite or ignorance, said that the Hebrew edition contained the same as the Greek and Latin editions, it is clear that they are either ignorant of Hebrew literature or that they deliberately lied so as to make fun of the gourd planters.

"EVERYBODY'S A CRITIC..."

Fast forward to Martin Luther, writing in September 1530. By this time, the Vulgate, much of it based on Jerome's translation, had taken on the same weight of authority that the Septuagint had enjoyed in Jerome's day. Challenging this authority – and inciting severe repression for it — was a growing number of translations in national languages, such as Tyndale's in English (for which he was executed in 1536 after a form of "rendition" from Antwerp), Lefèvre d'Étaples's in French (for which he was forced into exile), and Pécsi and Újlaki's in Hungarian (ditto).

Luther was luckier than the other major translators at the time. He wrote this letter while safely ensconced in Coburg Fortress under the protection of the Elector John Frederick II. His New Testament had been in print for six years and was a resounding, if controversial, success. The letter is to an old friend, Father Wenzel Link, and in it he denounces the perennial bugbears of the professional translator, the carping critics. The "bungler" he refers to is Hieronymus Emser, who had first denounced Luther's 1524 translation of the New Testament, then borrowed heavily from it for his own version published in 1527 (Robinson 1997b).

They say when you work in public, everybody's a critic, and that's certainly been true for me. All these people who can't even talk right, let alone translate, try to teach *me* how to do it! And if I'd asked them how to translate the first two words of Matthew 1:1, *Liber Generationis,* not one of them could've said jack, yet these fine journeymen would pronounce judgment on the whole Bible. St. Jerome faced the same thing when he did his Latin translation: everybody knew better than him how to do it, and people bitched and moaned about his work as weren't fit to shine his shoes. It takes a heap of patience to try to do any public service; everybody's got to be Mister Knowitall and get everything bass-ackwards, teaching everyone and knowing nothing. That's just the way they are; a leopard can't change his spots.

I'd like to see just one papist put his money where his mouth is and try his hand at translating one of Paul's letters or one of the prophetic books without using Luther's German language and translation. What fine-sounding

German we'd hear then! We've already seen what happens when some bungler from Dresden figures he'll "touch up" my New Testament (I refuse to utter his name in my books any more; he's got a higher judge than me now, and besides, he's well enough known as it is). He recognized that my German is sweet and good and knew plenty well that he couldn't do it any better himself, but still he wanted to drag it in the mud, so he rushed out and grabbed my New Testament, almost word for word as I had it, ripped out my preface and commentary and rubbed out my name, wrote his own name and preface and commentary in their place, and is now selling my New Testament under his name! Dear children, how it pained me when the governor in his ghastly preface condemned Luther's New Testament and forbade anyone to read it, while ordering everyone to read the bungler's New Testament – which is the exact same one Luther made!

You think I'm making this up? Go get both Testaments, Luther's and the bungler's, open them up in front of you, and compare them – it'll be pretty clear who translated both of them. The few places he changed and patched up, even though I may not always like the results, don't really hurt the text all that much, so that it's never really seemed to me worth the bother to attack it in print. But I did have to laugh at the high and mighty wisdom that trashes my translation and condemns it and bans it when it's published under my name, but makes everybody read it when it's published under some other name. Tell me, is it something to be proud of, to shove somebody's book in the mire, then to steal that book and publish it under your own name, and so to try and make a name for yourself with another man's work, which you despise? But God's his judge now. For me it's enough, and it makes me glad, that (as St. Paul too boasts [Philippians 1:18]) even my enemies need my work, and that Luther's book (though without Luther's name, under his enemies' name) is being read. What better revenge could I hope for?

The reader may be struck by the idiomatic American language in this translation, which is Douglas Robinson's and published in his splendid collection *Western Translation Theory: From Herodotus to Nietzsche*. In the first paragraph alone, one finds expressions such as "bass-ackwards," "bitched and moaned," "Mister Knowitall," and "not one of them could've said jack" (short for "jack-shit"). Is this a "good" translation of Luther, who was notoriously direct in his language? Is Robinson wrong to translate the first line so freely, to domesticate it so forcefully, or has he caught

Luther's tone and meaning? Compare it with the original German and with Gary Mann's more decorous translation from a Bible research website (Marlowe 2003):

Es heisst / Wer am wege bawet / der hat viel meister /also gehet mirs auch / Die jenigen die noch nie haben recht reden können / schweige denn dolmetschen / die sind allzumal meine meister / und ich mus ihr aller jünger sein / Und wenn ich sie hette sollen fragen / wie man die ersten zwey wort Matthei. j. Liber generationis / sollte verdeudschen / so hette ihr keiner gewust gack dazu zu sagen / und urteilen mir nu das ganze werck / die feinen gesellen. Also gieng es S. Hieronymo auch / da er die Biblia dolmetschet / da war alle welt sein meister / Er allein war es / der nichts kundte / und urteileten dem guten man sein werck die jenigen / so ihm nicht gnug gewest weren / das sie ihm die schuch hetten solle wisschen / Darümb gehört grosse gedult dazu / so jemand etwas öffentlich guts thun will / denn die welt wil meister Klüglin bleiben / und mus imer das Ros unter dem schwantz zeumen / alles meistern un selbs nichts können / das ist ihr art / davon sie nicht lassen kan.

It is said, "He who builds along the road has many masters." That is how it is with me also. Those who have never been able to speak properly (to say nothing of translating) have all at once become my masters and I must be their pupil. If I were to have asked them how to turn into German the first two words of Matthew, *Liber Generationis*, not one of them would have been able to say Quack! And now they judge my whole work! Fine fellows! It was also like this for St. Jerome when he translated the Bible. Everybody was his master. He alone was totally incompetent, and people who were not worthy to clean his boots judged the good man's work. It takes a great deal of patience to do good things in public. The world believes itself to be the expert in everything, while putting the bit under the horse's tail. Criticizing everything and accomplishing nothing, that is the world's nature. It can do nothing else.

SEVENTEEN HUNDRED PAGES OF PROPOSED CHANGES

Bible translation continues today as both a movement and an industry. The website of the international umbrella group United Bible Societies states that it is currently involved in translation projects into over 500 languages – 340 of them for the first time. The Bible is also endlessly re-translated into English, feeding a seemingly inexhaustible demand. A recent *New Yorker* article called "The Good Book Business" quoted research which found that "ninety-one percent of American households own at least one Bible – the average household owns four – which means that Bible publishers manage to sell twenty-five million copies a year of a book that almost everyone already has" (Radosh 2006).

Eugene Nida is one of the great contemporary figures in translation. As a theorist, he defined the "dynamic equivalence" approach, which emphasizes readability rather than word-for-word "formal equivalence." He also spent half a century on the road as a consultant to literally hundreds of Bible translation projects on behalf of the United Bible Societies. Nida's memoir *Fascinated by Languages* follows him across continents and languages as he discusses the linguistic, administrative, and political problems presented by such projects. In the following selection, Nida describes a truly participatory process of translation in Latin America – one can imagine generations of biblical translators spinning in their literalist graves – while laying out very clearly the debate between dynamic and formal approaches (Nida 2003).

Early in the twentieth century the Reina-Valera Bible in Spanish was revised by a secretary in the Spanish embassy in London and published in 1909 by the British and Foreign Bible Society, but a close comparison of this revision with earlier editions showed quite clearly that although the revisor was fully competent in Spanish, he was not sensitive to many of the theological issues involved. Furthermore, the Spanish of Latin America had departed significantly from the standards employed in Spain. As a result many words and phrases had little or no meaning for the average Spanish speakers in the western world.

Believers are usually reluctant to accept a revision of a text that has been used for a number of generations. In fact, the more old-fashioned a text seems to be, the more it appears to be closer to the original events of several thousand years ago. Furthermore, many people believe that their ability to understand a strange form of their own language is evidence that they have received from God a special gift for interpreting God's mysterious use of words. If the Bible is the very word of God, then it must contain the words of God, and therefore why should anyone change what God has said?

Other people, however, are not only frustrated by words they do not know, but they insist that if the words come from God, they should be in the language of the people of God. Was not that the purpose of Christ's coming into the world? So why hide the meaning in words that do not speak clearly to people today?

Even though there may be plenty of linguistic reasons for a revision, most people believe that a revision is justified only if the meaning of the text is clearer. But they also want notes, as well as introductions and better indexes in order to help them understand the text better. In addition, the format, including length of lines, size of type, punctuation, and paragraphing should represent important improvements.

Accordingly, we went from country to country, visiting the principal cities in Spanish-speaking Latin-America, speaking in churches and with individuals in order to learn what was needed and wanted. But we soon realized that we must have a more direct involvement of people, and so we cut important sections out of existing Bibles and pasted the pages on larger sheets of paper so that individuals and groups could indicate specifically what they thought should be changed in the text. The pages were sent to the local Bible Society and then on to me for study.

People sent more than 1,700 pages of proposed changes, and on the basis of a careful study of these recommendations a committee consisting of three presidents of seminaries, a specialist in rural churches, and a poet, worked out a set of principles and procedures for dealing with the various types of literature: history, legend, lyric poetry, wisdom sayings, prophecy, Gospel texts, and letters.

The mimeographing of the revised text during and after each session was a tremendous task, because there were several hundred pages to be typed, proofread, copied on old-fashioned mimeograph machines, and mailed to reviewers in Latin America and Spain. And at the beginning of each meeting of the revision team, the feedback from reviewers was studied.

We purposely arranged for the revision team to hold their sessions in different countries because this greatly helped people understand the international character of this enterprise. Once, however, we encountered a very unusual problem. A professor of Hebrew in one of the countries of South America came on his own initiative and announced that he should be a member of the revision team because all professors of Hebrew recognized him as the outstanding specialist in the Hebrew Bible. But he also told members of the revision team that if they did not accept his judgment on various issues, he was likely to have a heart attack.

When members of the team told me about the man's threat, I simply said, "Let him have an attack." I had recently read a research article on heart disease indicating that people who threaten a heart attack seldom have one. A couple of days later, our interim member of the team quietly left.

In this revision we purposely avoided radical changes, and we compensated for the changes in familiar verses by greater clarity, shorter words, larger type, more effective paragraphing, and helpful cross-reference notes. We were also delighted to have the help of Peter Denyer, a member of the Latin-American Mission, who proofread the texts, developed an exceptional cross-reference system, and prepared a first-class concordance published by the mission.

The success of this limited revision of the Reina-Valera text resulted in the later selection of an inter-confessional committee to produce a completely new text of the Scriptures in Spanish, in which due attention could be given to the style of language, important theological insights, and crucial helps for readers, for example, an index of key terms, notes about distinctive meanings, lists of parallel passages, section headings, and culturally distinctive elements.

Nida's memoir describes working in many exotic settings, from the jungles of Yucatán to the Inuit communities of the Canadian Arctic, with stops in Burma and the Pacific Islands. One of the strangest consultations occurred in the 1960s as the Roman Catholic Church under Pope John XXIII was going through a period of modernization.

Soon after the declarations of Vatican II that the liturgy and the three-year series of Scripture readings should be translated into the local languages of worshippers around the world, translation consultants were swamped with requests for help. From priests to bishops we received numerous requests for assistance – especially books dealing with principles of Bible translation and helpful commentaries published on various books of the Bible. These requests for help were both numerous and widespread, and so we concluded that this must represent a completely new policy of the Vatican. Accordingly, we invited some representatives of the Vatican, especially in the department of Propaganda Fidei, to meet with us in Crêt-Bérard, a conference center in Switzerland.

I was asked to head up the discussions, but I was opposed to the idea of prepared papers, because writers tend to defend their own views rather than explore the ideas of other people. Also, I thought it would be much better not to have a secretary or a recorder. We simply needed to talk about what was happening.

We began the two-day consultation by describing our experiences in various parts of the world and by asking quite frankly whether all this represented the policy of the Vatican. We indicated clearly that we wanted to respond positively to requests for help, but we needed to know if this would be misinterpreted in some circles.

To our immense surprise we learned that leaders in the Vatican knew nothing about requests for help from the United Bible Societies. They were as surprised as we had been, so what should we do? In some places there had already been considerable cooperation, but what form should this cooperation take in the future? Should we set up joint Protestant and Roman Catholic teams of translators? Should we make available existing texts of the Scriptures published by the Bible Societies? Should we have Roman Catholic translation consultants? What would be the implications of existing Scriptures being reviewed for an imprimatur? Anything and everything was on the table. I mentioned my experience with a group of Roman Catholic scholars in Hong Kong, and I wondered whether we could think in terms of joint teams of Roman Catholic and Protestant scholars preparing Bible translations for joint use.

Because our guests from the Vatican were as surprised as we had been, they scarcely knew how to answer, but they were anxious to talk about the incredible implications of such a development. The issue of proper names would inevitably be a problem, but the fact that within Roman Catholic and the Protestant traditions there are differences in the forms of proper names and in key terms might reduce considerably the emotional impact of new forms of names and new ways of talking about important theological concepts.

We also brought up such issues as the perpetual virginity of Mary, to which one Vatican representative responded, "That is part of our tradition, but it is not a part of the New Testament text." And we continued to talk about such issues as the brothers of Jesus and the various bulls against the work of the Bible Societies. Should such bulls be withdrawn or simply forgotten? The latter was obviously the better solution. By the second day there seemed to be no major road-blocks to launching a number of trial programs.

One of the Vatican representatives was so enthusiastic about the prospects that he immediately suggested giving wide-spread publicity to such a program. But I tried to point out that it would be much better to produce some joint texts and then inform people of the plans and policy. How could some of our Protestant friends in Latin America justify cooperation with people whom they regarded as "unsaved heretics"? But one member of Propaganda Fidei immediately responded, "You have your fundamentalists and we have our cardinals."

TRANSLATION FROM A PERFECT TONGUE

No one is ever likely to say, "If English was good enough for Mohammed..." Since Arabic was the native language of the Prophet, orthodox Muslim theologians ascribe a miraculous and unique character to the language of the Koran: it is only revelatory (i.e., divinely inspired) in Arabic.

The sacred nature of the language itself causes a problem for translators – and translation is necessary, because the vast majority of Muslims are not native Arabic speakers. You don't mess with it, even if (as many Muslim readers would agree) you find much of it obscure, repetitive and even internally contradictory. Some of the problems are illustrated by a colophon appended to a Spanish Koran translated from the sixteenth century, now in the public library of Toledo, Spain. A fascinating article by Consuelo López-Morillas of Indiana University puts it in context (López-Morillas 1983). At the time, as the Christian majority was busy destroying the vestiges of Islam in the country, fewer and fewer Spanish Muslims were able to understand Arabic and were forced to rely increasingly on translations. The translator, who was probably more of a copyist, sounds apologetic, and even goes so far as to quote a *hadith* (oral commentary) attributed to the Prophet to justify the translation.

> Here ends the first quarter of the glorious Qur'ān. One should not doubt it just because it is written in Christian letters; for he who copied it took it from another Qur'ān that was in its original Arabic language and set forth literally word by word. And he copied only the Romance [language] from it, to help him in his study of Arabic. And since it was lent to him by certain good people to copy in a specified time, which was short, and he hoped for God's grace to help him keep his promise and return it in the stated time, he wrote it in Christian letters. But the scribe bears witness that it is copied directly, just as he found it, and that he knows the letters of the Christians and of the Muslims and some Arabic. And he made bold to press on in his studying, as has been said, because of the short time that he had [the book] from the people who lent it; and the letters of the Christians are the most he dared to write in such a case. He begs that because it is in such letters it not be scorned, but rather respected; because being set down in this way it is more visible to Muslims who know how to read Christian, but not Muslim, letters. For it is true that the Prophet (peace be upon him) said that the best language was one that could be understood. This is obvious, although I confess that the perfect language is Arabic.

HOSTILE TRANSLATIONS: THE KORAN INTO ENGLISH

Like the Bible, the Koran has been translated into hundreds of languages, starting with Persian in the seventh century. In the West, many of these translations were frankly hostile enterprises – particularly during the fifteenth and sixteenth centuries, when the Ottoman Empire was expanding in eastern Europe. The late A.J. Arberry, in the preface to his own translation of the Koran, quoted some of his predecessors' commentaries. The first, published in 1649, is by the Scottish clergyman Alexander Ross, who, knowing no Arabic, translated it into English from André du Ryer's French version of 1647 – or as Ross's title page had it, "translated out of Arabick into French... and newly Englished, for the satisfaction of all that desire to look into the Turkish Vanities" (Arberry 1955).

> There being so many Sects and Heresies banded together against the Truth, finding that of Mahomet wanting to the Muster, I thought good to bring it to their Colours, that so viewing thine enemies in their full body, thou maist the better prepare to encounter, and I hope overcome them. It may happily startle thee, to find him so to speak English, as if he had made some Conquest on the Nation; but thou wilt soon reject that fear, if thou consider that this his Alcoran (the Ground-work of the Turkish Religion), hath been already translated into almost all Languages in Christendom (at least, the most general, as the Latin, Italian, French, etc.), yet never gained any Proselyte, where the Sword, its most forcible, and strongest argument hath not prevailed... Thou shalt find it of so rude, and incongruous a composure, so farced with contradictions, blasphemies, obscene speeches, and ridiculous fables, that some modest, and more rational Mahometans have thus excused it; that their Prophet wrote an hundred and twenty thousand sayings, whereof three thousand only are good, the residue (as the impossibility of the Moons falling into his sleeve, the Conversion and Salvation of the Devils, and the like) are false and ridiculous.

This was the only version most English-speakers had for almost one hundred years, and many of the succeeding translations, though more accurate and rendered directly from the Arabic, were equally hostile. What a difference, then, to read Arberry as he introduces his own translation, *The Koran Interpreted*. The title is significant, Arberry being sensitive to the orthodox Muslim view that the Koran is untranslatable. But Arberry, who was the Sir Thomas Adams's Professor of Arabic at Cambridge University from 1947 until his death in 1969, had a particular objective in mind, stating, "My chief reason for offering this new version of a book which has been 'translated' many times already is that in no previous rendering has a serious attempt been made to imitate, however imperfectly, those rhetorical and rhythmical patterns which are the glory and the sublimity of the Koran." Arberry reveals much about himself in the final two paragraphs of his preface:

> Using the language of music, each Sura is a rhapsody composed of whole or fragmentary leitmotivs; the analogy is reinforced by the subtly varied rhythmical flow of the discourse. If this diagnosis of the literary structure of the Koran may be accepted as true – and it accords with what we know of the poetical instinct, indeed the whole aesthetic impulse, of the Arabs – it follows that those notorious incongruities and irrelevancies, even those "wearisome repetitions," which have proved such stumbling-blocks in the way of our Western appreciation, will vanish in the light of a clearer understanding of the nature of the Muslim scriptures. A new vista opens up; following this hitherto unsuspected and unexplored path, the eager interpreter hurries forward upon an exciting journey of discovery, and is impatient to report his findings to a largely indifferent and incredulous public.
>
> During the long months, the dark and light months, of labouring at this interpretation, eclectic where the ancient commentators differ in their understanding of a word or a phrase, unannotated because notes in plenty are to be found in other versions, and the radiant beauty of the original is not clouded by such vexing interpolations – all through this welcome task I have been reliving those Ramadan nights of long ago, when I would sit on the veranda of my Gezira house and listen entranced to the old, white-bearded Sheykh who chanted the Koran for the pious delectation of my neighbour. He had the misfortune, my neighbour, to be a prominent politician, and so in the fullness of his destiny, but not the fullness of his years, he fell to an assassin's bullet; I like to think that the merit of those holy recitations may have eased the way for him into a world free of the tumult and turbulence that attended his earthly career. It was then that I, the infidel, learnt to understand and react to the thrilling rhythms of the Koran, only to be apprehended when listened to at such a time and in such a place. In humble thankfulness I dedicate this all too imperfect essay in imitation to the memory of those magical Egyptian nights.

A WOMAN'S POINT OF VIEW

Koranic translation and interpretation is the subject of a great deal of attention at the moment, often expressed in newspaper headlines about specific and highly emotive translation issues. For example, are martyrs (read: suicide-bombers) promised seventy-two virgins or a bunch of grapes when they get to Paradise? The answer may depend on whether you translate the Arabic *hur* as "houri," which has been the accepted translation for centuries, or as "white raisins," which linguistic analysis suggests was the word's meaning at the time the Prophet was dictating his thoughts. This particular question was raised by the German scholar Christoph Luxenberg (prudently, a pseudonym), whose research suggests that many passages in the Koran are derived from pre-existing Christian Aramaic texts, which is not reflected in the interpretations most widely distributed throughout the Muslim world.

As in other areas of religious translation, women have had little profile in translating or otherwise interpreting the Koran. That changed recently with the publication of Laleh Bakhtiar's *The Sublime Quran* (Bakhtiar 2007). In the preface, Bakhtiar tells a little about herself and about the methods she used in the new translation.

> The method used by English translators of the Quran to date is to start at the beginning of the sacred text and work through translating until the end. I used the same method in translating over thirty books before I earned a Ph.D. in educational psychology much later in life. Armed with this science, I began this translation as a scientific study to see if it was possible to apply these principles to a translation by finding a different English equivalent for each Arabic verb or noun in order to achieve a translation of a sacred text that has internal consistency and reliability.
>
> As I am unlettered, so to speak, in modern Arabic, I relied upon my many years of tutoring in classical Quranic Arabic grammar. It was at that time that I had become familiar with the al-Mujim al-mufahris. The Mujim lists every Arabic root and its derivative(s) found in the Quran as verbs, nouns and some particles (adverbs, prepositions, conjunctions or interjections). Each time a specific word appears, the relevant part of the verse containing that word is quoted with reference to Chapter and Sign (verse). They are listed under their three-letter or four-letter roots. I transliterated the words according to the system of transliteration developed by the American Library Association/Library of Congress 1997 Romanization Tables in preparing an accompanying Concordance. I then found a viable English

equivalent that I would not repeat for another Arabic word. I found that there are 3600+ different Arabic verbs and nouns, excluding most prepositions, that appear at least one time in the Quran. Only in some 50+ cases was it necessary to use the same English word twice for two different Arabic words. For example, there are two different Arabic words for parents, or the number "three," or the word "year," and three for the word "time."

For every Arabic verb's perfect (past tense), imperfect (present and future tense), and imperative form, the same basic English equivalent is used adjusted according to whether it is past, present or a command. A different English equivalent is used for a verbal noun, an active or passive participle, and a noun, again, adjusted according to its usage. The English equivalents for these verbs and nouns are then studied in context and, where necessary for correct meaning, an alternative equivalent that has not been previously used elsewhere in the text is used. This resulted in 5800+ unique English equivalents. I then added the some 50,000+ particles (adverbs, prepositions, conjunctions or interjections not listed in the Mujim) to complete the data base.

Beginning this process seven years ago with the words instead of the first sentence, I later learned that this was much the method, called formal equivalence, used in the translation of the King James Version of the Bible first published in 1611 CE. This translation, then, is one of formal equivalence in order to be as close to the original as possible. This is the most objective type of translation, as compared to a translation using dynamic equivalence, where the translator attempts to translate the ideas or thoughts of a text, rather than the words, which results in a much more subjective translation.

Another distinction between this translation and other present English translations arises from the fact that this is the first English translation of the Quran by an American woman. Just as I found a lack of internal consistency in previous English translations, I also found that little attention had been given to the woman's point of view.

While the absence of a woman's point of view for over 1440 years since the revelation began, clearly needs to change, it must be acknowledged that there are many men who have been supportive of the view of women as complements to themselves, as the completion of their human unity. To them, I and other Muslim women are eternally grateful. They relate to women as the Quran and Hadith intended. The criticism women have is towards those men who are not open to this understanding, who are exclusive in opposition to the Quran and Sunnah's inclusiveness.

Clearly the intention of the Quran is to see man and woman as complements of one another, not as oppressed-oppressor. Consequently, in the introduction and translation, I address a main criticism of Islam in regard to the inferiority of women, namely, that a husband can beat his wife (4:34) after two stages of trying to discipline her...

Bakhtiar explains her interpretation of Surah 4:34 in detail elsewhere in the book, basing her argument on formal equivalence (that the word in question, *idrib*, should be understood to mean "go away from" rather than "beat"), context ("the fact that the Prophet never beat his wives, clearly having understood the word in another sense"), and tradition ("noting that practices in Islam are based on what Prophet Muhammad did"). The concluding paragraphs in her preface provide a powerful explanation of why translation can make a huge difference in people's lives:

While I have personally been blessed by my contacts with the most understanding and compassionate of men in my lifetime, and I have never found myself in a situation of being physically threatened or beaten, reading about and hearing first hand stories of women who have, I felt the deep sense that I am essentially and spiritually one with them by my very existence. The question I kept asking myself during the years of working on the translation: How could God, the Merciful, the Compassionate, sanction husbands beating their wives?

The feeling, however, did not rise to the surface until the day I first publicly presented the results of this translation of the Sublime Quran at the WISE (Women's Islamic Initiative in Spirituality and Equity) Conference (November, 2006) where 150 Muslim women from all over the world had gathered to discuss the possibility of forming a Women's Islamic Council. I gave the logic as to why the word "to beat" in 4:34 has been a misinterpretation. At the end of the session, two Muslim women approached me. They said that they work in shelters for battered women and that they and the women in the shelters have been waiting for over 1400 years for someone to pay attention to this issue through a translation of the Quran. The heavy weight of responsibility suddenly fell upon my shoulders. I had to publish my findings as soon as possible to initiate a dialogue with the exclusivists.

Hopefully the initiating of a dialogue will further open the minds and awaken to consciousness and conscience those men who place their hand on the Word of God giving themselves permission to beat their wife.

I ask for the forgiveness of the One God for any errors in this translation, at the same time that I ask for His blessings.

CHAPTER FIVE

Govspeak: Translating the official version

One of the greatest fears of international lawyers is that translators will "scuttle"
the intent of the parties by attempting to clarify clauses that are intentionally
vague, obscure or even ambiguous.
— SUSAN SARCEVIC in "Legal Translation and Translation Theory:
  A Receiver-Oriented Approach" (Sarcevic 2000)

Governments have always had to deal with language barriers, often within their own borders in the case of multilingual states or empires. The Chinese government (dynasties come and go, but the civil service is eternal) has been employing translators for almost three thousand years, particularly during periods of imperial expansion or other moments of engagement with the world outside the Middle Kingdom. When the government is the client, source documents can range from tax forms to legislation, from international treaties to expense invoices, and from the most public of speeches to the most secret of intelligence. As long as the state has its reasons, it will also have its translators.

WE WON, YOU LOST

The very notion of an "official" translation implies a power relationship. Consider article L of the Treaty of Tientsin (1858) following the so-called Opium War by the Western powers against China:

> All official communications addressed by the Diplomatic and Consular Agents of Her Majesty the Queen to the Chinese Authorities shall, henceforth, be written in English. They will for the present be accompanied by a Chinese version, but, it is understood that, in the event of there being

any difference of meaning between the English and the Chinese text, the English Government will hold the sense as expressed in the English text to be the correct sense. This provision is to apply to the Treaty now negotiated, the Chinese text of which has been carefully corrected by the English original.

The power of the victor has seldom been expressed more blandly and brutally than that.

TRANSLATION AND EMPIRE

Most imperial translating is part of the tedious business of administration, but history records a few more interesting translation projects taken on by colonial or military officials. Consider Sir George Grey (1812–98), who had a long career in the service of the British Empire, serving as governor of South Australia, the Cape Colony, and (twice) New Zealand, where he eventually capped his career as premier. He was also a translator and informal ethnologist, amassing the first great written store of knowledge about the indigenous peoples of New Zealand. During his first term as governor there (he arrived five years after the signing of the Treaty of Waitangi, the translation of which became hugely controversial in the twentieth century), Grey took it upon himself to learn the Maori language in order to deal more directly with the new "subjects of Her Majesty," some of whom were intermittently in open revolt against the colonial government. But he soon decided that even some level of fluency was not enough (Grey 1855).

> To my surprise, however, I found that these chiefs, either in their speeches to me or in their letters, frequently quoted, in explanation of their views and intentions, fragments of ancient poems or proverbs, or made allusions which rested on an ancient system of mythology; and, although it was clear that the most important parts of their communications were embodied in those figurative forms, the interpreters were quite at fault, they could then rarely (if ever) translate the poems or explain the allusions, and there was no publication in existence which threw any light upon these subjects, or which gave the meaning of the great mass of the words which the natives upon such occasions made use of; so that I was compelled to content myself with a short general statement of what some other native believed that the writer of the letter intended to convey as his meaning by the fragment of the poem he had quoted or by the allusions he had made. I should add that

even the great majority of the young Christian natives were quite as much at fault on these subjects as were the European interpreters.

Clearly, however, I could not, as Governor of the country, permit so close a veil to remain drawn between myself and the aged and influential chiefs whom it was my duty to attach to British interests and to the British race, whose regard and confidence, as also that of their tribes, it was my desire to secure, and with whom it was necessary that I should hold the most unrestricted intercourse. Only one thing could under such circumstances be done, and that was to acquaint myself with the ancient language of the country, to collect its traditional poems and legends, to induce their priests to impart to me their mythology, and to study their proverbs. For more than eight years I devoted a great part of my available time to these pursuits. Indeed, I worked at this duty in my spare moments in every part of the country I traversed and during my many voyages from portion to portion of the Islands. I was also always accompanied by natives, and still at every possible interval pursued my inquiries into these subjects. Once, when I had with great pains amassed a large mass of materials to aid me in my studies, the Government House was destroyed by fire, and with it were burnt the materials I had so collected, and thus I was left to commence again my difficult and wearying task.

The ultimate result, however, was that I acquired a great amount of information on these subjects, and collected a large mass of materials, which was, however, from the manner in which they were acquired, in a very scattered state – for different portions of the same poem or legend were often collected from different natives, in very distant parts of the country; long intervals of time, also, frequently elapsed after I had obtained one part of a poem or legend, before I could find a native accurately acquainted with another portion of it; consequently the fragments thus obtained were scattered through different note-books, and, before they could be given to the public, required to be carefully arranged and rewritten, and, what was still more difficult (whether viewed in reference to the real difficulty of fairly translating the ancient language in which they were composed, or my many public duties), it was necessary that they should be translated.

Having, however, with much toil acquired information which I found so useful to myself, I felt unwilling that the result of my labours should be lost to those whose duty it may be hereafter to deal with the natives of

New Zealand; and I therefore undertook a new task, which I have often, very often, been sorely tempted to abandon; but the same sense of duty which made me originally enter upon the study of the native language has enabled me to persevere up to the present period, when I have already published one large volume in the native language, containing a very extensive collection of the ancient traditional poems, religious chants, and songs, of the Maori race, and I now present to the European reader a translation of the principal portions of their ancient mythology and of some of their most interesting legends...

With regard to the style of the translation a few words are required: I fear in point of care and language it will not satisfy the critical reader; but I can truly say that I have had no leisure carefully to revise it; the translation is also faithful, and it is almost impossible closely and faithfully to translate a very difficult language without almost insensibly falling somewhat into the idiom and form of construction of that language, which, perhaps, from its unusualness may prove unpleasant to the European ear and mind, and this must be essentially the case in a work like the present, no considerable continuous portion of the original whereof was derived from one person, but which is compiled from the written or orally delivered narratives of many, each differing from the others in style, and some even materially from the rest in dialect.

I have said that the translation is close and faithful; it is so to the full extent of my powers and from the little time I have had at my disposal. I have done no more than add in some places such few explanatory words as were necessary to enable a person unacquainted with the productions, customs, or religion of the country, to understand what the narrator meant. For the first time, I believe, a European reader will find it in his power to place himself in the position of one who listens to a heathen and savage high-priest, explaining to him, in his own words and in his own energetic manner, the traditions in which he earnestly believes, and unfolding the religious opinions upon which the faith and hopes of his race rest.

YES, MINISTER

Grey was an unusual man in that he was someone with real power who was also a translator. In real life, or at least in real politics, that is rarely the case. Translators working for politicians often find themselves caught between their professional responsibility to translate their client's words accurately and their moral responsibility to tell the truth. Jean Delisle, one of the foremost historians of translation, provides an example in his *Translators through History* (Delisle and Woodsworth 1995).

The lawyer Eugène-Philippe Dorion (1830–72) was an important figure in official translation in Canada during the years immediately preceding and following Confederation (1867). He was highly acclaimed by his contemporaries for his knowledge of ancient languages, as well as English, French and some native languages. Appointed head of the French translators' bureau, he improved the quality of language in French versions of legislation, but he sometimes had to bow to the will of politicians. One of the founding fathers of Confederation, Sir Georges-Etienne Cartier, exercised his authority and insisted that he translate the term "Dominion of Canada" as *Puissance du Canada* in the *British North America Act*, the constitutional legislation by virtue of which modern Canada was created. The translator found it pretentious to call a nonindustrialized colony of three-and-a-half million inhabitants a *"puissance."* He was not alone in this opinion. However, his outstanding linguistic ability and authority in the field of translation were outweighed by the dictates of a minister. Common sense and a translator's judgment could not override the influence of a politician. The expression remained unchanged until the 1950s. After that time its use became less and less frequent, until the Constitution Act of 1982 got rid of it once and for all.

Translators are thought to have little alternative but to respect the powers that be – especially if those powers hold the purse strings. The translator's *droit à la parole* is, after all, the right to render someone else's ideas for the benefit of a third party. The translator is even more constrained by obligations to remain trustworthy, keep official secrets and remain employable for repeat performances. Thus, translators have power only by delegation, and only for as long as they can be trusted.

I KNOW, LET'S GET *MACHINES* TO DO IT!

The early days of research into machine translation (M.T.) were largely driven by governments. John Hutchins' *Early Years in Machine Translation: Memoirs and Biographies of Pioneers* is a fascinating collection of texts by or about the pioneers of this field, starting in the late 1940s and taking in the work of teams in the U.S., the USSR, France, Japan, Czechoslovakia, Italy, and the U.K. (Hutchins 2000).

Here are two excerpts from the book, written by an American and Russian respectively, which give a sense of the excitement of those years, but also of the very different experiences of people working under opposing political systems. In the first, Victor H. Yngve writes about the research done at the Massachusetts Institute of Technology (MIT), and the early computers they had at their disposal (Yngve 2000).

I am often asked how I ever happened to move into linguistics from physics. The reader will see that the shift was a gradual and quite natural move from physics through MT to linguistics. I perceived my early full-time commitment to MT and its renewal every year or so in the beginning as exciting and adventuresome, but entailing considerable career risks. I realized acutely that each year away from physics would make it that much harder to return to the forefront of research there. I have never regretted the move.

As part of my research assistantship at the University of Chicago I was involved in preparing instrumentation and running experiments for detecting the incoming cosmic radiation in the stratosphere using high altitude balloon flights and airplane flights. The instrumentation was designed to detect and record high-energy particles capable of triggering several Geiger counters in a row simultaneously while penetrating up to 22 cm. of lead. The means for detecting and recording the coincident electrical pulses from the counters were similar to techniques found in the literature on the new automatic electronic computers, the so-called giant brains of the late 1940s.

It seemed to me that these new machines might be useful for other purposes besides computing – perhaps for playing chess, searching a library file, or translating languages. Of these, translating seemed potentially the most important, for it might help to eliminate some of the barriers between countries in a post-war world...

I became convinced that linguistics studied stable and repeatable phenomena like the phenomena found in cosmic-ray physics, and that the phenomena were every bit as complex and interesting, and even more important. I was convinced that under the methods of the structuralists the study of linguistic phenomena could be eminently scientific. Furthermore, the possibility of a linguistics methodology following strict structural procedures not relying on knowledge of the meaning suggested the possibility of a mechanizable translation methodology that did not rely on the machine understanding the meaning of what it was translating, for it was clear (wasn't it?) that a machine could never understand meaning, something that even the linguists were hard-pressed to deal with...

One of the first things I turned to [when he moved to MIT in 1953 to work full-time on machine translation] was to test the proposition that a solution of grammatical and syntactic problems would also be a solution for considerably more than half of all the multiple meaning problems and that a specialized field glossary could cope with most of the rest.

For this purpose a German book review of an American book on mathematics was secured. A secretary was asked to prepare vocabulary cards for the review, one card for each different word appearing in the review. Different inflected forms of the same stem were to count as different words. I then took these cards and, not having read the book review or the book being reviewed, chose one correspondent for each German word and wrote it on the card for that word. For those words that had a special sense in mathematics, the mathematical sense was chosen so as to simulate the effect of a specialized field glossary. But for many of the grammatical words such as *der* and *sein,* no one translation would be adequate. For these, the original German word was retained as the 'translation.' Furthermore, the grammatically significant endings for many words were also retained untranslated and added to the translated stems. Words and portions of words translated into English were rendered in all caps; the untranslated words and endings were rendered in lower case. German compounds were hyphenated in the translation.

A "translation" of the book review was then prepared using these cards so as to simulate the output of a machine doing a word-for-word translation. The original German word order was of course retained. One sentence from the resulting "partial translation" follows as an example:

Die CONVINCINGe CRITIQUE des CLASSICALen IDEA-OF-PROBABILITY
is eine der REMARKABLEen WORKS des AUTHORS.

Readers of the partial translation who knew no German could grasp the subject matter from the translated stems but were generally unable to get much of an idea of what was being said about that subject matter. However, readers who knew a little German grammar were able to understand quite well and fairly rapidly what was being said. This was thought to simulate the result of the machine having solved the grammatical and word-order problems. From the great difference between these two types of readers in their ability to understand the translation, it was concluded that a solution to the grammatical problems was well worth the trouble. Furthermore, the experiment seemed to confirm that if specialized field glossaries were used, very few multiple meaning problems would remain.

Some consideration was given to the possibility that partial machine translations would be useful in themselves if readers were prepared with a short course in German grammar. I estimated that the historic Whirlwind computer, designed and built at MIT, could be programmed to translate 20,000 words per hour using a 10,000 word dictionary.

BETWEEN THE DEVIL AND THE KGB

Igor A. Mel'cuk came to machine translation from a different direction, as a linguist. Here, in an article based on an interview with John Hutchins, he describes some challenges that his American counterparts didn't face (Mel'cuk 2000).

My contact with MT came already while I was a student of Spanish. It was early spring in 1954, cold, slushy, horrible weather, and I was in a rush to go home when I was suddenly stopped in the street by someone I knew – another student of my department. He started telling me something really bizarre: he had a girl friend, a mathematician who was working with someone else on something called "machine translation," and they were looking for someone from one of the linguistics departments who could speak French and help them. The organizer of the project was Professor A.A. Ljapunov, a wellknown mathematician, and since he spoke French, he wanted the first MT to be done from French into Russian, so that he could control the research. I had no idea what MT could be, I had not heard about computers at all (at the time there were perhaps only two or three in the whole country), but I was curious and I went to see this girl Natasha Ricco. There were actually three of them altogether: her two colleagues were graduates in mathematics, and one of them was Olga Kulagina. They explained to me quickly and precisely what it was about. For me it was ideal: I loved languages but I hated philology, I loved logic but there was none in our courses; and this was a chance to be logical with languages. I started immediately, working with Olga on an algorithm for translation from French into Russian. The first runs were done in the fall of the same year (1954), about six or eight months after the IBM-Georgetown experiment by Paul Garvin and Peter Sheridan in the previous January.

We wrote up what we had done and a paper was published in *Voprosy Jazykoznanija* in 1956; it was probably the first paper on MT in the Soviet Union (Kulagina and Mel'cuk 1956). Our boss Ljapunov wanted me to work for him but he could not hire me at his own Institute of Applied Mathematics (Matematiceskij Institut imeni V.A. Steklova) again because I was Jewish, and the institute was a state and military oriented body. Only non-Jewish postgraduates were allowed to work there. However, he eventually managed to get me a position in the Institute of Linguistics of the Soviet Academy of Sciences (Institut Jazykoznanija) on an understanding between himself and the administration that I was to be his employee – in fact I was even paid by him because he had transferred an official job and its salary from his own institute. I began at the Institute of Linguistics in July 1956, where I stayed 20 years before I was expelled from the USSR...

At one point, almost jokingly, I said that "automatic, or machine, translation (at least in its linguistic aspect) subsists even without a machine." Actually, in the circumstances we lived, we had no computers available, so we were virtually forced to treat MT as a thought-experiment. In any case, I believed then that it was extremely important to describe language as if for an ideal computer. It is a way of ensuring good rigorous formalization of what you are describing. I am not against a practical approach to MT, and would willingly participate in such research and development, but in Russia at the time there was no such prospect. For a linguist what is much more important is the idea of thinking in formal terms – and MT gives you that. I would never have discovered the significance of modeling language without working on machine translation. In theoretical discussions you can postulate whatever you want without any controls, but in MT everything is controlled by the principle of the applicability to a computational problem. This does not mean testing ideas by formulation in a computer program. In fact, for some time I have believed that you should not even try to write algorithms. For example, a dictionary can be criticized without knowing how people apply it, just by looking at correspondences and saying if they are right or wrong, if they are complete or not. There are plenty of algorithms for using a dictionary, but the quality of the dictionary itself is absolutely independent of them...

One day I was summoned to the vice-director of my institute; he had with him an official, obviously from the KGB, and they asked whether I had police clearance to see secret documents. Of course, I had not; they said I had to get one quickly; the KGB man would come back the next week. Evidently they had a very important document in my area of competence which they wanted me to evaluate. To get the clearance I had to go to another institute of the Academy of Sciences. The next day I encountered this formidable old lady, the head of what was known as Section One (*Pervyj Otdel*). She was an Armenian, beautiful like a Roman empress, who promised that she would prepare a file and that I would hear from her in about five months. Next week I explained the delay: "Oh no, we cannot wait five months!" Then I realized that although they could not tell me details they could tell me whether it was a manuscript or something published. It was "half-published, multiplied." Was it on machine translation? "Oh yes." What country is it from? That they could not say. I said I believed I knew everyone in this field, and that I have seen all the documents, and so I said that if they could show me just a piece of the document I could tell whether I knew it or not. I reeled off the groups I knew about: Oettinger's at Harvard, the Texas group, the one in Washington, a group in France, the TITUS group in Dusseldorf, etc. and said I knew all their publications. After sending me out of the room for a while, they decided to show me just a corner of the paper. I recognized immediately the color, the way the paper was printed, and said "I have it! Not only do I know it perfectly, but I have it! Wait a second and I'll bring it to you and you can say whether it is the same." I returned with the publication, which I had received by ordinary mail from [the French MT pioneer Professor Bernard] Vauquois.

"It cannot be true!" They opened their folder and it was exactly the same, but covered in stamps and seals. "You are telling us it came over the mail?" Of course, it is university publishing and it is there for the asking. "Thank you very much, comrade Mel'cuk. You are free to go." I believe it must have cost someone his job, or maybe his vacation in the Crimea. They did not want me to translate it, just to say whether it was important or not. Probably it had been received through some circuitous route by some KGB officer who did not know French. And now they knew it was of no value, anyone could get a copy.

EUROPE, EUROPA, ΕΥΡΩΠΗ, AN EORAIP...

Translating official text into one language is hard enough, but multiple target languages multiply the challenges geometrically. Emma Wagner describes the part that her translation unit at the European Commission played in a competition to find a slogan for Europe, and particularly the problem of ensuring accountability in an environment of conflicting loyalties (Chesterman and Wagner 2002).

This problem is well illustrated by an interesting project we were asked to undertake recently: translating the *Devise pour l'Europe* (Motto for Europe). This was a competition organized by the French newspaper *Ouest-France;* secondary school classes throughout Europe were invited to submit a European motto. The 10 best mottoes per country – 150 in all – were sent to us for translation into all the eleven official languages, so that a shortlist could be produced by an international panel of journalists. The end result was to be a single motto for Europe: something along the lines of: "United for peace and democracy," "Our differences are our strength," etc. It would have to work in all 11 official languages plus Latin. Translation was needed to enable the judges to understand the entries submitted, and also to disguise the national origin of each entry. The organizers did not want the judges to know which country the mottoes had come from – they were to be judged on content, not nationality.

When we translated the 150 best mottoes, we came up against a number of loyalty problems. Firstly, it was a competition, so the translations had to be "fair" – not an improvement on the original entries. I would interpret this as a duty of loyalty to the client: the organizers of the competition.

At the same time, we had to be loyal to the authors – the schoolchildren who had submitted the original mottoes. We must not do them a disservice by producing pedestrian translations of their efforts. We had to ensure "linguistic equality" – that mottoes written in lesser-known languages such as Greek and Finnish had as good a chance of winning as those in the widely known languages like French and English.

Naturally we also had to be loyal to the readers: to ensure that the translated mottoes would be effective in their own right and would convey a message without sounding foreign.

It became clear that we would also have to explain objectively why some entries were untranslatable. This I saw as a matter of loyalty to the translation profession: I had to find ways of explaining untranslatability to a lay audience made up of the competition organizers and Eurosceptic journalists who would be only too happy to pick holes in our translations.

The untranslatable mottoes included acrostics (where the initials make up a word) like this one submitted by schoolchildren in the United Kingdom:

Equality
Unity
Reform
Opportunity
Peace
Europe.

It would not be impossible to invent an equivalent motto in all languages, but it would be re-invention, not translation. For example, here is a French translation (close to original):

Egalité
Unité
Réforme
Ouverture
Paix
Europe

German translation (less exact):

Einheit
Umwelt
Reform
Optimismus
Partnerschaft
Achtung

The German version is a re-invention, not a translation. It introduces *Umwelt* (environment) and *Achtung* (respect) which do not feature in the original English motto, and has *Partnerschaft* (partnership) instead of "peace." The word for "peace" in several Germanic languages begins with an "F" (Danish and Swedish: *fred;* German: *Frieden*) but there is no "F" in "Europa," so this important concept has to be omitted, as does "equality" (*Gleichheit* in German).

Then there were some mottoes that were untranslatable because they had been submitted in (sort of) English:

> Original (from Austria): *YOUrope*
> Original (from Holland): *Europe = You are up*

There were also plays on existing catchphrases that could be translated perfectly well into some languages but not into all of them:

> Original (from Spain): *Haz Europa y no* la Guerra
> English translation: *Make Europe not war* (allusion to "Make love not war")
> French translation: *Faites l'Europe, pas la guerre*

This translates well into the Romance languages, but not into the Nordic and Germanic languages because they do not have a single verb like *make* that applies to Europe, love and war.

Rhymes were quite a challenge, and could not always be reproduced in all languages:

> Original (from the Netherlands): *Europa is trots, het staat als een rots*
> English translation (literal – rhyme not possible): *Europe is proud, it stands like a rock*
> French translation (exact equivalent, reproduces rhyme): *l'Europe est fière, solide comme la pierre*

Problems arose with unsuitable content: some mottoes referred to the new millennium (not the theme of the competition), while others contained factual mistakes such as references to fifteen stars on the European flag (there are twelve), or had undesirable political connotations, as in the following example:

> Original (from Austria): AEIOU: *Alle Europäer in Optimaler Union* (All Europeans In Optimal Union). This is an attempted overhaul of the old Habsburg motto *Austriae Est Imperare Orbi Universale* (Austria should rule the whole world) and arguably unwise in this context.

We had several weeks to prepare for the project, so like all dutiful project coordinators I tried to find out about recommended methods for translating slogans and mottoes. No theories, guidelines or "body of knowledge" appeared to exist. Once we had started the job, however, some of the translators suggested that one useful theoretical concept that we could use was Christiane Nord's distinction between *documentary* and *instrumental* translation, where documentary translation "shows what the original says" and instrumental translation "does what the original tries to do." To help untangle some of the loyalty conflicts I have described, and face up to the untranslatability problems, we devised a simple solution. We divided the original mottoes into two classes, D and A (we didn't have a class B or C):

> Class D – defective motto – untranslatable or unsuitable – *documentary* translation will do;
> Class A – viable motto, worth making the effort of *instrumental* translation (re-creating a rhyme, for example).

So the first step was to analyze and classify the mottoes. Then we had to ensure that all the 70 translators involved in the project had understood and would follow the Class A / Class D strategy in the same way. On the whole, they did, somewhat to my surprise. It seemed more efficient to channel their creative talents into translating the viable mottoes, rather than trying to turn dross into gold. Also to my surprise, the organizers of the competition agreed to this approach, and were grateful for our input on the relative merits of the competition entries. They even sent a TV crew to film us discussing the mottoes (visibility at last!) and invited me to act as consultant to the competition judges, explaining the translation problems we had encountered and the viability of the mottoes in all languages. One particular problem I encountered, as mentioned above, was that of demonstrating untranslatability and explaining the documentary / instrumental approach to the competition judges. It would have been pointless to use those words, because they are not generally understood – instrumental sounds as if violins should be involved somewhere. *Overt/covert* would not be applicable either. *Overt* might have its uses, but covert translation sounds so underhand. So when I was speaking to the "Motto for Europe" judges, I compromised by talking about *fairly literal* translations of the defective mottoes, and *creative* translations of the viable ones...

The winner was *Europe: Unity in diversity,* but no one had actually submitted that motto. It is an interesting case of what I call the "eclipse of the original," where the translations take over from the original... and then the original has to be changed to match the translations.

This is how it came about:

1. A German-speaking class submitted the motto *Einheit der Vielfalt.*
2. My colleagues translated this into:

   French: *Unité de la diversité*
   English: *Unity in diversity* (because the literal translation, Unity of diversity, is meaningless)

   ... and all the other languages.

3. The international panel of journalists that produced the shortlist of seven was not allowed to know the original language because that might create national bias. In effect they discussed everything in English and French. Their discussion went like this: "The French translation is not correct. It should be *Unité dans la diversité.* Let's put that on the shortlist."

4. The final jury of VIPs chose *Unity in diversity* as the winning motto, and agreed that the German should be changed to *Einheit in Vielfalt* to bring it into line with the other language versions. They also felt that the word *Europe* should feature. So it became *Europe: Unity in diversity.* In answer to the question "Who proposed it?" we can say "Everyone and no one. It is a representative motto and an expression of the common will of Europe's young people."

At the time of writing, the motto still has the status of a kind offer by the competition organizers, the French newspaper *Ouest-France,* and it has not been officially adopted by the E.U. institutions. Here it is in all the official languages plus Latin and Irish:

ES	Europa: Unidad en la diversidad
DA	Europa: Forenet i mangfoldighed
DE	Europa: Einheit in Vielfalt [note: the final version was In Vielfalt geeint]
EL	Ευρώπη: Διαφορετικοί αλλά ενωμένοι
EN	Europe: Unity in diversity

FR	L'Europe: l'Unité dans la diversité
IT	L'Europa: L'Unità nella diversità
NL	Europa: Eenheid in verscheidenheid
PT	Europa: Unidade na diversidade
FI	Eurooppa: Erilaisina yhdessä
SV	Europa: Förenade i mångfalden
Latin	Europa: In varietate concordia
Irish	An Eoraip: Aontacht san iolracht

CHAPTER SIX

L1on to G1on and back again: Business and technical translation

A fully localized program, insofar as it presents an interface to users, will also make use of images and metaphors for usage that are appropriate to that user community. This is not simply a translation of the text. An icon of an American mailbox, for example, may be completely puzzling to people in a different environment. The worst case I've seen was a Pause button with the image of two animal pawprints… Obvious, and mildly amusing to a native English speaker; utterly baffling to others.

— MARK DAVIS in "Globalization: Resistance Is Futile" (Davis 2003)

U ntil recently, the only translations that got much respect or academic attention were theological, literary, or scholarly. Today, however, pretty much every area of human endeavour requires translation, and each new technical or commercial advance creates a need for specialized translators. Globalization (G1on) and localization (L1on) are upon us: as a *Star Trek* character famously put it, resistance is futile.

WHEN HOMOGENIZATION MEETS DOMESTIFICATION
The dominant position of English on the global stage is a subject of considerable discussion in many circles, not just among translators. But it is not a simple phenomenon going inexorably in one deterministic direction, as Esperança Bielsa points out in her essay "Globalisation as Translation: An Approximation to the Key but Invisible Role of Translation in Globalisation" (Bielsa 2005). In fact, Umberto Eco's notion of translation as negotiation – described in chapter 3 – comes to mind.

Globalisation has caused an exponential increase of translation. The global dominance of English has been accompanied by a growing demand for translation, as people's own language continues to be the preferred language for access into informational goods. An area of significant growth in the translation industry over the last two decades has been the activity of localisation, through which a product is tailored to meet the needs of a specific local market (Cronin 2003: 13) [Michael Cronin's *Translation and Globalization* (Routledge, 2003)]. In an informational economy characterised by instantaneous access to information worldwide, the objective of the localisation industry becomes simultaneous availability in all the languages of the product's target markets (2003: 15). Translation values and strategies in localisation and e-localisation (web site localisation) are not uniform but combine elements of domestification and foreignisation to market products that have to appeal to their target buyers but, at the same time, often retain exoticising connections to the language of technological innovation (for an example, see Cronin 2003: 16–17)...

An analysis of translation as a key infrastructure of globalisation offers a way of exploring the articulation between the global and the local on a concrete, material level. In particular, it allows us to conceptualise and empirically assess how cultural difference is negotiated under globalisation and how present trends towards cultural homogenisation and Anglo-American domination are mediated at the local level through strategies of domestification and hybridisation.

THE RISE OF THE *AUTORISERET TRANSLATØR*

To some degree, the business world has been globalized for centuries. As long as people have had to write contracts and invoices for foreign products, other people have had to translate them. Here, Cay Dollerup describes the gradual professionalization of business translation in his native Denmark (Dollerup and Appel 1996).

In Denmark, the first professional translators were employed by the State in 1635: they worked at Elsinore where they had to translate into Danish the lading documents of foreign ships which paid the "Sound Dues," at that time a major source of revenue for the Danish Crown. The translators were few and translated indiscriminately from all languages, with nautical terms and the words for export articles as their main area, thus indicating that normally word-for-word translation served the purpose. The title *auto-riseret translatør* was introduced in 1782. I suggest that this is the general pattern in Europe: the professional translators appear when trade, legislation, bilingual administration and the like demand that words and documents must be understood in more or less the same way in different cultures and can be inter-subjectively (and naively) referred to as "the same" with the same implications for people speaking different languages.

In the 19th century, then, foreign language acquisition and teaching gain ground and become important. It is a problem in our context that foreign language teaching and foreign language acquisition tie up with the ability to translate so that it is impossible to find evidence of any translation teaching per se. It must have been an element of foreign language teaching, although national variations were doubtless great.

In Denmark, professional translators founded a school, *Translatørskolen*, around 1910 which operated courses (in translation) on a commercial basis. They attracted mostly people already employed in business, trade or law. At this particular school, where I attended a few classes back in 1960, teaching was rigidly prescriptive and carried out by individualists. The school ceased operating around 1970 when its functions were finally transferred to a state institution, the Copenhagen Business School. The point to note is that the decisive factor in establishing the teaching of translation is a recognised social need for this to be done: in this case first by the professionals, whose motivation has also been to improve the status of the profession, and, subsequently, by society at large, i.e. the State.

TIME, COST, QUALITY: YOU CHOOSE

Translation can be a big-budget item in a business project, sometimes costing far more than the writing or distribution costs. Calculations about the trade-offs between quality, cost, and speed of delivery can make all the difference between profit and loss – for both the supplier of the translation and the client. In his "Checking, Revision and Editing," John D. Graham discusses some of the compromises that have to be negotiated in commercial translating (Graham 1989).

All translators are torn between the two irreconcilable extremes: quality versus quantity. Since economic survival is dependent upon quantity, the number of pages takes on a great deal of significance – especially for the freelance translator. However, quality is also required. Bearing in mind the purpose for which the translation is required, the translator will also have to decide which of these two extremes is of greater importance: the quality of the finished version or the quantity produced. Quality takes time and costs money. Bad translations, however, can also cost money.

As a rule of thumb, it can be said that average run-of-the-mill commercial texts for company-internal consumption can best be translated with quantity in mind, accuracy of content being of more importance than the formulation or style. Paradoxically, literary translators have to produce quality – though not necessarily Nobel prize literature quality – although their livelihood depends upon quantity. Translators themselves have the greatest influence over the quality of their translations. For this reason, before they hand their translated text over, they should think of two things:

- One fine day, their text may be scrutinised in court by the recipient's solicitors.
- Once a clanger is dropped, the translator's reputation is gone (and very often the reputation of all translators at the same time). The old rhyme says it all:

Many critics, no defenders,
Translators have but two regrets;
When they "hit" no-one remembers,
When they "miss" no-one forgets.

Once out of the translator's hands, the text is bound to be checked or criticised by someone. In other words, like any product, it will be submitted to some form of quality control to ensure that it meets the function for which it was intended. This is quite simply a systematised extension of the principle that two heads are better than one. This quality control function can be undertaken by a variety of persons at a variety of levels and may involve one or more of the following steps: checking, revision and editing...

There is no need for the translator to fear the verdict or comments of the checker, reviser or editor unless he knows that he has handed in a poor job and then he deserves to be afraid. The checking, revising and editing functions are a safeguard of quality to the user of the translation and the target reader and, at the same time, a safety net for the translator.

TRAINING FOR THE REAL WORLD

The process of professionalization has meant that more and more translators are graduates of translation schools, most of which are attached to universities. Margherita Ulrych, of Italy's University of Trieste, reminds us that students should be equipped with practical business skills as well as the tools of the translation trade (Ulrych 1996).

> A training programme for translators will ideally aim to develop a series of skills and competences that are relevant to both their future profession and educational status. Translators should be proficient linguists, or rather text-linguists, in two or more languages including their mother tongue, as well as cultural mediators, competent writers and editors. They will therefore need not only language and content knowledge but also courses specifically designed to enhance their socio-cultural awareness and encyclopaedic knowledge. They also require the cognitive and meta-cognitive skills that will enable them to evaluate their expanding competence and to monitor their performance in relation to a broad range of text-types and fields of discourse. Practical hands-on experience with currently available technological aids has, besides, become an essential component of translation pedagogy today.

> All these skills and competences will, however, remain purely academic if they are not related to real-world criteria. A professionally and educationally cogent training programme for translators should, therefore, present translating as an activity which takes place within a social context and should be based on a careful and up-to-date assessment of their multi-faceted future profession. It should, moreover, cater for client-related skills since a significant part of translators' future professional lives, whether they opt for in-house or freelance translating, will be spent in establishing sound interpersonal relations with authors, publishers and requesters.

FOCUS ON THE CUSTOMER

Geoffrey Kingscott, a distinguished technical translator, has thought long and hard about the differences between various types of translating, and their implications for training professional translators. In his essay "The Impact of Technology and the Implications for Teaching," he notes that although technical translation accounts for by far the biggest proportion of translation work in the world today, "many contemporary translation courses were started from within university language departments, and all too many reflect the somewhat literary bias of traditional university language teaching." The final sentence in this passage is worth repeating (Kingscott 1996).

> It could be said that business and technical translation is really one aspect of technical communication, and should be taught as such. It is not enough to bolt a few technical elements on to an essentially linguistic course. Technical translation involves a lot more than introducing a Language for Special Purposes element.
>
> In traditional translation teaching there tends to be great stress on the correct rendering of the source message. In technical communication there is much more emphasis on the target message, and the source message must, if necessary, be reworked to suit the particular application. "Reader-oriented writing," they call it in technical communication. Not all source-language technical texts are produced by professional technical writers, and some fail to be as reader-oriented as they should be. However, it is the responsibility of the technical translator, who is a professional, to write as a target-language technical writer would, taking into consideration the likely reading ability of the user of the manual, the technical writing culture of the target-language country, the emphasis to be given to different aspects (warning notices, task sequences, etc.) and so on...
>
> The watchwords in technical writing are clarity and readability, and these priorities must be carried over into technical translation. It is essential that students be taught how to write clearly in their own mother tongue. However, even today the greatest complaint from employers of translators, particularly of those coming out of university translation courses, is not, as one might expect, the lack of domain-specific technical knowledge, but the inability of the students to write their own language well.

BEGINNERS' PERILS: CONTRACTS

The real world can be a cold, hard place when you are just starting out. In his essay "Death of a Ghost: A Case Study of Ethics in Cross-Generation Relations between Translators," Arnaud Laygues provides a fascinating case study from Finland of how a young translator was exploited by a more experienced colleague (Laygues 2001).

Disparities in the status of translators stem from many factors, irrespective of whether the translators are specialized, literary, scientific, general, staff or freelance. One dimension nevertheless seems to be common to all categories: some translators are just starting and others have been working for many years. The case we will be studying here is the epitome of an attitude based on this difference. The problem is that novice – often young – translators are vulnerable to senior translators and publishers who have been on the market for a long time and who make the rules of the game. The relationships between the two parties determine the conditions in which the new generation will take over – including the ethical conditions.

[The case study] we are concerned with is extremely recent. Since it is the guarantee of anonymity that has allowed me to obtain the relevant details reported here, all actors will be represented by a letter.

There are three main actors involved. It all started when the translator (Mr. K.) of a recognized writer (Mr. V.) decided to establish his own publishing company and to offer the translation of Mr. V.'s latest novel to another translator, since his new occupation did not leave him with sufficient time to translate the novel himself. A young translator (Ms. L.), not known in literary circles, agreed to translate the 500-page novel as the translator in her own right. She later found out that she was only a co-translator with the publisher. The translation was made from Finnish into French. The fact that Finnish is a "minority language" adds an important dimension to the case: since Finnish is rarely translated into French – compared with English, Spanish or German – the network of translators and publishers involved is fairly small. The young translator worked in Finland while the publisher – and later co-translator – was in France. They communicated mainly by e-mail.

The novel in question had received a prestigious prize in Finland and aroused much public interest. These turned out to be significant factors since Ms. L.'s strong desire to translate the novel blinded her to the working conditions. Finally, it is important to note that the young translator had not had any specific training in translation but had done a few poetry translations that were well received. This raises the question of the role of translator training.

The chronology of the facts is as follows:

FACT 1: In October 1999, the author of the book to be translated, Mr. V., put Ms. L. in touch with the publisher. Ms, L. verbally promised the author that she would translate the text in a manner that would respect its original quality. The publisher asked her to translate the novel (500 pages). She waited for him to send her a contract. As she did not receive a contract, she understood there was a financial problem and looked for potential translation grants.

FACT 2: Ms. L. proposed that the publisher apply for a grant from the Finnish Ministry of Culture. The publisher, Mr. K., advised her to ask for FIM 80,000 (8000 GBP) but Ms. L. realized this sum would never be granted and asked for FIM 54,000 (5400 GBP) for nine months of work. The author informed the publisher that Ms. L. was still expecting a contract.

CONTRACT 1: In December 1999, Ms. L. received a contract stating how the grants would be shared if obtained: the publisher and the translator would get 85% and 15% respectively. She told Mr. K. that this clause was illegal since the grant would be linked to her name. At any rate, the money was not granted and they had to search for other sources of funding. In the meantime Ms. L. translated two chapters but did not send them to the publisher.

FACT 3: The publisher sent Ms. L. an e-mail stating that when he was young the conditions were worse and that as she was a novice translator there was no guarantee of the quality of her work. He was apparently trying to impress her, but this nearly made her give up entirely. Similar messages were sent with increasing frequency toward the end of their work together.

FACT 4: In April 2000, Ms. L. found out that the publisher had applied for a grant elsewhere and that in the application she was only mentioned as a co-translator. This grant would be obtained on publication of the book. Another condition for the grant was the existence of a contract.

FACT 5: Meanwhile the publisher asked Ms. L. to send him 50 pages so that he could apply for another grant from a cultural institution in France. The publisher first submitted, without revision, the 50 pages that had already been translated by Ms. L. and then later sent in the same 50 pages with the modifications he had made. The grant was denied because of excessive translation mistakes. Ms. L. found out from a third person that the version revised by Mr. K. contained more mistakes than her original version.

CONTRACTS 2 AND 3: The publisher proposed two contracts: one with Ms. L. as the translator with a deadline of September 15th, the other with her as the primary translator and the publisher as co-translator, without a deadline, specifying that Ms. L. will have 10 days to read and accept the revisions made to her version.

FACT 6: Ms. L. agreed to sign these contracts, even though one of them was pre-dated (December 1999); she understood that this manipulation of the dates was necessary for the publisher to get the grant.

FACT 7: From December to April, Ms. L. had hardly worked at all on the translation, since she was not sure she would be paid. She thus had 6 months left to translate 500 relatively difficult pages.

FACT 8: In May 2000 Ms. L. met the co-translator/publisher for the first time. Mr. K. asked her to send him the translation one chapter at a time. She accepted and did so for 10 chapters, then stopped sending her work since she needed to "stand back" so as to make her text consistent.

FACT 9: In July 2000, Mr. K. informed Ms. L. that the contract had been violated since she was not sending him the translation one chapter at a time. Ms. L. considered this clause to be non-binding and thought the contract was still valid. She stopped all communication with the co-translator and sent the whole translated text on September 15th. She did not receive the payment that had been agreed upon (1200 GBP).

FACT 10: Mr. K. claimed that he refused to open the diskettes sent by Ms. L., although it was obvious that he had the text in his possession since he informed Ms. L. that the corrections would be done by a third person.

FACT 11: At an art festival where the translation – had it been finished – should have been presented, Ms. L. learned that the publisher had presented himself to the organizers as the sole translator.

At the time of writing the book has still not been released, the translator has not received the second part of her payment, and she does not know whether her name will appear on the book.

From the start of collaboration, the status of the various participants was not well defined. From October 1999 (Fact 1) to April 2000 (Fact 4) Ms. L. believed she would be the sole translator. The change of status seems to be due to the application for grants; it was a purely tactical change and Mr. K. made the decision without telling Ms. L. about it (Fact 4). At that point, the publisher/translator assigned himself the task of revising the "raw material" so as to make a stylistically acceptable novel out of it. The task distribution defined in Contract 3 was as follows: "Translator: translation and writing of the primary text; Co-translator: proof-reading and formatting of the final text" (my translation).

This cooperative arrangement may be described as "separate." Unlike a translation made by two translators sitting at the same desk or translating simultaneously, this translation was achieved in two steps. Unfortunately, studies that deal only with the "lone translator" do not take into account this growing tendency toward teamwork in professional translation.

Contract 3 was not well written; it did not mention any deadline; the co-translator did not have any obligations; above all, the contract was not sufficiently detailed: there was no specification of how often the translator had to submit material to the co-translator, and this is what finally led to disagreement about the status of the contract (Fact 9).

Ms. L. refused the first contract because she considered it illegal. One might think that she then knew about the ethical status of the person she was dealing with, and she should have rejected the idea of working with him at that stage. She nevertheless agreed to sign two contracts. Contract 2, between her and Mr. K. as the publisher, assigned her the task of translating the book and set out general conditions (deadlines, rights, remuneration). It was a standard contract, suggesting that Ms. L. was the sole translator of the novel. This contract was terminated by Mr. K. as soon as he received the first version of the translated text. Contract 3 distributed the tasks between translator and co-translator in the terms quoted above. In this contract, Mr. K. was not the "manager" of the publishing company but rather a translator on the same level as Ms. L. He was subject to the same conditions and was to receive same remuneration. Note that Mr. K. was not subject to any deadline in Contract 3 whereas a deadline was clearly specified for Ms. L. in Contract 2. Mr. K. thus held a "time advantage" over Ms. L.

Note also that Contract 3 was pre-dated (Fact 6): it was the one Mr. K. needed in order to optimize his chances of receiving a grant. By agreeing to sign, the young translator made two mistakes: she made herself an accomplice to the publisher by signing a false document, and she validated a contract that stated that she had already worked on the translation from December to April. The contract deadline was impossible to meet, even if her actual deadline was not (Fact 7). This gave the publisher a potential reason for claiming breach of contract.

Ms. L. apparently did not notice the advantages that Mr. K. granted himself. There was a clear imbalance between the tasks of the two translators, even though they were supposed to receive the same fees. Ms. L. had to translate the 500 pages while Mr. K. was only proof-reading and doing what is vaguely described as "formatting" (*mise en forme*, Contract 3). It seems that since Ms. L. was a novice translator with little self-confidence, Mr. K. granted himself a translator's pay for work that was mostly his responsibility as a publisher, and this was in addition to his regular salary. He thus enjoyed a clear financial advantage over Ms. L. ...

The concept of visibility – or rather absence of visibility – is extremely useful when analyzing the isolation of the primary translator. Koskinen (2000: 99) divides the concept into three main types: textual visibility (within the text itself), paratextual visibility (through prefaces, notes, the name on the cover of the book, etc.) and extratextual visibility (visibility in the profession). The case studied here can be analyzed according to these three categories. Of course, here we are dealing with the translation of a novel, a literary object, and this type of translation allows the efficient use of visibility tactics for ethical purposes. This is not to question Koskinen's and Pym's comments to the effect that this strategy is more questionable when dealing with other types of translation.

The contract assigns the co-translator the task of "stylizing" the text translated by the primary translator (Contract 3). The role of the co-translator is thus implicitly to hide all traces of his colleague, since the latter is apparently not supposed to submit a sufficiently correct text in French. This is quite different from working together; the young translator could not even contemplate proposing a "resistant" translation (Venuti 1995) as she knew there would be another translator to make improvements to her style (Contract 3). In fact, she was very careful not to stray from the original:

given that she was only the primary translator, she would not be in control of the final distance. The co-translator then strayed so far from the text that the result was considered to have betrayed the original (Fact 5). The young translator accomplished her part of the contract by remaining source-oriented and thus, to some extent, producing a resistant translation, knowing that the co-translator was there to honour the target language. We see here that it is possible to resist while remaining invisible.

The young translator's paratextual visibility is just as uncertain. Nowhere in the contract was it specified how she would be named in the book. The only indication is that she had the right to ask not to be named; she had the right to "erase herself," to decide not to accept responsibility or credit for her work. Apparently she did not have the right to the privileged position provided by the preface, nor did she have any guarantee of being recognized in the book's promotion. Fact 11 gives a clear idea of Ms. L.'s paratextual visibility. By announcing to the festival that he was the sole translator, and thus removing all extratextual visibility from his young collaborator, Mr. K. also obviously removed her paratextual visibility.

The young translator officially had a double status: translator and co-translator. When analyzing her real situation, which is invisible, unrecognized, unpaid or badly paid, another type of status comes to mind: that of the "ghost writer." This English expression can be compared with its French equivalent le nègre ("negro"), a metaphorical and relatively pejorative term to refer to "a person who anonymously writes or outlines books signed by a famous writer" (Le Robert 1994 – my translation). This latter term is based on an explicit image of the slave in colonialist France (the word first appeared figuratively in 1757). Invisibility is the very condition of the literary nègre/ ghost's function. This function can be adapted to the field of translation. Insofar as the primary translator, who produced what can be considered the translation itself, is "erased," their status is functionally that of a nègre/ghost of the co-translator. If this condition has not been freely chosen, it results in exploitation by the stronger (the visible and recognized part) of the weaker (the invisible and unrecognized part). This exploitation is possible as soon as cooperation is transformed into domination.

The young translator told me that she was prepared to renounce her salary if the co-translator had acknowledged the validity of her translation and if he had shown more respect for her. She had enjoyed starting her career with a well-known text by a recognized author: when she started, she was primarily motivated by the quality and fame of the novel. Ms. L. did need that money to live on, though. Why do many young translators accept to work without any absolute guarantee of appropriate payment? Let me suggest that there are other ways of remunerating a translation, ways that are well known by those who attach so much value to money. Bourdieu defined these ways as "symbolic remuneration" (*contre-prestation symbolique*), all the more symbolic when the financial situation is unequal. Symbolic remuneration in this case meant being able to publish such a text so young, and the promise of entry into the relatively closed circles of the French publishing industry. Those were the aspects that interested the young translator; they may have blinded her to the weaknesses of the contract she was signing.

There is, however, an ingredient that the co-translator/publisher forgot to add to this symbolic remuneration: acknowledgement and respect of his young colleague as a translator in her own right. Is the co-translator/ publisher really to be blamed for this? The conditions that he set out seemed fair to him. He listened to the young translator's complaints and replied, "You're young, I also suffered when I was your age!"

BEGINNER'S PERILS: TRANSLATION TESTS

Today, the best source of practical advice, collaboration, and commiseration for translators is the Internet, with its growing selection of forums, networks, and weblogs. Here the author of the blog About Translation, Riccardo Schiaffino, provides sage advice on the issue of translation tests requested by prospective clients (Schiaffino 2006).

Often when we contact a translation company (and sometimes when a translation company contacts us), we are asked to do a translation test, or sample translation, as a preliminary to possible collaboration with them.

Many translators object to doing translation tests for free, on various grounds, from the fact that other professionals do not do free tests (which is not exactly true, as many lawyers and other professionals do provide free consultations, after which you can decide whether to retain them or not), to the fact that translation tests are allegedly used by unscrupulous agencies to stitch together the translation of an entire book done for free (which I have always thought a translator's urban legend, as this is something people always hear but never actually see first hand, and also because any agency that would attempt a stunt like that would soon be out of business, as the resulting quality of such a patchwork would certainly be abysmal).

Another objection is that translation tests mean little, and that translation companies should rely instead on the work experience, education, or other indicators of a translator's worth, which is a valid objection, but would not help one gain work from an agency who has decided to use translation tests in their screening process: normally, if you don't do the test, you also don't work for them.

In my opinion, the best objection to doing free translation tests is that one has no time for that: if you already have enough work, doing a translation test for free is probably not the best investment of your time.

If one decides to do the translation tests, there are several things to consider:

1. The test should be of an acceptable length (normally no more than 500 words or so).
2. Read carefully, and follow any instructions given together with the test: when I worked as a manager in the translation department of a major business software company, we used translation tests as a part of our screening process. We never asked to translate more than 250 to 350 words, but we normally sent out tests in which the words to be translated were clearly marked within longer texts. Failure to follow the instructions (by, for example, translating more than we had asked) was a serious mark against our candidates, since it was indicative that these translators would not be good at following instructions in a real work environment, either.
3. If you accept to do the test, do your best, and treat it as a real work assignment: put your best foot forward.
4. Do not leave alternate translations: you would not do that in a real work assignment, and you should not do it in a test (any alternate translations left in a test would normally be marked as an error).
5. Do not add translator's notes, unless specifically requested to do so in the instructions: I've seen many apparently acceptable tests fail because the translation notes made clear that the translator had not, in fact, understood the meaning of some sentence or term.
6. Do not have someone else translate the test for you: I've seen it done,

and more often than not cheats are quickly found out, if not during the test evaluation, eventually with the first work assignment.

Finally...

7. Do not use Babelfish to do the test (happened: we once received a test which looked really terrible. We began to joke that Babelfish probably would not do it worse, so we ran the test through Babelfish, just to see how much worse a free MT program would do it... turned out it did it exactly the same, as the would-be translator had used it to do the test).

VERBING THE PHARMACEUTICALS

On another blog, Anne Catesby Jones discusses some of the difficulties that technical English presents to the working translator (Jones 2006).

The English language is alive and kicking. The problem is that it keeps kicking me!

Aside from the obvious vocabulary changes due to the emergence of an extraordinary array of new objects and processes, whether in daily life (satellite TV in remote parts of China) or highly specialized situations (biotechnology bots of various sorts), English is undergoing changes in usage that I believe are the true headache for a translator. It is usually possible to discover the meaning of an unusual word by finding either glossary definitions or clear context on the billions of Web sites that have been made accessible by search engines, not to mention the age-old method of talking to the author. Usage, on the other hand, is a more slippery matter, so slippery that even when the translator has access to the author of a document, the result of a consultation may not yield a translatable unit like a definition.

What I would like to discuss are some specific instances of usage that I have come across in translating standard operating procedure documents in the pharmaceutical industry that particularly gave me pause. I translate primarily into Spanish, but I will not be proposing any translation solutions here for any particular language. What I am addressing are what I feel to be difficulties in parsing English, a task that is independent of the ultimate target language. Specifically, I am going to address three kinds of usage that I have found to be prevalent and troublesome: conversion of the parts of speech, a virgule placed between two words and the ellipsis.

Perhaps the part of speech conversion that is most commented on is verbalization, noun-to-verb conversion, also called "verbing" (an example itself of the phenomenon). We find that things are to be centrifuged, autoclaved, pipetted, chromatographed or filtered. All of these are verbs that originated in nouns describing an instrument or a process, and the only one not usually found as a verb in common dictionaries is autoclave. Verbalizations of this kind seem natural to me, a transformation of the instrument or process into a verb makes language more concise, making it unnecessary to say "process in the centrifuge," "sterilize in the autoclave," "dispense with the pipette," "analyze using chromatography," or "pass through a filter."

What does not seem quite as natural is a transformation based on the object of the action, for example with the word "gown." "The associate shall gown" does not mean that the worker will put on an actual gown, but that the worker will put on the required sanitary clothing and accessories. In the documents I handled, the verb replaced the phrase "don the gown," in which an archaic verb would have persisted. While disconcerting at first, it was understandable. What stumped me was this instruction: "If there is no data, NA it." As it turned out, the idea was for the person to write NA (N/A or Not Applicable) in the space provided for writing the data. The object of the action became the name of the action itself, as with the gown.

In any case, these conversions are constantly used in English and may or may not be directly translatable. It may be necessary to determine what the instrument does, what the process consists of, or what must be done to the object, all of which have been masked in the conversion of the part of speech. It could be that rather than dispensing with the pipette there is aspiration with the pipette, for example. The on-line *Translation Journal* recently published a useful article by translators Hernandez and Cabrera on this topic, available at the Accurapid Website, http://accurapid.com/journal/31conversion.htm.

Another usage that has become prevalent is placing a virgule, perhaps better known as a slash (/), between two words. The trend may have started with the usage "and/or," which is almost universally condemned. There is no translation for "and/or" because it is a term of unfathomable meaning. The term "and/or" purports to achieve concision, yet in phrases such as "quality degradation and/or bioburden contamination" just "or" is sufficient. It seems to me that part of the issue in "and/or" phrases is that the relationship between the elements is really of a hierarchical nature in which one element could be an example of another. If there is bioburden contamination, by definition there is quality degradation. What the writer meant was "quality degradation, as for example, by bioburden contamination," not "quality degradation or bioburden contamination or both," which is the long version of an "and/or" phrase.

As evidence from another field, I offer this from a World Trade Organization document:

> Interpretation of "and/or"
>
> 7.81 The interpretations of the parties are also in a sharp contrast with each other regarding the meaning of "and/or" in Article 6.2. As noted above, according to Pakistan, a subject domestic industry consists of producers of (i) like products, or (ii) directly competitive products, or (iii) both like products and directly competitive products. In contrast, the United States argued that Members are permitted to identify a "domestic industry" as an industry producing a product that is: (i) like but not directly competitive; or (ii) unlike but directly competitive; or (iii) both like and directly competitive. –WT/DS192/ R, 31 May 2001 (01-2567).

Due to space restrictions, I will refer you to the WTO website for the discussion on the interpretation of "and/or." The consequences of the lack of meaning of "and/or" in this case affected an important part of world trade, the cotton trade.

Then there is the usage in a situation of elements that are not subsets of each other, as in the instruction "place on a table and/or rack." Here the issue is really of a physical impossibility: you cannot place the same object on a table and a rack at the same time. I could give many more examples, but what I am trying to emphasize is that the translator is faced with a real problem, not just a stylistic quibble, as some would like to classify the "and/or problem." That there are millions of examples of "and/or" being used does not mean that the users are being clear...

The final kind of nail I feel driving into my skull is the nail of ellipsis. In the phrase, "line to permeate," where is the article to tell me that "permeate" is a noun and not a verb? How should I know that a "pre-integrity test" is a test of integrity before a given process or step? And an "aseptic fill," which is not filling anything? Rather, is it a test performed to verify that the aseptic level has been maintained? Would you want to generate a nonconformance? Of course not! You want to generate a nonconformance report. A "tempera-ture EN" was explained to me as a device with an Equipment Number that is used to measure temperature. And the engineer triumphantly informed me that "temperature is not a noun!" Another example:

> An HPLC injection valve is placed in-line between the tee and the column for sample introduction... The flow through the column is changed by adjusting the length of the restriction capillary or by vary-ing the flow rate from the HPLC slightly.

HPLC is High Pressure Liquid Chromatography or Chromatograph. How can there be something from the High Pressure Liquid Chromatograph or Chromatography? Obviously, it is from the HPLC system, valve or device.

I could continue, but my purpose here is to assure my colleagues, who will forever be accused of treason, that English is like any other language: a language in constant change, whose users will do what they please, style-books and scolding editors notwithstanding.

DANISH BEET DIGGERS, GERMAN SOIL CULTIVATORS

Although the term "technical translation" might suggest otherwise, a good under-standing of both source and target cultures is an essential part of the job. Jens Hare Hansen gives some examples in his article "Translation of Technical Brochures" (Hansen 1997).

> Most of the time brochures are translated on the assumption that the important thing is reproducing the denotative contents. The translation of technical brochures, however, demands far more from the translator than is usually supposed. I aim to show that a long series of conditions must be taken into consideration. The main thing is that the source text is tied to a certain culture or socioculture, and that, consequently, one must take into account that the cultural conditions and relevant marketing conditions are different in the target-language culture.
>
> Even though the Danish and German languages are closely related, and even if the Danish and German cultures are equally closely related, there are differences in the way that brochures are linguistically formulated.

There is a tendency to express illocutions differently in the two languages. Things are often said more directly in Danish brochures. This means, for example, that the directive aspect is clearer to be seen. This can be illustrated by the following examples:

> *Det er klogt at vælge Agrometer fra starten* (= It is wise to choose Agrometer from the beginning)
>
> *Den næste roeoptager bør også være en Tim* (= The next beet digger should also be a Tim)
>
> *Derfor er Hydrema det sikre valg* (= That's why Hydrema is the right choice)
>
> *Tim er de bedste* (= Tim machines are best)
>
> *Køb dansk, når det er bedst!* (= Buy Danish – when it is best)

That sort of very direct speech acts can also be found in German brochures, but here they are much rarer. The German producers are to a certain degree more modest, as they normally do not explicitly assert that they produce the best machines, neither do they talk directly about *the right choice*. When German concerns want to throw themselves into relief compared to the competitors, this is normally done in relation to certain technical conditions/problems, which may be seen in the following example:

> *Heute wissen wir, daß die Bodenbearbeitung häufig übermechanisiert ist. Pflügen oder Grubbern, Bearbeiten und Säen verlangen sowohl bodenbiologisch wie betriebswirtschaftlich einen hohen oft zu hohen Preis. Die vernünftige Alternative ist die Komplett-Bodenbearbeitung mit der* DUTZI.

In the English translation of the brochure the quotation is translated into:

> Today, agricultural specialists are aware of the overmechanisation of soil cultivation. Ploughing or conventional cultivation, tillage and sowing have their price, in many cases a high one. Not least as far as soil biology and economy are concerned. All-in-one soil cultivation by using the DUTZI is the sensible alternative.

DUTZI describes their own product as a machine which is well suited to solve the problems that might arise. As it is clear from the texts, DUTZI also says that it is *wise to choose* especially *their* machine, and that DUTZI machines *are best,* but the message is less directly formulated than in the Danish examples, which have been quoted above.

Danish brochures have more direct statements than the German ones. In Danish sales brochures you will often find directive speech acts like *Save manpower, Save fodder* and *Try Us.* Obviously German brochures want to say the same things, but here they normally do so in a sort of language which is typical for technical language. In German, for example, they mention that the machine implies *Verminderungen des personellen Aufwandes,* which means that it *reduces manpower requirements.* Instead of writing *Save fodder* the German brochures typically have *Es wird Kraftfutter gespart* (= Fodder is saved), *Das Kraftfutter wird optimal ausgenutzt* (= Concentrates are utilized to an optimal degree), or *Die Futterkosten werden gesenkt* (= Fodder costs are reduced). The superficially representative German sentences will, as is shown above, become directive through inferencing.

Danish brochures tend to use more informal language, including many colloquial expressions and puns. Direct address is more often used in Danish brochures than in German ones. They say, e.g. *You will not have to leave your driver's seat; The well-being of your cows is important, if... ; You will reduce your fuel consumption to about ⅓* and *Did you know that... ?*

German brochures are normally kept in a more impersonal style, where the third person singular or plural is used. Therefore they mostly describe technical aspects, and hereby they may point to the fact that certain *functions can be performed directly from the driver's seat.* Instead of writing *The well-being of your cows is important, if...* , the German brochures tend to stress that a certain *technique will lead to a greater output.* While the Danish texts can quite well use *You save fuel,* the German expression will more often be that *the use of the machine will result in the saving of fuel,* or that it has a *low energy dissipation.* In Danish brochures it will be all right to write *Did you know that...* Such a use would be uncommon in German, where a technical thing is described without questioning whether the receiver knew of it.

TEAM MEMBER OR COG IN THE G10N MACHINE?

In a large proportion of today's translations, the text – an instruction manual for an automobile, a menu for a restaurant, subtitles for a film, etc. – is merely an adjunct to another product, and a component in a larger process generally known as "localization." Here, the distinguished translation theorist and teacher Anthony

Pym discusses the skill set and competences needed to manage localization projects that must include translators (Pym 2006).

We use the term "localization" to refer to a general set of discourses inform- ing cross-cultural text production and adaptation in the fields of software, product documentation, web technology, and some international news services. We find those discourses within what is sometimes also known as the "globalization, internationalization, localization and translation industries" (GILT for short). Although those four long "-ion" terms are all somehow necessary to describe what those industries do, or what kind of communication they are engaged in, the four are rarely used together, and the acronym GILT has not really caught on (perhaps due to some kind of well-deserved guilt). In the place of those four terms, we most usually find the one word "localization," which at least has the serious virtues of not being an acronym and is not too long, especially when reduced to the form "L10N." The term definitely comes from the industry, rather than from esoteric theory or the felt needs of training institutions. It has leaped out from places where money is made and jobs are created. That might be a good reason for our interest in it. But can the one term really represent the whole complex of interrelated communication processes (the thing that GILT was supposed to cover)? Can the part really stand for the whole? If not, what price do we pay for this convenient reduction?

Standard definitions of "localization" usually come accompanied with definitions of the terms associated with it (the ones sharing the space of the GILT industries). Here, for example, are those offered by the Education Initiative Taskforce of the Localization Industry Standards Association:

- LOCALIZATION involves taking a product and making it linguistically and culturally appropriate to the target locale (country/region and lan- guage) where it will be used and sold.
- INTERNATIONALIZATION is the process of generalizing a product so that it can handle multiple languages and cultural conventions with- out the need for re-design. Internationalization takes place at the level of program design and document development.
- GLOBALIZATION addresses the business issues associated with taking a product global. In the globalization of high-tech products this involves integrating localization throughout a company, after proper

internationalization and product design, as well as marketing, sales, and support in the world market.

We might thus say that there is one general process called "globalization" (here understood at the level of the individual company), of which "internationalization" and "localization" are parts. In order to globalize, you first make your product general in some way ("internationalization"), then you adapt ("localize") to specific target markets ("locales"). The terms are by no means as standard as they may appear (Microsoft uses them very differently, especially for degrees of internationalization). Yet they encapsulate a whole logical process, a coherent view of the ways in which cross-cultural marketing can be carried out in an age of information technology and international capitalism. Together, those terms can form a whole. If the one word "localization" should simply represent that whole, it might thus be a matter of mere convention, and little more need be said. Yet things are not that simple. For example, we have described this whole as a "process of communication," but exactly who is communicating with whom through a localized product? What are the effects of the massive amounts of technology that stand between any sender (perhaps now a "developer") and any receiver (now a profiled "user")? Or again, more worryingly, what is the precise role of "translation" within this wider whole? The term "translation" is indeed part of the GILT tetra; but it has no place alongside the reductions L10N or i18N (for "internationalization"). No one talks about "To9N." Translation is definitely not cool enough for a neologism.

We suggest that these simple questions, if pursued, reveal that the whole known as "localization" is far more fragmentary and problematic than it might first appear. Many of its visions are in fact of no more than parts.

It is easy enough to recognize a "translation competence," and to break that down into aptitudes, skills and knowledge that a translator should have in order to be a competent translator. An institution can then use that model in order to set about training translators. The same could be said of the various kinds of interpreters, whose professions correspond to different kinds of interpreting competence. But how can we think in those terms with respect to localization? Who or what is a competent localizer? Impossible to say – localization is carried out by teams.

When we ask this kind of question, we quickly discover that the localization industry is not configured in the same way as the traditional markets for translators and interpreters. Its training needs cannot be approached in the same way. If localization is a competence, it is certainly not one in that same way that translation and interpreting are.

Localization processes certainly do exist, at least as logical steps that a product has to go through in order to be localized successfully. Here, for example, is a basic process model for the localization of software:

- Analysis of Received Material
- Scheduling and Budgeting
- Glossary Translation or Terminology Setup
- Preparation of Localization Kit (materials for the translators)
- Translation of Software
- Translation of Help and Documentation
- Processing Updates
- Testing of Software
- Testing of Help and Publishing of Documentation
- Product QA and Delivery
- Post-mortem with Client.

There is a certain competence involved in getting all these things to happen in a timely and coordinated way (or better, controlling the chaos when they all happen together). That competence is called "project management", and it is useful for any kind of work that involves teams and projects. (Note, in passing, that localization work can also involve long-term maintenance or up-date programs as well as projects, for example in the case of multilingual websites.) Within this localization process, there is work for people competent in terminology, revising, testing, software engineering, and yes, translation. But all those things are usually done by different people. There is no one person there who acts as an all-round "localizer." In its very nature, the localization project requires a significant division of labor. And it is in this structural and very necessary division that we might locate the underlying reason for the fragmentary visions of the process as a whole.

Some might object that project managers do indeed see the whole, and that *their* competence should properly be described as "localization." However, do project managers generally see what happens in the reception of the product, or in the rendition of all the languages? Managers often have to coordinate work into languages they do not know. Do they consistently see anything beyond times and quantities? Do they have time to do so? There are many variables involved, and the project management we most like in theory will certainly require all the visions we can muster, especially those involving translation. But one must seriously doubt whether project managers really require, in the eyes of the industry, competencies other than those associated with good business skills.

One must then also doubt the industrial virtues of anything like a localization competence. What industry requires, and what various training institutions can supply, are sets of skills and aptitudes, some of which may involve translation.

WOLVES, EAGLES, AND JAPANESE PATENTS

The business and technical translation market is full of niches, and therefore fertile ground for people prepared to become specialists. Czech-born, California-based and husband to a Japanese wife, Steve Vitek is a thoughtful writer on language and translation. He has several specialties, one of which is translating patents from Japanese, German and several other languages. In his article "The Changing World of Japanese Patent Translators," he writes not only about technological changes in the patent translation field but also about the community – he argues convincingly that there is one – of patent translators working in California. In this extract from the article, he starts with a description of Japan Patent Office's bilingual website and ends with a reflection on the influence of the Internet on freelance workers (Vitek 2001).

> The Japanese part of this website is not very useful for patent lawyers in this country unless they can read Japanese because everything is in Japanese, including the instructions on displaying and downloading. If you make a mistake, for instance by typing in the wrong number of digits or the wrong sequence, the website will display fourteen (count them ?????????????) angry question marks, which is the only help that is offered to novice users by the JPO. If you still can't figure out the proper sequence, an angry spirit dwelling in the innards of the JPO site will display 28 question marks in two rows (The Help File is of no help, of course, like all Help Files. I always visualize an angry Japanese face that is looking reproachingly at me when I see those question marks). Another problem with this site is that the default display form is low resolution, and the default printing is also in low resolution, possibly to save storage space for zillions of Japanese patents that need to

be stored and thrown at non-Japanese patent lawyers in legal disputes dealing with infringement of existing patents. It is possible to change the format by clicking on the "display again" button and display and print the text at high resolution. However, this will display and print only selected blocks of text and it is almost impossible for some reason to print the entire text at high resolution on any of my printers. I usually print out the whole text at low resolution and then go back to view or print out at high resolution the portions that are not clearly legible in my text. In spite of the shortcomings of this website, as far as I know, this is the most comprehensive collection of Japanese applications for patents and utility models available online for free. In the Japanese part of the website, Japanese patents are listed from the year Showa 46 (1971) for unexamined (Kokai) patents and from the year Taisho 11 (1922) for examined (Kokoku) patents.

But My Favorite Website for Foreign Patents is the EPO Website

The second website, one that is frequently used by U.S. patent lawyers (I found out about this website one day when I was identifying Japanese patents in a lawyer's office), is the website of the European Patent Office (EPO) at http://www.espacenet.com. If for some reason your browser refuses to take you there, go to my website at http://www.japanesetranslators.com (or http://www.pattran.com), click on buttons: HELPFUL LINKS → EUROPEAN PATENT OFFICE → PATENT SEARCH (bottom line) → ACCESS esp@cenet via the EPO. This will take you to the QUICK SEARCH page. This is an extremely useful page for me because I can use it not only to search for and to display the patents that I need to translate, but I can also search here for other information in a number of languages. For example, I can type the words narrow-band beam expander or a German compound word such as Kabelsatz in the field Simple Text to display hundreds of patents in various languages that I can use as reference to track down the proper term for a certain technique. Several hundred to thirty thousand or so patents will be usually identified in one hit, although the system can display only the first five hundred patents. Or I can type the name of the company in the field Company name to display other patents filed by the same company. Because Japanese and German companies file the same patents in America and in Europe in English and in various European countries also in other languages, I can sometimes find a very similar patent dealing with a very similar technique which has the precise terms that I am looking for in

English or another language. This sometime saves my life when a Japanese patent uses transcription into katakana (one of two Japanese alphabets used, along with Japanese kanji characters, which are of Chinese origin). The problem with transcription of foreign words into Japanese is that since the original spelling is lost in Japanese, you either know what the original word was, or you don't. And if you don't, it may be very hard to figure it out from the mutilated form resulting from a transliteration that fits the Japanese phonetic system, which has only a limited number of sounds. And because the transcription provides no indication as to which language the original word was in or whether it is a personal name or a common word, it can be very difficult to track down such a word.

Will Japanese Patent Lawyers Ever Learn That "Anaguro" Is Wrong?
In addition, Japanese patent lawyers who write patent applications also sometime make mistakes and they frequently transcribe foreign words incorrectly. This is sort of understandable because a foreign word is just a foreign word to those busy Japanese patent lawyers and they don't really care what the correct spelling is as long as they know what the word means. I remember for instance how an in-house Hitachi patent lawyer (let's not name names here – I have not sunk that low yet) kept using in an old Hitachi patent application the word "anaguro" instead of "anarogu" which is the correct transcription for the English word "analog." Obviously, analog is a very easy word to figure out, even if the transcription is wrong. But what about for example the word "purikahsahtoh"? It did ring a distant bell when I saw it recently in a patent opposition brief, but since I had not dealt with patents in this field (spinning techniques for multi-filament fibers) for several years, I could not remember what it meant. But when I ran a search on the EPO website for other patents filed by the same company, after about a minute of clicking on patents published in English, I realized that these were two words: "purikahsah," which sounded at first like the name of an African king to me, meaning "precursor," and that the second word "toh" is "tow." Without the EPO website, I would have had to pore over a number of Japanese-English and monolingual dictionaries for a long time, trying different spelling combinations before arriving at the correct term, although I would have recognized the term immediately of course ten years ago or so when I was dealing with this field daily.

English Summaries on the EPO Website Can Also Be a Lifesaver

If I type the number of the patent application in the field View a patent application, the EPO site will display an abstract in English first, usually from 50 to several hundred words. This abstract is very useful not only because it gives me the terms that a Japanese native translator, possibly a specialist in the field (whose English, however, is often not very good) would use in this translation, but also because the text in English also displays the names of the inventors transcribed into English. As every Japanese patent translator knows, transcription of Japanese names is a major hassle and it makes very good sense to have other people do this work for us, especially if they do it for free and Japanese is their native language. I use the EPO website not only to locate highly legible, easily searchable copies of Japanese patents, but also for German and French patents, most of which are also provided with an abstract in English...

Lonely Wolves Are Turning Into Lonely Eagles

Most translators of Japanese and German patents that I have met over the years tended to be very individualistic and highly opinionated people who became freelance contractors because they enjoyed the freedom that is available, at a cost, to those of us who run a freelance business. Those who lived in large metropolitan areas, as I did in the eighties and early nineties, had the luxury of being able to live the lifestyle of their choice while at the same time they could also meet other translators at regular meetings of groups of translators not far from their home. Translators who lived far away from major metropolitan centers did not have the advantage of being able to network with their colleagues as frequently.

The Internet has changed also this part of the equation. The lonely wolves who used to live and work as freelance translators mostly in urban areas some 15 years ago have often dispersed to other parts of the country where the real estate costs are much lower and parking spaces are much easier to find. When I think of the group of Japanese translators that used to meet in the house of Donald Philippi in San Francisco several times a year until Don passed away in 1993, only a couple of them are still living in the San Francisco area. (There are three interesting interviews with Don Philippi, who became the mentor of many Japanese translators on the West Coast in the eighties, on Don Philippi's memorial Web page http://www.jai2.com/dlpivu1.htm. These interviews were conducted by Fred Schodt in 1984.)

Some have moved to other parts of California, some to the Pacific Northwest, others to the East Coast, Japan, and even Australia. We can all communicate by e-mail or phone if we want to, but for some reason, we never seem to find the time to do that. Many of the lonely wolves who used to congregate every now and then in packs of translators, partly because this made it easier to hunt down the prey (translation work) have turned into lonely eagles. Eagles don't need to hunt in flocks because they have an excellent view from high up in the sky. We can see most of what we want to see from the Internet – our new and very useful vantage point. So much so that we don't seem to talk much to each other any more. Some translators talk to other translators on online forums such as the Honyaku, LANTRA-L, or FLEFO, some just lurk (i.e., read messages without ever posting), and others simply don't have time for chitchat any more. This new, "informed isolation" is to me a destructive part of the development brought about by the Internet.

AND IF THE "ORIGINAL" IS ACTUALLY A TRANSLATION? FINDING THE ANCHOR LANGUAGE

Earlier this year I was trying to track down a quote about translation when – in one of those serendipitous moments that make research such fun – I came across a book called *Language and Translation in International Commercial Arbitration: From the Constitution of the Arbitral Tribunal through Recognition and Enforcement Proceedings* (Várady 2006). Idly browsing, I was hooked by the description of a complicated case involving a disputed grain deal, a Commercial Court in Uzbekistan, an import-export firm based in Geneva, and a London-based trade association. It became clear that the field of commercial arbitration – already a complicated one in a single language – turns into Alice's looking-glass world when it begins to cross linguistic borders. The author of the book, Tibor Várady, is an eminent professor of law who works as an arbitrator in five languages. Here he illustrates a particular problem that arises in international arbitration cases; like a trial lawyer, he begins with a reflection from daily life before moving on to the linguistic point at issue:

I do not think I have had a day in my life speaking one language only. When I was a small child, three languages were spoken in my street: Serbian,

Hungarian, and German (German later disappeared from my hometown). I went to Hungarian school, but most people I met outside the school were Serbs or Croats. I studied in Belgrade in Serbian, but had a Hungarian roommate. Later I studied in the United States, but within the community of international students I often switched to German or French, and had some Hungarian friends too. I am living now in Hungary, teaching in English, and I am mixing Serbian and Hungarian with my Serbian wife.

In a multilingual daily life, the concept of translation is becoming somewhat volatile. Translation (or interpretation) in its conventional sense is a rare occurrence. There is typically a language shared by all participants of the conversation. Sometimes it is the language of the majority; in some – not so rare – cases, it is a language that is not the first language of any of the participants. Are we just communicating directly, or translating from our (hidden) first languages? In such a situation, translation becomes detectable by way of imperfections. A few days ago, we were talking English in a group of five, and somebody in the group, trying to show that he was stunned, said, "Good Virgin Mother!" What he was aiming at was, "Good Lord!" But he translated verbatim "Szűzanyám!" – the Hungarian equivalent. I know, of course, that this kind of experience is not some exclusive privilege of those whose life has been tied to several languages. People who use English only, often also have conversations with people who have a hidden first language behind their English. What I am trying to speak about is not the phenomenon in general, but the consequences of the phenomenon in a very specific domain where choice of words may literally cost millions. This is the domain of international contracts, and of the scrutiny of these contracts by courts and arbitral tribunals.

In the domain of international transactions, contracts are often drafted in a language that is not the native language of any of the parties to the contract. A Danish principal and a Greek agent may very well choose English as the language of their agency agreement. A Croatian seller and a Polish buyer may execute a sales agreement in German. In a sales transaction, the draft is typically presented by the seller – rather than by the native speaker. Circumstances may prompt the seller to present the draft in a language other than his/her native language. One could say that in such situations, the original signed by the parties is actually a translation, and the language from which such translation was made remains hidden. I would use the term "anchor language" for the language that remains hidden. The question emerging before courts is whether this anchor language is or is not relevant. If we have an original of the contract and an imperfect translation of it, the court can certainly reach back to the original in order to establish what the parties actually wanted – both in order to determine whether a breach occurred, and what consequences should follow. Can one also reach back to the anchor language?

In a case I had contact with, the contract was drafted by an English seller in French, and it was signed by the French buyer as presented. Hence, the anchor language was English. It was stated in the arbitration clause that the arbitrators have no power to award "dommages par conséquence". This did not make much sense. "Dommages par conséquence" means just "damage as a consequence" – and of course every damage is a consequence of something. Applying what was actually written in the French contract would have meant not to award any damages. But it was also clear that behind the French term there was a hidden English anchor, which in all likelihood referred to "consequential damages," a specific type of (indirect) damages, which are sometimes, indeed, excluded.

In another case – between a Hungarian and a U.K. party – the arbitration clause (or purported arbitration clause) in the "Mutual Agreement" read: "In case of controversial matters the parties determine the selected court, which operates next to the Chamber of Commerce in Budapest." The question arose about whether this was a valid arbitration clause. Arbitration agreements bestow considerable powers on the decision-makers, hence it is logical to set quite stringent criteria. What the text appears to say is that the parties wanted to confer their dispute to a court that is in the vicinity of the Budapest Chamber of Commerce. This is quite baffling. If one takes into account, however, that the anchor language of the contract is Hungarian, one could also heed the fact that the Hungarian term for arbitration is "választottbíróság" and the literal translation of "választottbíróság" is "selected court" (or "chosen court"). One should add that "which operates next to" is probably a maladroit translation of "mellett szervezett." The official name of the Court of Arbitration at the Hungarian Chamber of Commerce and Industry contains the term "mellett szervezett," meaning "organized at," or "attached to," [the Hungarian Chamber of Commerce and Industry]. This case reached the Budapest Court of Arbitration. An oral hearing was held, but the U.K. respondent failed to appear (although duly notified). The absence of the U.K. party made it more difficult to clarify the intentions of the parties. In the English language award rendered in 2002, the arbitrators raised the question of whether a valid arbitration agreement existed, and stated: "This leads to the difficult question of the limits of the power of the arbitrators in seeking the 'true intent' of the parties beyond (or even in spite of) what the parties actually wrote. It is the opinion of the arbitrators, that the arbitration agreement must possess in itself a minimum level of coherence in order to serve as a foothold for a search after the true intentions of the parties." Referring specifically to the "selected court" language, the arbitrators stated further on: "The wording of the arbitration clause does not make much sense otherwise but on the assumption that this is a translation of a Hungarian draft – which translation actually conveyed the words, more so than the meaning."

In real life international commercial contracts, it happens with some frequency that a mistranslation becomes part of the original. In many cases this will not yield true misunderstandings that might influence the outcome of the dispute, but in some cases, genuine dilemmas emerge. Observance of the hidden anchor language may indeed help the arbitrators to understand the true intentions of the parties. But the issue is not a simple one.

As far as the contract between a Hungarian and a U.K. party is concerned, it is quite obvious that the English native speaker party did not devote much attention to the language of the contract. It happens – unfortunately with some frequency – that contracts are concluded without sufficient scrutiny. Normally, the party that failed to devote attention to the wording but signed the contract will be bound by it. The party will be bound by what is written in a clause, even if he/she failed to scrutinize it (despite having had the opportunity to scrutinize it). The situation is somewhat different when one has to reach towards an anchor language in order to establish the proper meaning of a contractual provision. If the literal translation offers a plausible option as it stands, the party who has no command of the anchor language may possibly insist on this option, arguing that he/she was misled (led to trust the meaning flowing from the literal translation). Bona fide reliance on the literal meaning may block an examination of the anchor language. In the case referred to above, however, it would have been difficult for the U.K. party to argue that it did not know that "selected court" actually stood for arbitration. It would also be quite difficult for the English speaking party to explain what it did have in mind. Explaining any other meaning would have been quite difficult. It just would not sound plausible to argue that by saying that "[t]he parties determine the selected court, which operates next to the Chamber of Commerce in Budapest," the parties actually meant to submit disputes to some court which is identified by being in the proximity of the Budapest Chamber of Commerce. Even though arbitration clauses have to be interpreted with more caution, in this Hungarian case it is difficult to see any plausible interpretation, which could have blocked resort to the anchor language.

There are, indeed, cases in which the original is a translation that conveys the words rather than the meaning. In such cases, dependence on the anchor language appears to be more sensible than letting the literally translated word determine the meaning. Reliance on the anchor language may be compared with reliance on legislative history. Legislative history – like the anchor language – takes us back to the environment in which the rules were crafted, and where it may be easier to re-discover the intended meaning. Reaching for the hidden anchor language mandates caution, but it is a rational device of contract interpretation when contracts are being shaped in a multilingual environment.

You do not need to speak several languages to be a good judge. But in today's multilingual legal environment, you cannot be a good judge without knowing something about translation.

....

Questions not answered by a writer cannot be answered by the translator: what is obscure in the original is likely to be even more obscure in the translation.

— ALAN DUFF in *The Third Language: Recurrent Problems of Translation into English* (Duff 1981)

CHAPTER SEVEN

Lost and found: Translating poetry

The translator's starting point is not language in motion, which is the poet's raw material, but the fixed language of the poem. It is a frozen language, and yet it is quite alive.

— OCTAVIO PAZ in the UNESCO *Courier* (1986)

After *traduttore, traditore*, and possibly surpassing it since the success of the eponymous movie, the world's most quoted translation aphorism may well be Robert Frost's quip "Poetry is what gets lost in translation." (Actually, he may have said "Poetry is the first thing that gets lost in translation," which is rather different.) Another eminent poet, Josef Brodsky, counter-quipped that "Poetry is what is gained in translation," but then part of his fame rests on his widely admired translations of his own poems from his native Russian into English. The debate about the "do-ability" of poetry translation is almost as much fun as the activity itself.

FROST WILL NOT QUITE DO

W.H. Auden knew something about the subject, having translated a wide range of texts, from Mozart operas to Icelandic epics. He responded to Frost's famous quote in schoolmasterly style (Auden 1962).

> Frost's definition of poetry as the untranslatable element in language looks plausible at first sight but, on closer examination, will not quite do. In the first place, even in the most rarefied poetry, there are some elements which are translatable. The sound of the words, their rhythmical relations, and all meanings and association of meanings which depend upon sound, like rhymes and puns, are, of course, untranslatable, but poetry is not, like

music, pure sound. Any elements in a poem which are not based on verbal experience are, to some degree, translatable into another tongue, for example, images, similes and metaphors which are drawn from sensory experience. Moreover, because one characteristic that all men, whatever their culture, have in common is uniqueness every man is a member of a class of one – the unique perspective on the world which every genuine poet has survives translation. If one takes a poem by Goethe and a poem by Holderlin and makes literal prose cribs of them, every reader will recognize that the two poems were written by two different people. In the second place, if speech can never become music, neither can it ever become algebra. Even in the most 'prosy' language, in informative and technical prose, there is a personal element because language is a personal creation. *Ne pas se pencher au dehors* has a different feeling tone from *Nicht hinauslehnen*. A purely poetic language would be unlearnable, a purely prosaic not worth learning.

POSSIBLE, DIFFICULT, IMPOSSIBLE

Ezra Pound decided that some poetry is translatable, some isn't, and some can be approximated. In his "How to Read," he described the three categories of poem he had in mind, and how their translation can be approached (Pound 1954).

MELOPOEIA, wherein the words are charged, over and above their plain meaning, with some musical property, which directs the bearing or trend of that meaning.

PHANOPOEIA, which is a casting of images upon the visual imagination.

LOGOPOEIA, which is "the dance of the intellect among words," that is to say, it employs words not only for their direct meaning, but it takes count in a special way of habits of usage, of the context we expect to find with the word, its usual concomitants, of its known acceptances, and of ironical play...

The melopoeia can be appreciated by a foreigner with a sensitive ear, even though he be ignorant of the language in which the poem is written. It is practically impossible to transfer or translate it from one language to another, save perhaps by divine accident, and for half a line at a time. Phanopoeia, can, on the other hand, be translated almost, or wholly, intact. When it is good enough, it is practically impossible for the translator to destroy it save by very crass bungling, and the neglect of perfectly well-known and formulatable rules. Logopoeia does not translate; though the attitude of mind it expresses may pass through in paraphrase. Or one might say, you can not translate it "locally," but that having determined the original author's state of mind, you may or may not be able to find a derivative or an equivalent.

RESTORING BORGES, WEARING NERUDA

Some translators have a privileged window into the lives of great artists and the creation of great art. One of these is Alastair Reid, who has translated some of the world's greatest poets, as well as writing essays, children's books, and poems of his own. The following is from his collection of essays, *Whereabouts: Notes on Being a Foreigner* (Reid 1987).

The two writers who have dominated the literary scene in Latin America are Borges and the Chilean poet Pablo Neruda, who died in late 1973. What is most curious about their coexistence is how little they have to do with each other as writers, how seldom they met or even mentioned each other as men, how drastically different their work is, and yet how Latin-American each is, in his separate way. Borges' collected work is as sparse and spare as Neruda's is abundant and ebullient, metaphysical as Neruda's is physical, formal as Neruda's is free-flowing, dubious as Neruda's is passionately affirmative or condemnatory. Where Neruda is open and even naive, Borges is subtle and sceptical; where Neruda is a sensualist, Borges is an ascetic; where Neruda writes of tangible, physical experience, Borges' fund of experience is purely literary – he looks on reading as a form of time travel. Although Borges roots his stories in Buenos Aires, Latin America is for him something of a metaphor, a geographical fiction. Neruda, quite to the contrary, celebrates, in hymnic joy or rage, the inexhaustible particularity of the Latin-American continent. For him, language is largesse, and his human concern made his political commitment inevitable...

For some years now, I have been translating poems of both Borges and Neruda, coming to know both men well and their work even better, for one never enters the being of a poem as completely as when one is translating it. It is an odd exercise of spirit, to enter another imagination in another language and then to try to make the movement of it happen in English. Untranslatability that no ingenuity can solve does arise, which is to say that some poems *are* untranslatable. (I keep a notebook of these untranslatables, for they are small mysteries, clues to the intricate nature of a language.) To a translator, Borges and Neruda are exigent in different ways. Borges learned English as a child, read voraciously in English, and has been influenced in the formal sense more by English writing – Stevenson, Kipling, Chesterton, Anglo-Saxon poetry, and the English poetic tradition – than by Spanish literature. In his stories, he tends to use English syntactical forms and prose order – making his Spanish curiously stark but easily accessible to English translation. Indeed, translating Borges into English often feels like restoring the work to its natural language, or retranslating it. In his poems, Borges leans heavily on English verse forms and on many of the formal mannerisms of English poetry, so that translating his poems calls for technical ingenuity and prosodic fluency, precision being all-important. His poems are so thoroughly objectified, however, that no great leaps of interpretation have to be made in translating them. It requires only the patience to refine and refine, closer and closer to the original. Neruda's poems present absorbingly different problems, though not just in their extravagance of language, their hugely varying themes and forms; what distinguishes them is their special tone, an intimacy with the physical world, the ability to enter and become things. (Neruda was commonly referred to in the conversation of his friends as *el vate*, the seer.) To translate his poems requires one to enter them and wear them, on the way to finding a similar tone in English. Neruda's larger poems have a vatic intensity that is difficult to contain in credible English, and has its closest affinities with Whitman, an engraving of whom always sat on his writing table. But his more personal lyrics are within closer reach of English, and, given linguistic luck, are not unre-creatable. Translation is a mysterious alchemy in the first place; but it becomes even more so in the experience of entering the language and perception of two writers who have read human experience so differently and have worded it in such distinct ways – of becoming both of them, however temporarily.

It is interesting to compare the fate of these two writers in translation. Borges has earned such attention in English, and the body of his work is so comparatively small, that translating him in his entirety is a feasible project. (This has not been entirely to Borges' advantage, for some of his earlier critical writing, which would have been better left in the decent obscurity it enjoys in Spanish, goes on being dragged into English.) The interest in

Borges has one advantage, however, in that his work has been translated by many hands, giving English readers a choice of versions, and a chance to realize what every translator must: that there is no such thing as a definitive translation. Something of the same is true of Neruda's work, and it has benefited particularly from the variety of its translators, since he was so many different poets himself; but, however assiduously he is mined, his work is so vast that only a fraction of it is likely to come satisfactorily into English. He waits, in his fullness, in Spanish. For that reason, I am discouraged from continuing to translate Neruda; but every now and then a poem of his so startles and absorbs me that its equivalence begins to form in English, and I make a version, for the awe of it. Translation becomes an addiction in one special sense: one can always count on it to take one again and again to the threshold of linguistic astonishment.

WHEN POETRY BECOMES POYITRY

Brian Holton has published many translations of classical and modern Chinese literature into both Scots and English. Here he explains why one might translate into a "non-metropolitan language" like Scots in the first place (Holton 2004),

> If we choose to translate into Scots, the first question will always be "Why not English?" – though you wouldn't ask a Dutchman or a Dane, "Why not German?" At least with translation there is a series of clear answers to "Why Scots?":
> * because this text demands non-metropolitan language;
> * because we hear this authorial voice in Scots;
> * because another tongue would impede or destroy the flavour of the original;
> * because with this text the translator is happier in this tongue.
>
> And this is to ignore for the moment wider issues such as:
> * every tongue needs to grow;
> * living languages are stretched best by cross-cultural contact;
> * translations challenge the scope and accuracy of tongues;
> * social/ political/ cultural factors demand the use of this tongue rather than that;
> * the translator ignores/ subverts/ colludes with social/ political/ cultural factors.

Next, he puts the theory into practice, explaining why, to his multilingual ear, Scots "works" better than English as a language for translating some of the poems of the Chinese poet Yang Lian.

With Yang Lian, however, it seems to me that the essential hameliness (familiarity and intimacy) of the Scots paradoxically enhances the strangeness at the heart of his poetry, just as the ordinariness of his poetic diction in Chinese contrasts with the oddness of his vision. What Scots seems to bring out is an earthiness, an immediacy and a strength which, together with the spikier rhythms of the Scots, can transmit Yang's voice more powerfully than English versions have so far been able to. This is how he looks in Scots:

WHAUR THE DEEP SEA DEVAULS

blue's aye heicher yet   same as yir weariness
hes walit the sea   same as a bodie's glower gars the sea
get twice as dreich

gaun back same as aye
ti the wrocht stane lug whaur the drumbeats is smoorit
peerie coral corps   a yowdendrift

gairie spreckles on deid fish
same as the lift at bields yir ilka want

gaun back ti the meiths   same as the enless gaun back
ti the scaurs   storm heids aa about ye
yir pipes weirdit ti skirl on efter yir daith   tunes o corruption i the
           howe o the flesh

whan blue's been kent at the last   the mishantert
sea   millions o caunles   blinters an devauls.

WHERE THE SEA STANDS STILL

blue is always higher   just as your weariness
has chosen the sea   just as a man's gaze compels the sea
to be twice as desolate

going back as ever
to that carved stone ear where drumbeats are destroyed
where tiny coral corpses   fall in a snowstorm

gaudy speckles on dead fish
like the sky that holds all your lust

go back to the limit   like limitlessness
going back to the cliffs   stormheads all around
your pipes doomed to go on playing after your death   tunes of
        corruption deep in the flesh

as blue is recognised at last   the wounded
sea   a million candles   stands dazzlingly still.

This is not the ornate and elegant poetic diction of, say, eighth-century Tang poetry, whose effortless ease and grace are not easily rendered into European tongues. (The linguistic need to clumsily insist on explicit markers for tense, gender, number, etc., is a dead weight that cramps the sinewy allusiveness and simplicity of classical Chinese verse to such an extent that there are few poets who survive the exchange with anything like their native grace.) This is strong, muscular poetry, with a pronounced Beijing accent and a profound sense of place; perhaps these are some of the qualities shared by Scots, and perhaps this may explain why these versions work. But in the end, it's all down to your ear, and your grasp of your ain (own) tongue, as well as your grasp of the other language.

For good measure, here is the poem in the origional (Yang Lian 1999):

大海停止之处

蓝总是更高的　当你的厌倦选中了
海　当一个人以眺望迫使海
倍加荒凉

依旧在返回
这石刻的耳朵里鼓声毁灭之处
珊瑚的小小尸体　落下一场大雪之处

死鱼身上鲜艳的斑点
像保存你全部性欲的天空

返回一个界限 像无限
返回一座悬崖 四周风暴的头颅
你的管风琴注定在你死后
继续演奏 肉里深藏的腐烂的音乐

当蓝色终于被认出 被伤害
大海 用一万枝蜡烛夺目地停止

VOLTAIRE'S "TO BE OR NOT TO BE"

Some of the most poetic language in the English language is, of course, found in the plays of William Shakespeare. Shakespearean translation has a long history, with some eminent practitioners. One of the earliest was François-Marie Arouet (1694–1778), better known as Voltaire, who spent two years in England after enduring his second stay in the Bastille. He wrote approvingly in his *Letters on the English* (Lettres Philosophiques) about England's traditions of tolerance and freedom of speech but was less impressed by certain aspects of English culture (Voltaire 1919). He uses Hamlet's most famous soliloquy to illustrate his exegesis; I have taken the liberty of truncating it.

> Shakespeare boasted a strong fruitful genius. He was natural and sublime, but had not so much as a single spark of good taste, or knew one rule of the drama. I will now hazard a random, but, at the same time, true reflection, which is, that the great merit of this dramatic poet has been the ruin of the English stage. There are such beautiful, such noble, such dreadful scenes in this writer's monstrous farces, to which the name of tragedy is given, that they have always been exhibited with great success. Time, which alone gives reputation to writers, at last makes their very faults venerable. Most of the whimsical gigantic images of this poet, have, through length of time (it being a hundred and fifty years since they were first drawn) acquired a right of passing for sublime. Most of the modern dramatic writers have copied him: but the touches and descriptions which are applauded in Shakespeare are hissed at in these writers; and you will easily believe that the veneration in which this author is held, increases in proportion to the contempt which is shown to the moderns...
>
> You will undoubtedly complain, that those who have hitherto discoursed with you on the English stage, and especially on the celebrated Shakespeare, have taken notice only of his errors; and that no one has

translated any of those strong, those forcible passages which atone for all his faults. But to this I will answer, that nothing is easier than to exhibit in prose all the silly impertinences which a poet may have thrown out; but that it is a very difficult task to translate his fine verses. All your junior academical sophs, who set up for censors of the eminent writers, compile whole volumes; but methinks two pages which display some of the beauties of great geniuses, are of infinitely more value than all the idle rhapsodies of those commentators; and I will join in opinion with all persons of good taste in declaring, that greater advantage may be reaped from a dozen verses of Homer or Virgil, than from all the critiques put together which have been made on those two great poets.

I have ventured to translate some passages of the most celebrated English poets, and shall now give you one from Shakespeare. Pardon the blemishes of the translation for the sake of the original; and remember always that when you see a version, you see merely a faint print of a beautiful picture. I have made choice of part of the celebrated soliloquy in *Hamlet*, which you may remember is as follows:

> To be, or not to be? that is the question!
> Whether 't is nobler in the mind to suffer
> The slings and arrows of outrageous fortune,
> Or to take arms against a sea of troubles,
> And by opposing, end them? To die! to sleep!
> No more! and by a sleep to say we end
> The heart-ache, and the thousand natural shocks
> That flesh is heir to!...

My version of it runs thus:

> Demeure, il faut choisir et passer à l'instant
> De la vie à la mort, ou de l'être au néant.
> Dieux cruels, s'il en est, éclairez mon courage.
> Faut-il vieillir courbé sous la main qui m'outrage,
> Supporter, ou finir mon malheur et mon sort?
> Qui suis-je? Qui m'arrête? et qu'est-ce que la mort?
> C'est la fin de nos maux, c'est mon unique asile
> Après de longs transports, c'est un sommeil tranquille...

Do not imagine that I have translated Shakespeare in a servile manner. Woe to the writer who gives a literal version; who by rendering every word of his original, by that very means enervates the sense, and extinguishes all the fire of it. It is on such an occasion one may justly affirm, that the letter kills, but the Spirit quickens.

How well did Voltaire do in translating this most famous of Shakespeare's speeches? The following is a literal back-translation of this passage, which does not attempt to reproduce the tight rhyme scheme that Voltaire felt was proper for serious theatre. While he covers much of the philosophical and plot-related ground of the original (although giving it an anti-religious spin), audiences relying on Voltaire's translation would have had a very different sense of *Hamlet*, both as a character and a theatrical experience.

> Hold, one must choose and move in an instant
> From life to death, or from being to nothingness
> Cruel gods, if you exist, enlighten my courage
> Must I grow old, bowing to the offending hand?
> Bear it, or put an end to my misfortune and my fate?
> Who am I? Who holds me back? and what is death?
> It is the end of one's troubles, my only refuge
> After long travails, peaceful slumber.

SING IN ME, MUSE!

Even in translation, great poetry inspires great passion – one is tempted to say, "if it doesn't, it isn't." Passion seems to be one of the hallmarks of Burton Raffel's many translations and commentaries: he positively radiates enthusiasm for sharing the poems that he enjoys, from the Anglo-Saxon epic *Beowulf* to the poems of the Indonesian writer Anwar Chairil. The following is from his book *The Forked Tongue: A Study of the Translation Process* (Raffel 1971):

> Greek poetry comes to me entirely in English; I cannot refer to any original texts, and have trouble deciphering even the alphabet when anyone else does so. However, when Butcher and Lang [in *Greek Literature in Translation* (Longmans, 1945)] tell me that Homer's *Odyssey* opens:

> Tell me, Muse, of that man, so ready at need, who wandered far and wide, after he had sacked the sacred citadel of Troy, and many were the men whose towns he saw and whose mind he learnt, yea, and many the woes he suffered in his heart upon the deep, striving to win his own life and the return of his company.

– I feel confident that... there is some flavour here, but the immense, towering reputation of the poet could not possibly be justified if this were how he sounded to those able to read and savour precisely what he wrote. Or this:

> The hero of the tale which I beg the Muse to help me tell is that resourceful man who roamed the wide world after he had sacked the holy citadel of Troy. He saw the cities of many peoples and he learnt their ways. He suffered many hardships on the high seas in his struggles to preserve his life and bring his comrades home.

This brisk Homer comes courtesy E.V. Rieu [Penguin Books, 1946]. There is no nonsense about this version, and no pretense of poetry; here is the story, bare and straight, take it or leave it. I doubt that there is much to choose from, as between these two versions. It seems to me to depend on how you like your poetry watered down; if you can stay awake, I suspect that the Butcher and Lang rendering gives a little more of something somewhat like Homer himself.

But then there is:

> Sing in me, Muse, and through me tell the story,
> of that man skilled in all the ways of contending,
> the warrior, harried for years on end,
> after he plundered the stronghold
> on the proud height of Troy.
>   He saw the townlands,
> and learned the minds of many distant men,
> and weathered many bitter nights and days
> in his deep heart at sea, while he fought only
> to save his life, to bring his shipmates home.

This is Robert Fitzgerald's new translation [Doubleday, 1961] and no one is likely to fall asleep reading such lines. This is indisputably poetry. And if it is not representative of Homer, as I will blindly swear it must be, then that does not make any real difference either. Homer-Homer, or Fitzgerald-Homer, it is good, it is very good indeed.

THE TRANSLATOR'S BOND

Of course, that opens a can of poetic worms – it actually *does* make a difference to many readers whether it is Homer-Homer or Fitzgerald-Homer. Which brings us right back to the debate about translating for literal equivalence or for sense. The poet and translator Dante Gabriel Rossetti (1828–82) had this to say about it, referring to a "bond" between the poet and his or her translator that imposes certain constraints on the latter (Rossetti 1919):

> The life-blood of rhymed translation is this, – that a good poem shall not be turned into a bad one. The only true motive for putting poetry into a fresh language must be to endow a fresh nation, as far as possible, with one more possession of beauty. Poetry not being an exact science, literality of rendering is altogether secondary to this chief aim. I say literality, – not fidelity, which is by no means the same thing. The task of the translator (and with all humility be it spoken) is one of some self-denial. Often would he avail himself of any special grace of his own idiom and epoch, if only his will belonged to him; often would some cadence serve him but for his author's structure – some structure but for his author's cadence; often the beautiful turn of a stanza must be weakened to adopt some rhyme which will tally, and he sees the poet revelling in abundance of language where himself is scantily supplied. Now he would slight the matter for the music, and now the music for the matter; but no, he must deal to each alike. Sometimes, too, a flaw in the work galls him, and he would fain remove it, doing for the poet that which his age denied him; but no, – it is not in the bond. His path is like that of Aladdin through the enchanted vaults: many are the precious fruits and flowers which he must pass by unheeded in search for the lamp alone; happy if at last, when brought to light, it does not prove that his old lamp has been exchanged for a new one – glittering indeed to the eye, but scarcely of the same virtue nor with the same genius at its summons.

NO EASIE ART

Wentworth Dillon (1633–85), the fourth Earl of Roscommon, was a popular poet in his day, and a well-known translator of Homer and Virgil. In 1684 he published his "Essay on Translated Verse," a monumentally discursive work whose rhyming couplets seem to go on forever, but which yields up a few useful nuggets for today's translator (Dillon 1685). First, Dillon's assessment of the translator's place and value in the artistic hierarchy:

> 'Tis True, Composing is the nobler Part,
> But good Translation is no Easie Art:
> For tho' materials have long since been found,
> Yet both your fancy and your Hands are bound,
> And by Improving what was writ Before,
> Invention Labours Less, but Judgement more...

Second, he provides some useful advice about how to choose an author if you are trying to decide whom to translate:

> Examine how your Humour is inclin'd,
> And which the Ruling Passion of your Mind;
> Then seek a Poet who your ways does bend,
> And choose an Author as you choose a Friend;
> United by this Sympathetick Bond,
> You grow Familiar, Intimate and Fond.
> Your Thoughts, your Words, your Styles, your Souls agree,
> No Longer his Interpreter, but He.

CHAPTER EIGHT

Collusion, collision, conversation:
The author/translator relationship

It's a strange business, translation. Impersonation of an author is not yet a chargeable offence in the courts of philosophy, but it's a doubtful and slippery affair.

— BRIAN HOLTON in his translator's notes for *Where the Sea Stands Still: New Poems* (Yang Lian 1999)

T he relationship between translators and the authors they translate can be as intimate as a marriage or as perfunctory as an emailed "cc:". The relationship is actually rather one-sided. Few authors will ever have occasion to read a translator's work with anything like the attention the translator puts into theirs, and fewer still are actually capable of judging the quality of the translation. On the other hand, translators often feel their close reading of the original text gives them a unique and privileged access to the author's mind. Certainly, translators' memoirs often provide fascinating insights into the lives and work of certain authors.

"FAR CANAL" IS *NOT* A DISTANT WATERWAY
The author's side of the relationship is described here by the Australian novelist Shane Maloney, whose series of thrillers featuring ministerial adviser Murray Whelan include *Something Fishy*, *The Big Ask*, and *Nice Try*. Maloney may be monolingual but he is clearly multi-idiomatic, with a fine appreciation of the nuances in the different variants of English. He put this appreciation to good use in his article "When Language Gets Your Unicorn's Goat" (Maloney 2004).

The republic of letters has always been an international community. And for the majority of us, those not fortunate enough to be fluently multilingual, access to that community comes by way of translation. It is through an interpreter that we encounter the words of the great figures of world literature – Tolstoy, Boccaccio, Dumas, Kafka and that blind Argentinian joker with the unpronounceable surname.

When we read a book in translation, we know we're not getting the full deal. We implicitly accept that something inherent in the original is lost, even if we don't know what. We place our trust in the translator and plough ahead with our reading. As long as the text captures our imagination, its foreign origins need not intrude.

Likewise, when it comes to feeling validated as a writer, there's nothing quite so affirming as being published in a foreign language. After all, what can compare with seeing your work rendered entirely unintelligible by a person you've never met from a place you've never been.

My initiation into the world of translation began with a stream of recommendations and queries from my American publisher. Initially, these were concerned with minor modifications, a little light tinkering at the margins. Spelling needed to be brought into line with American usage (-ise endings became -ize, colour became color). False cognates and unfamiliar diction had to be ironed out ("shopping-trolley" vs "grocery cart" and "diary" vs "calendar"). And certain unfamiliar items of vocabulary required clarification.

Could I please provide meanings and possible replacements for the following terms? Franger. Duco. Shoot through. Op shop. Furphy. Laminex. Ruckman. Fibro. A piece of piss. An unreconstructed Whitlamite.

Only after attending to this basic housekeeping did we finally get down to nuts and bolts, the cross-cultural crux of the matter. American usage required that "footpath" become "sidewalk."

Get stuffed, I declared, or words to that effect. We don't have sidewalks in Australia. We have footpaths. And while I could find no compelling reason to die in a ditch for the sake of the franger and the dunny, there was no way that I was going to allow Murray Whelan to take a hike down some goddamn American sidewalk. Next thing, he'd be eating Oreo cookies, drinking Miller Lite and voting Republican.

In due course, a mutually acceptable version was hammered out, one that retained as much Australian idiom as might reasonably be grasped by the average American reader. Of which, my U.S. publisher persuasively argued, there are many millions.

At least the Americans consulted me. With the Finns, there was no correspondence whatsoever. Presumably, this is because Helsinki has a good supply of unreconstructed Whitlamites who know the difference between a franger and a furphy. Or perhaps because the translator guessed that my grip on the Finno-Ugric branch of the tree of languages is tenuous at best, limiting my capacity to make constructive suggestions. Whatever the case (and for those interested, Finnish has 15 cases including the partitive, the accusative, the allative, the instructive and the comitative), a book in Finnish simply arrived one day. The only part I could decipher was my name. And that was because it was printed on the cover. The title read Hyvä Yritys. I've still got no idea what that means, but it sounds pretty snappy so they obviously got the tone right...

My first and only contact with my Japanese translator took place at the book launch. We exchanged business cards and signed each other's copies. Conversation was minimal. To tell the truth, I am not sure that Mr. Yakusha speaks English, although I would like to believe that he reads and writes it to a high degree of proficiency. As to his translation, all I can say for sure is that the script runs back to front and right to left. While this does not strictly conform to the original, it is perhaps an improvement.

Likewise, the book itself has been shaped to the culture. For a start, it has been miniaturised, shrunk to pocket size for ease of reading on a crowded subway. Advertising flyers are inserted between the pages, promoting obscure products at discount prices. And like a kimono, it comes wrapped with an obi.

Given the opportunity, I'd like to have exchanged expletives with Yakusha-san. Purely on a professional basis, of course, in order to satisfy my linguistic curiosity. Some of the characters in my books, members of the Australian political class, do quite a lot of swearing, and I cannot help but wonder how this was managed in Japanese, a language with a premium on politeness.

Even my tactful circumlocutions must have presented a huge challenge to Mr. Yakusha. For example, the exclamation "far canal!" could easily have proven problematic for somebody who did not immediately recognise it as a phonetic rendering of the vernacular pronunciation of a popular oath. Was it mistakenly rendered as "distant waterway" instead of "%&@#*&!"?

But however tenuous our lines of communication and whatever uncertainties I may harbour as to their competence, I hold all my translators in high esteem. Not only have they undertaken a task well beyond my own capacities, they have done so under conditions of virtual anonymity. They do the work, I get my name on the cover. And so I salute them as my silent partners, my co-authors.

Especially that bloke in Finland. To him I say "Hyvä Yritys, pal. Love what you've done with the umlauts."

BETRAY ME, PLEASE

A few people know both roles. One such is Michel Tremblay, who is by far Canada's most-translated playwright. Asked whether he agreed that translation is betrayal, he replied (Craig 1993):

> I am very well aware of it, because I have done it myself, translating Tennessee Williams' *Orpheus Descending*, for example. I know too well that it is much better in English. But we cannot say "no" to world literature. It's wonderful to be betrayed in the language of another person.

KAFKA'S THOUGHTS, LEVI'S KNOTS

Primo Levi was one of the twentieth century's most remarkable writers, and much of his work is available in translation from the Italian. He was ambivalent about being translated, as he made clear in his *L'altrui mestiere*, translated as *Other People's Trades* by Raymond Rosenthal in 1991 (Mendel 1998):

> It is worth saying a word too about the condition of a writer who finds himself being translated. Being translated is neither an everyday nor a holiday activity, indeed it is not an activity at all. It is a semi-passivity, similar to that of the patient on the operating table or on the psycho-analyst's couch, rich however in violent and contrasting emotions. An author who is confronted by one of his own pages translated into a language he knows, feels in turns – or at one and the same time – flattered, betrayed, ennobled, x-rayed, castrated, planed down, violated, embellished, killed. One rarely remains indifferent to a translator, known or unknown who has poked his nose and

his fingers into your viscera; you would willingly send him, by turns or at the same time, your heart – suitably wrapped – a cheque, a crown of laurel or one's seconds.

Levi was a translator himself, whose work included two books by the French anthropologist Claude Lévi-Strauss into Italian, *Le regard éloigné* and *La voie des masques*. In the early 1980s he published a translation of Kafka's *The Trial*. In a postface to the translation, Levi commented on his approach (Mendel 1998).

> I do not believe that there is much affinity between Kafka and me. Often, during the process of this translation, I have had the feeling of collision, of conflict, of the immodest temptation to unravel, in my own way, the knots in the text; in sum, to correct, to exploit the dictionary choices, to superimpose my own way of writing on Kafka's. I have tried not to yield to this temptation.
>
> Since I know that there is no such thing as the "right way" to translate, I have trusted more to instinct than to reason, and I have adhered to a line of interpretative correctness, as honestly as possible, even if not always coherent from page to page, because not all the pages present the same problems... Although I noted, for example, the obsessive effect (perhaps intentional) provoked by the lawyer Huld's opening speech, which is prolonged relentlessly for ten pages, with no paragraphs, I took pity on the Italian reader and introduced some interruptions. In order to preserve the flow of the language I have eliminated some limiting adverbs (all but, much, a little, approximately, about etc.), which German tolerates better than Italian. On the other hand I have made no attempt to thin out the accumulation of terms of the family "to seem" – likely, probable, discern, be aware, as if, apparently, like and so on; they seemed to me typical, even indispensable, in this account which tirelessly uncoils events in which nothing is as it seems. For the rest, I have made every effort to temper fidelity to the text with fluidity of language. Where in this notoriously tormented and controversial text there were contradictions and repetitions, I have conserved them.

The above excerpt from Levi was translated by the late David Mendel, himself a fascinating character – an eminent cardiologist who was also a writer, and had a brief but close friendship with Levi before the latter's suicide in 1987. His assessment of

Levi's Kafka, and particularly his explanation of how Levi came to write it, is enlightening about both the man and the international publishing business.

In my view, Levi's lack of affinity with Kafka is important but not crucial. More deleterious is his attempt to clarify, correct and embellish the text, superimposing his own way of writing on Kafka's. He wrote "I have tried not to yield to this temptation." But alas, he too often succumbs.

The changes Levi makes are so contrary to the aims of modern translators of literature and to his own previously stated goals, that one must ask why he undertook the translation.

Levi was asked by the publishers, Einaudi, to translate *The Trial* as one of a series of classic novels translated by modern novelists. He had learned a "barrack room" German in the camps, and then studied the language at the Goethe Institute in Turin. He spoke the language well, but he was by no means bilingual. He said in an interview reported in *Tecnologie chimiche* in December 1983 "I am doing translations from the German just to keep in practice." Many translations are made by people who realise that in so doing, their understanding of a foreign language will be increased. His failures seem less due to incomprehension than to positive decisions on technique. He yielded to the temptation to interpret instead of sticking to translation.

Levi translated the book just before he retired from his work as an Industrial Chemist. People on the brink of retirement are usually preoccupied by doubts about how they will manage on a reduced income. Though translation fills the mind rather than the purse, he might have been seeking to enlarge his possible sources of future income. It was not until a year or two after his retirement that his fame spread world-wide and gave him an assured income...

Cesare Cases, that shrewd critic of Levi's work, wrote in *L'Indice* (December 1987), "That he found himself translating *The Trial* is due to one of those unhappy situations into which an author may stumble if he does not know how to defend himself well enough from pressure from his friends" (my translation). Whatever the explanation, the translation, though workman-like, does not measure up to his own explicit criteria, to his own high literary standards or to modern requirements.

The late and incomparable James Thurber once met a fervent French admirer. "I am fortunate," said the admirer, "because I speak English well enough to appreciate – and to love – your stories. But," he went on, "I have also read them translated into French and, believe me, they are even better in French." Thurber, with his usual modesty, gave an understanding nod. "I know," he said. "I tend to lose something in the original."

— MOURA BUDBERG in her essay "On Translating from Russian" (Budberg 1971)

MAKING A MARKET

While some translators are solitary creatures whose relationships with others are essentially one-on-one, others become part of a literary "scene." Denys Johnson-Davies got to know many of the important writers in Arabic over the years, and was both a translator and a champion of their work. Shortly after his arrival in Cairo in the late 1940s, he became friendly with Edwar al-Kharrat, an outstanding figure in the development of modern Egyptian fiction (Johnson-Davies 2006).

Edwar has all along been a great encourager of younger talents, many of which were first introduced to a wider public through the magazine *Gallery* 67, which he edited. These include such writers as Ibrahim Aslan, Mohamed El-Bisatie, and the late Yahya Taher Abdullah. His small flat in Zamalek – made small by the abundance of books – where I first met him in the 1940s, is a regular meeting-place for budding writers. One evening – I recollect that Mustafa Badawi, who taught Arabic at Oxford University, was in Cairo on a visit – a number of younger writers were present. That evening it was brought home to me how the translator from a language such as Arabic differs from one who translates from say French or German. The latter relies upon publishers to choose the books they wish to have translated. Would the translator be interested in such-and-such a novel? What sort of fee would he or she require? This approach of course doesn't operate where Arabic is concerned. There is no publishing house in London employing anyone interested in modem Arabic literature or capable of reading Arabic. As an Arabic translator, therefore, having read a book that I feel deserves to be translated, I can either sit down and translate the work in question in the hope that, when the time comes, I will find a publisher for it, or I must have at my disposal a publisher who has sufficient confidence in my judgment and will publish anything I care to translate – as happened with the Heinemann Arab Authors series. I know that many Arab writers – and Tayeb Salih has expressed this opinion to me openly – feel that attempts should have been made to find mainstream publishers for Arabic works of fiction. In the case of Tayeb himself, I was grateful to have the Arab Authors series at my disposal, otherwise his novel *Season of Migration to the North* might well have remained unpublished. At least, through its own merits, the novel later achieved translation into a number of languages beside English, and has even now found its way into the prestigious Penguin Modern Classics. As a translator's main concern is to be assured that his efforts are going to be rewarded by seeing the book in print, I have always sought to find a publisher who could be relied upon to look favorably on translations from the Arabic. However, it required Naguib Mahfouz to win the Nobel prize for an American publisher of the caliber of Doubleday to take him on. Today publishers are primarily businesspeople and are loath to take risks, particularly with a book translated from Arabic. English readers, it is known, keep away from any translated book, be it even from French. Consider, for example, the work of the Lebanese writer Amin Maalouf, who writes in French. The rights to a novel of his that had sold over a million copies in France were bought by Quartet Books in London, and the resulting English edition sold a mere two thousand copies. Arabic translators thus, in many ways, have both greater power and more responsibility than their French counterparts, for they take upon themselves not only the role of translator but also that of the person deciding what should be translated. By choosing to translate X, you are seen as rejecting both Y and Z (who may well be just as good, or even better than X).

That the role of the Arabic translator is both difficult and unenviable was brought home to me that evening that I spent at Edwar al-Kharrat's flat with several of Cairo's younger writers, one of whom suddenly demanded of me: "Who are you to choose what writers you translate?" I was taken aback by the question and was grateful to Edwar when he intervened and asked the young man: "So what do you want him to do if not to make the choice himself?" The young man answered: "He should go to the Ministry of Culture and get a list of the books that should be translated." This reply evinced general merriment, for it is well known that the establishment has its own favorites, and these are not necessarily the best. Edwar continued by pointing out that in the end it was I who was going to have all the work of translating the book, so why should I translate a book that might not be to my liking? Also, being English, was I not better qualified to judge which book would be likely to be well received by the English reader? I was grateful to Edwar for answering for me, aware as I am of the feeling that must inevitably exist among many writers who have not had their work translated for one reason or another. It is a sad fact that it is only by being translated that the Arab writer has a chance of achieving any serious recognition and at least the possibility of some real monetary reward. It should also be borne in mind that translating Arabic fiction is poorly rewarded in financial terms – if one practiced translation in order to supplement one's income, one would be better off using one's time giving private English lessons. This is not something that is generally appreciated...

I remember Tewfik al-Hakim, on one of my visits to his office, opening the drawer of his desk and producing a check, which he waved in front of me. It was from Heinemann, the publishers of the Arab Authors series, and was for six months royalties: a total of £3.60. "It would be a real shame to cash this," he joked. "I think I'll get it framed so I can hang it up."

CONSULTING WITH VARGAS LLOSA

Gregory Rabassa's *If This Be Treason: Translation and its Dyscontents, A Memoir* is an enjoyable collection of reflections on his profession, and on the authors with whom he has worked. In his chapter on Mario Vargas Llosa, Rabassa describes his relationship with the novelist, and the difficulties of translating the genre known as "magic realism" (Rabassa 2005).

There is an extremely fascinating character in *The Green House,* the Japanese-Brazilian smuggler and badman Fushia, who runs his sector of the jungle with a cruel and iron hand. Years after the novel was written Vargas Llosa went into politics and ran for president of Peru. Like so many young liberals in Latin America (and elsewhere), with the years he has drifted rightward and was the candidate of the oligarchical upper class that has run things there whenever the army has allowed them to. The country was in a chaotic state and Mario's populist opponent, the Japanese-Peruvian Alberto Fujimori, promised everything and trounced him. He went on to betray the people's hopes and backslid into the usual corrupt dictatorship. My immediate thought was that here was Fushia wreaking his revenge on Mario for having created him as such a baleful figure in the novel.

With this novel Vargas Llosa became one of that group practicing what would be called, for better or for worse, magic realism. I found him closer to Asturias than to Cortázar, but that could have been due to a similarity in terrain. There is nothing otherworldly in *The Green House*, although the characters, this-worldly as they are, have the proportions of monsters and, also, the atmosphere of the story is overloaded with tension, and tension is the stuff of magic. Given all this, I had to tread carefully, not choosing words that would be completely magical in tone or picking ones that would be too drably realistic. The original helped in this because Mario had just the right words and if I sensed and chose the right English ones I was home.

Mario looked over my work as I went along and would offer suggestions. Most were appreciated, especially where it had been some jungle peculiarity I had missed. At times, however, he would latch on to what he thought was a mistake and offer a correction. His limited English had simply kept him unaware of the fact that my word was nothing but a synonym for the one he was suggesting. He was wary of the novel's becoming too exotic in tone and I had to tell him that it would be hard for a North American not to find exotic even the most banal aspects of Amazonian existence and that if the translation was to be true there was little that could be done to offset that impression. I also reminded him that the Spanish reader in Madrid, or even in Lima, would find it no less so. Here was a case of magic realism by definition, as what was real in Iquitos would come off as something magical in northern climes. I am sure that if Fushia could have read the book as his biography he would have found nothing unreal about his surroundings or even, perhaps, about his own strange self.

A few years later Cass Canfield [the literary agent] came back with another Vargas Llosa novel to be translated: *Conversación en la Catedral* (Conversation in The Cathedral). You will note that *Catedral* is capitalized in Spanish and that both *Cathedral* and the article are in English. This is because the locale in question is not the cathedral of Lima at all but a bar across the way that takes its name from it. This made for great trouble in maintaining the capitalized article in reviews and notices, given the fact that no one was aware of that circumstance without having read the book.

Fingerspitzengefühl, *a nice German word, meaning sensitivity, instinct, but literally fingertip feeling, that is what one is after, and supposing the original text is good, the translation never comes out quite as good as one could wish. Perhaps that is only as it should be; and the text that can actually be improved by translation is not worth translating in the first place.*

— ANTHEA BELL in "Translator's Notebook: Delicate Matters" (Bell 2006)

HEROINE WORSHIP

I wish I could say that I had a relationship with the Belgian novelist Amélie Nothomb, but that would be, as Huckleberry Finn put it, a "stretcher." I had no communication at all with her during the several months I spent translating her wonderful *Sabotage Amoureux*. It was only much later that I spoke to her on the telephone... once. Despite the circumstances (see below), it was a thrill. I also treasure a fax passed on by her agent, in which Amélie called me "charmant et talentueux." A bit pathetic on my part? Maybe so, but I think my reaction was fairly common: literary translators are frequently in awe of the writers they translate – or if not them personally, then of their work. It is why we often go to such lengths to get them published (I don't mean get *ourselves* published – it is *their* book) in our own language. The following is from an article of mine called "Sabotage, eh? Translating *Le sabotage amoureux* from the French into the Canadian and the American" (Wilson 2003).

> "La petite peste de la littérature française" – that was what first caught my eye. The place was Vancouver, Canada, the year was 1993, and the words were a headline in the French-Canadian newsmagazine *Actualité*. Amélie Nothomb had just published *Le sabotage amoureux,* and the magazine had run a two-page spread about her and the new novel.
>
> I remember idly wondering how best to translate the headline, and settled on "the brat of French literature." It certainly fit the mischievous, 22-year old face in the accompanying photograph. (Neither the face nor the image has changed much in the intervening years.)
>
> If the title and photo caught my attention, the article sold me on the book. Who could resist the premise: a multi-national gang of children re-fighting World War II in Beijing's diplomatic compound during the era of the Gang of Four. I ordered the book, enjoyed it hugely, and started telling my friends about it... Which was thoroughly unsatisfying, since you can't

really have a discussion about a book other people can't read. Vancouverites are far more likely to speak Cantonese or Punjabi than French, and few of my friends there read French comfortably, or at all.

I knew that literary translations usually lag the original by several years, which seemed a pity. *Le sabotage amoureux* was only one hundred and ten pages long, and the vocabulary seemed pretty basic. So I decided to translate it. At two hours a day, *Petit Larousse* at my side, it took two months. I duly showed it to my friends, most of whom liked it as much as I did. And that was that. I liked what I'd done, but always assumed that someone, someday would translate it properly.

Fast-forward to 1998...
As it happened, *Sabotage* never did get translated into English by anyone else. In fact, five years passed before anything by Amélie could be read in English. I didn't much care for the spiky, unsympathetic *Les Catilinaires* (published in English as *The Strangers Next Door*, translated by Carol Volk): it seemed an unfortunate choice to introduce her to English-speaking audiences. After a few inquiries, I got in touch with the agency that represents French publishers in North America, the French Publishers Bureau, in New York. The English-language rights were still available – a sad commentary on the North American market for literary translations, but a pleasant surprise for me.

From there it was relatively easy to find a small Canadian publisher willing to take it on: Vancouver's Hurricane Press (owned, conveniently, by my younger brother). That had a happy knock-on effect a few months later, when the Bureau placed it with New Directions, the American literary publishers, who had wanted to publish Nothomb for years...

Copy-editing generated few surprises, and the process of graphic design – which authors usually have little to do with – was fun. When it got to the American publisher, however, I re-discovered some of the subtle differences that operate above and below the 49th parallel. Standard Canadian English sounds very much like standard American; but it still retains vestiges of its more recent connection with Britain. New Directions' editor David Savage did his work with a discreet, sensitive touch, but we had differences on some very subtle issues of syntax and tone.

You can see it on the first page of the book, where the narrator rides her horse on The Square of the Great Fan, "appelé plus vulgairement place

Tiananmen." I had translated the phrase as "known more commonly as Tiananmen Square"; David felt it should be "more commonly known as Tienanmen Square." In a note to him about this and other questions, I wrote, "I'd prefer 'known more commonly as' because her construction feels a bit more high-falutin' than simply 'more commonly known as'." The latter sounded to me like a cop describing someone's use of an alias ("AKA John Doe"), rather than the way an erudite European would describe one of the world's great squares.

I got my way on this passage in the Canadian edition, but not in the American one. It's no big deal, but it still bothers me a little, and I still think it matters. As Amélie herself says later on in the book, "Rien n'est moins innocent que le syntaxe." (Comparing notes with Adriana Hunter, the highly accomplished translator of *Stupeurs et tremblements*, I found I got off lightly – her American publisher didn't even do her the courtesy of discussing the changes they eventually made.)

And finally, Amélie herself
It was 6 in the morning when the phone rang.

"Allo," she said, in her lightly accented English. Then, hearing my sleep-muddled reply, "Oh, I'm sorry – it is not the same time as New York?"

Nope. Actually, Vancouver is three time zones behind New York, the result of distances that many Europeans can't quite imagine. But I was thrilled to finally hear Amélie's voice and get her opinion on the final draft that we'd sent for her approval.

"La petite peste de la litterature française" was charming and very complimentary of the translation, but she had a few things on her mind. The biggest issue for her was the title. Neither the Canadian nor the American publisher liked the literal translation, "Loving Sabotage." They both thought that "In the City of Electric Fans" would work better, advertising both the exotic and the quirky virtues of the text. I was ambivalent, but had the feeling that there was something clunky about "loving sabotage" as a phrase. It doesn't sound quite... right, though at the same time it isn't wrong.

Amélie, however, was adamant. *Sabotage* had by that time been published in 10 languages, and she'd noticed that the versions with literal translations of the title did well (bestsellers in Germany and Italy, for instance), while other solutions didn't (Holland, which went for the fans – *Vuurwerk en Ventilatoren*). I quote from a fax she sent her publicist:

Ce n'est pas du narcissisme d'auteur... Qu'on ne vienne pas me dire qu'en anglais ça sonne bizarre (grand argument passe-partout des traducteurs): en français aussi, cela sonne bizarre, et c'est précisément pour cette raison que cela marche! [It isn't a question of author's narcissism... Don't tell me that it sounds strange in English (the translator's default argument): it sounds strange in French too, and that's precisely why it works!]

So "Loving Sabotage" it was, and is.

....

If the translation of a well known, well thought of work appears dull to you, don't assume the accolades were misplaced, try another translation.

— ESTELLE GILSON in the theatre blog *CurtainUp* (1998)

CHAPTER NINE

When I hear the words "Translation Theory...":
Translation studies

I try to avoid the jargon of "target language;" I am an old infantryman, and we dogfaces were taught to shoot at a target and, ideally, kill it.

— GREGORY RABASSA in *If This Be Treason: Translation and Its Dyscontents, A Memoir* (Rabassa 2005)

Cognition. Structuralism. Derrida. Functionalism. Dynamic equivalence. Sapir-Whorf Hypothesis. Formal equivalence. Semiotics. Schleiermacher...

Still with me? The very term *translation theory* conjures the comment variously attributed to academics, senior British Treasury officials and Irish prime ministers: "Fine, so it works in practice. But does it work in theory?"

I was inclined to dismiss theory before I began this anthology. But writers like the ones presented in this chapter changed my mind. The thing to remember is that translation theory is part of the wider field of translation studies, a vast and eclectic area of scholarship that draws from a wide variety of disciplines and from researchers in many countries. The best of it makes you think again about texts you thought you knew, as the translator not only becomes "visible" but is subjected to the equivalent of a full MRI scan. Gender, politics, and ideology receive a much-needed airing, providing fuel for passionate polemical battles. While too much of the scholarly writing about translation is turgid academic-speak, it is safe to say that the field is also well served by lively and engaging minds who express themselves very well indeed.

LET THEORY BE YOUR FRIEND

In my experience, the translation theorist Andrew Chesterman is spot-on when he says the following (Chesterman 1997):

> Many practising professional translators are suspicious of theory, or may be of the opinion that there is no such thing as a theory of translation anyway. Translator trainees, too, often feel that what they need is simply more practice, not high-flown talk about abstract theory.

But Chesterman doesn't buy it.

> In response to such claims, I argue that a translator must have a theory of translation: to translate without a theory is to translate blind.

Chesterman has long made it his business to show the practical value of theory. The book *Can Theory Help Translators? A Dialogue Between the Ivory Tower and the Wordface* grew out of his correspondence with Emma Wagner, a translation manager at the European Commission whom we met in chapter 5. A surprisingly lively read despite the title, the book covers many aspects of the relationship between translation theory and translation practice, including the translator's identity and changing historical role, the issue of "visibility," and professional standards. Wagner's first words in the text vividly evoke the divide between the two worlds (Chesterman and Wagner 2002):

> "Translation theory? Spare us…" That's the reaction to be expected from most practising translators. Messages from the ivory tower tend not to penetrate as far as the wordface. (The wordface is the place where we translators work – think of a miner at the coalface.)

Wagner (EW) then provides an example from her own work environment, and asks Chesterman (AC) how theory might help make a better translation. His response gives a useful look at some of the conceptual tools used in translation theory, as well as the use of machine aids to translation.

> EW: This example is a sentence from a European Commission recommendation on action to help "SMEs" (small and medium-sized enterprises). This is a routine document addressed to politicians and bureaucrats, but even they deserve translations that are more readable than Translation A:

French original text:

Le rapport biannuel sur la coordination des activités en faveur des PME
et de l'artisanat rendra compte des progrès accomplis notamment
grâce à l'établissement et à la comparaison de données sur le taux
de participation des PME aux programmes communautaires tant en
nombre de projets qu'en volume budgétaire et à l'introduction, le cas
échéant, de mesures spécifiques susceptibles d'augmenter la participation des PME.

Translation A:

The twice-yearly report on the coordination of activities to assist SMES
and the craft sector will detail the progress achieved, particularly
through compiling and comparing data on the participation rate of
SMEs in Community programmes – in terms both of the number
of projects and the budgetary volume involved – and through the
introduction, where appropriate, of special measures to increase the
participation of SMEs.

A more readable translation would be something like this:

Translation B:

Our success or failure will be measured by the twice-yearly report on
action to help small businesses. This will show exactly how many of
them are involved in Community programmes – both the number of
projects, and the financial volume they represent. The report will also
chart the impact of any special measures that might boost applications from small businesses.

Which theoretical tools do you think Translator B used (consciously or otherwise) to arrive at Translation B instead of Translation A?

AC: Experienced professional translators use all kinds of conceptual tools in
a routine way, without actually thinking of them, although they may have
learned to use them consciously during their training. Here are some of the
most common ones.

Transposition

This means changing the word class. "Transposition" is one term used for this idea (since Vinay and Darbelnet, 1958), but different theorists use different names (sorry). This seems to be an unknown idea to Translator A. True, that translator does try to get rid of a couple of nouns (*the progress achieved, particularly through compiling and comparing data*), but this only leads to a misinterpretation: it sounds as if the progress will be achieved by compiling data. Most of the French nouns come out faithfully as English nouns, and so on. But there is nothing sacred about word classes in texts like this. In English, verbal forms are generally preferable to the heavy abstract nouns so common in French, and introducing more verbs (as Translator B has done) makes it much easier to produce an acceptable version, less cluttered with nouns and prepositions. Translation A, on the other hand, is rather like what a good machine translation program could produce... What would your Systran program produce, I wonder?

EW: OK, here it is:

> Raw Machine Translation:
> The biannual report on the coordination of the activities for the SMEs and for the craft industry will give an account of the progress achieved in particular thanks to the establishment and thanks to the comparison of data on the rate of participation of the SMEs in the Community programmes both in number of projects and in budgetary volume and in the introduction, if necessary, of specific measures likely to increase the participation of the SMEs.

AC: Yes, no evidence of transposition here. Conceptual tools are, after all, only accessible to human brains – by definition! Strange, though, how some (less professional) translators seem to translate like machines. Here are some more useful concepts for human translators.

DEVERBALIZATION. This is a key term in the training used at the ESIT institute of interpretation and translation in Paris. It means simply that a translator or interpreter has to get away from the surface structure of the source text, to arrive at the intended meaning, and then express this intended meaning in the target language. (I will bypass here the deconstructionist arguments that there is no objective meaning there in the first place. Translators have to believe that there is something there, after all...) In other words, deverbalization is a technique used to avoid unwanted formal interference: professional translators need to process the intended meaning in their own words, rather than try to mechanically manipulate source-text structures. What has Translator A done? In most cases, he or she seems to have processed the source structure bit by bit, twisting it into some form of grammatical English, without stopping to ask what the hell this is actually supposed to mean. I'd love to ask them: if you had this idea to express in English, but no French source text to distract you, would you really express it like this? Are these words in the translation "your own words"? Would you really choose to have such a long subject? Would you yourself use an expression like *the introduction, where appropriate*? Do you actually like using such complicated noun phrases? More importantly: do you think your readers find such a style pleasant to read, easy to understand?

ICONICITY. Roughly speaking, iconicity is the matching of form and meaning, so that the form reflects the meaning or the experience that is being described. It is a well-known pragmatic maxim of clarity that iconic expressions are easier to process than non-iconic ones. For instance, *Switch on after plugging in* is not iconic. *Plug in before switching on* is iconic, because the order of information expressed matches the order of the events described.

Another aspect of iconicity is illustrated by your example: chunking, i.e. the way the information / meaning / message is broken up into digestible pieces. Translator B has chosen to split the French sentence into three chunks, each encoding a distinct idea, so that the form (three sentences) reflects the semantic structure: (1) there will be this report; (2) it will do this; and (3) it will do that. Nice and clear.

Sometimes it can be difficult to find an iconic solution that can be combined with the need to deverbalize. So let's appeal to the concept of relevance.

RELEVANCE. Readers of the translation will usually be different from the readers of the original, and will have different cognitive backgrounds etc., they will have different ideas about what is relevant to them. The translator's job is to translate what is relevant: this may mean explaining or adding or omitting things occasionally. One scholar, Ernst-August Gull (2000), puts the point in a way that links it nicely with the deverbalization concept: what the translator has to do in order to communicate successfully is to arrive at the intended interpretation of the original, and then determine in what respects the translation should "interpretively resemble" the original in order to be consistent with the principle of relevance for the target audience with its particular cognitive environment. Other scholars have proposed a related concept: the maxim of "sufficient degree of precision" (see Honig and Kussmaul 1982; Schaffner 1998). Good professional translators go to the level of precision needed, not beyond it.

Another way of making this same point is to use the idea of IMPLICITA-TION. This conceptual tool is the technique of making information implicit: not everything needs to be explicit, not even everything that was explicit in the original. The opposite procedure is of course EXPLICITATION. There are examples of both in your French text:

> Implicitation: *notamment grâce à l'établissement et à la comparaison de données sur* → (the report) will show (reports always do compile and compare data, so there is no need to say it)

> Implicitation: *des PME et de l'artisanat* → small businesses (*artisanat* "craft trades" can be omitted; show me a craftsman who's in *big* business)

> Explicitation: *des progrès accomplis* → success or failure

> Explicitation: PME → small businesses

But doesn't all this mean that the translation changes the style of the original? Well, in what respects should the style remain the same, do you think? If a translation (of a non-literary text) ends up being clearer than the original, so what? IMPROVING THE ORIGINAL is another useful concept.

EW: Yes – though not many translators have the confidence to suggest improving the original.

These "conceptual tools" are excellent, and very interesting. So obviously translation theorists *can* help us, once they overcome their fear of being prescriptive. Why are these concepts useful? Because they provide labels for things that good translators do instinctively (at the same time "coining a common language in which we can talk about translation," as

I put it earlier). The guidelines embodied in transposition, deverbalization, iconicity and relevance are very sound.

I can't resist the urge to point out that a descriptive approach would not do anything to correct dull unreadable stuff like Translation A, which is typical of much of the output of bored professional translators with no self-esteem and a sneaking suspicion that no one will read their translation anyway. Translation B (produced by me) represents what I would have prescriptively instructed Translator A to produce if I'd had an opportunity to revise their translation. Did I use the tools of transposition, deverbalization, iconicity, relevance, explicitation and implicitation? Deverbalization, certainly (how can one translate without it?). Explicitation and implicitation are a conscious part of translation too. The others I obviously used subconsciously...

BELOVED BANGLA

In 2001, Gayatri Chakravorty Spivak gave the keynote speech to a conference of translators at India's National Academy of Letters, the Sahitya Akadami (Spivak 2005). Spivak is both a working translator and a major intellectual, a pioneer in feminist and post-colonial studies since the early 1970s, who has sometimes been accused of opaqueness in her academic work (she has – I hope at least semi-humorously – referred to herself as a "practical Marxist-feminist-deconstructionist"). Yet there is nothing opaque about the speech excerpted below. Its deceptively modest title, "Translating into English," does not begin to suggest its cultural and historical sweep – nor her evident delight in language.

I am a translator *into* English, not just *from* specific languages. Because of the growing power of English as a global lingua franca, the responsibility of the translator into English is increasingly complicated. And, although I chose my examples in order to avoid cultural nationalism, it is of course true that the responsibility becomes altogether more grave when the original is not written in one of the languages of northwestern Europe.

For a variety of reasons, the market for quick translations from such languages is steadily on the rise. Since the mid-1970s, it has been enhanced by a spurious and hyperbolic admiration not unrelated to the growing strength of the so-called international civil society. In the 1970s, extra-state collective action in Europe, Latin America, Asia, and Africa concerned itself with issues such as health, the environment, literacy, and the like. Although their relationship with the nation-state was conflictual, there was still a relationship. Gradually, with the advance of capitalist globalization, this emergent force was appropriated into the dominant. These earlier extra-state collectivities, which were basically nongovernmental entities, often with international solidarity, were now used to undermine the constitutionality (however precarious or utopian) of the state. Powerful international NGOs (nongovernmental organizations) now control these extra-state circuits globally. Indigenous NGOs typically have a large component of foreign aid. This self-styled international civil society (since it is extra-state) has a large cultural component, especially directed toward gender issues. It is here that the demand for translation – especially literary translation, a quick way to "know a culture" – has been on the rise. At this point, we translators into English should operate with great caution and humility.

Yet the opposite is often the case. Meenakshi Mukherjee, the well-known feminist Bengali scholar of English literature, has spoken to me of a person – she did not mention the name – who has recently turned her or his hand to translating from the Bengali. Upon repeated questioning about her or his proficiency in Bengali, this would-be translator has given the same answer: *"bangla parte jani"* (I can read Bengali). We all know of such cases.

It is time now to mention the other obvious point – the translator must not only make an attempt to grasp the presuppositions of an author but also, and of course, inhabit, even if on loan, the many mansions, and many levels of the host language. *Bangla parte jani* is only to have gained entry into the outer room, right – the front gate.

I am at the moment engaged in translating Mahasweta Devi's novel *Chotti Munda ebong tar tir* (Chotti Munda and his Arrow) published in 1980. In the last paragraph that I translated I made a choice of level when I came across the phrase *mohajoner kachhe hat pa bandha.* "Arms and legs in hock to the moneylender," I wrote. "In hock" is more in the global lingua franca than in the English that is one of the Indian languages. Sujit Mukherjee, the brilliant Indian translator from Bengali into English, and I had a running conversation about such choices. But "mortgaged" would have been, in my judgement, an error of level, and would have missed the pun, "being tied up or trussed," present in the original. Not that "in hock" catches the pun.

But "hock" is sufficiently confusing in etymology to carry the promise of nuances. The translator must play such games.

Lower down in the paragraph, I'm less satisfied with my treatment of the phrase *hoker kotha bollo na Chotti?* as "Didn't Chotti speak of 'rights'?" *Hok*, in Bengali, a *totshomo* or identical loan from the Arabic *al haq*, is not rights alone but a peculiar mix of rights and responsibilities that goes beyond the individual.

Anyone who has read the opening of Mahasweta's novel knows that the text carries this presupposition. I have failed in this detail. Translation is as much a problem as a solution. I hope the book will be taught by someone who has enough sense of the language to mark this unavoidable failure.

This for me is an important task of translation, especially from languages that are dying, some fast, some slow, for want of attention. In our particular circumstances, we translators from the languages of the global South should prepare our texts as metropolitan teaching texts because that, for better or for worse, is their destiny. Of course, this would make us unpopular, because the implicit assumption is that all that "third world" texts need is a glossary. I myself prepare my translations in the distant and unlikely hope that my texts will fall into the hands of a teacher who knows Bengali well enough to love it, so that the students will know that the best way to read this text is to push through to the original. Of course not everyone will learn the language, but one might, or two!

Later in the speech, Spivak deftly weaves political history into her exploration of Bengali's development, particularly the influences of nationalism and religion. Yet the passage is also about a specific problem: how to translate accurately two words in a poem – a poem which itself deals with what happens when two languages rub up against each other.

... Through the centuries of the Mughal Empire in India (1526–1857) and the corresponding Nawabate in Bengal, Bengali was enriched by many Arabic and especially Persian loan-words. Of course Bengali is derived from Sanskrit, which was by then "dead," so the relationship is altogether different. But learned and worldly Bengali gentlemen were proficient in Arabic, and especially Persian – the languages of the court and the law. The important entry of the British into India was by way of Bengal. It is at least the generalist's assumption that the British played the Bengali Hindus with promises of liberation from the Muslim empire. William Jones's discovery that Sanskrit, Greek, and Latin were related languages even gave the Hindus and the English a common claim to Aryanism, a claim to intertranslatability, as it were. And, from the end of the eighteenth century, the fashioners of the new Bengali prose purged the language of the Arabic-Persian content until, in Michael Madhusudan Dutt's (1824–73) great blank verse poetry, and the *Bangadarshan* (1872–76) magazine edited by the immensely influential novelist Bankim Chandra Chattopadhyaya (1838–94), a grand and fully Sanskritized Bengali emerged. Its Arabic and Persian components became no more than local color. This was the language that became the vehicle of Bengali nationalism and subsequently of that brand of Indian nationalism that was expressed in Bengali. The medium was simplified, expanded, and diversified into the contemporary Bengali prose that is the refined edge of my mother tongue, which I learned in school, and which did not allow me to translate *murtad* and *dorra*.

A corresponding movement of purging the national language Hindi of its Arabic and Persian elements has been under way since independence in 1947. Such political dismemberments of language have become part of Partition Studies – as Serbian separates from Croatian, Czech from Slovak, and Cantonese is dismissed as a mere dialect of Han. The political production of internal translation requires a different type of analysis, which I will touch upon in my conclusion.

If the Arabic and Persian elements were purged out of Bengali, how do I encounter them as a translator today? I encounter them as part of a general movement in Bangladesh to restore these components. This is not to be confused with an Islamicization of the language, since there can be no question of transforming the Sanskrit base of Bengali. Indeed, Mazhar uses the Sanskrit-based vocabulary of Bengali with considerable flair. One may call this an attempt persistently to mend the breach of a partition that started – as I have indicated in my generalist tale – long before the named Partition of India in 1947. It is to restore a word-hoard that went underground.

What was created as East Pakistan in 1947 became independent as Bangladesh in 1971. Although there was an important political and military conflict that brought this about, it would not be incorrect to say that one strong factor of the mobilization of what was to become Bangladesh was the issue of language. And indeed the naming of the new nation as Bangladesh was to shrink an older cartography. Bangladesh (Banglaland) is the name of the entire land area whose people use Bangla, or Bengali; or Bangla is the name of the language of the entire people of the land or desh called Bangladesh. Before the independence-partition of 1947, this would have been the entire British province of Bengal including today's Indian state of West Bengal and the modern nation-state of Bangladesh, whose geographical descriptive could be East Bengal – in Bengali Paschim and Purbo Banga. Banga is the ancient name of a tract of land somewhat larger than the British province of Bengal. Thus the proper name of a pre-modern area and kingdom, displaced into the name of a Nawabship, translated into the colonial proper name of a province, expanded beyond a language area into the governmental abstraction of a presidency – is now modernized to designate, not a language-area but a bounded nation-state metonymically claiming the whole...

If the establishment of a place named Bangladesh in a certain sense endorses the partition of 1947 – the language policy of the state, strangely enough, honors that other partition – the gradual banishment of the Arabic and Persian elements of the language that took place in the previous century – and thus paradoxically undoes the difference from West Bengal. The official language of the state of Bangladesh, 99 percent Muslim, is as ferociously Sanskritized as anything to be found in Indian Bengali.

It is over against and all entwined in this tangle that the movement to restore the Arabic and Persian element of Bengali, away from its century-old ethnic cleansing, does its work. And it is because I grew up inside the tangle that, in spite of my love of Bengali, I could not translate *murtad* and *dorra* – though I could crack *ashamoyer* with Nietzsche.

I am only a translator, not a Bengalist. I can cite only two names in this movement: Akhtaruzzaman Ilias (1943–1998), the author of *Chilekothar Sardar* and the fantastic *Khoab-Nama;* and Farhad Mazhar, whose poem I was about to translate when I launched into this lengthy digression. It may be claimed that these writers do a double bluff on the Sanskritized linguistic nationalism of Bangladesh.

At the meeting of the Sahitya Akadami I was immediately sidetracked into a translation of the word *huda* (about which more later), as an Arabic-origin Urdu word foreign to Bengali and a learned etymologico-philosophical disquisition (a pale imitation of which I would be able to provide for Sanskrit-origin Bengali words) from a distinguished professor of Urdu from Kashmir. None of the Indian Bengalis could offer a translation.

Murtad and *dorra* can be translated as "apostate" and "whiplash." *Huda* so overwhelmed the discussion that they remained un-Englished at the Akademi meeting. I have withheld this information for so long because, as I was moving through various European and Asian countries, revising, I kept wondering how I would get to find the English equivalents! A chance encounter – someone reading Bengali web in Bangkok airport, must be Bangladeshi! – provided them at last...

Translating these two words in Mazhar, I was also suggesting that the burden of history and paleonymy are added to this double bind. Arrived here I often hear, Not everybody can be so well prepared! Is there ever such a refusal of craftspersonly expertise for European-language translation? I suggest we pay no attention to such excuses and proceed to the next poem, where another kind of history is invoked.

This poem refers us not to Bengali in the history of the nation-state but in the internationality of Islam. As already mentioned, Bengali is not of Arabic/Persian origin. It is not taken seriously as a language of Islam. During the war that established Bangladesh, soldiers of the then West Pakistan regularly taunted East Pakistani soldiers and civilians as not "real" Muslims, no more than the force-converted dregs of Hinduism. In this frame, Mazhar addresses Allah, as follows:

Bangla Is Not Yours

You've built the Bangla language with the crown of
my head and the roof of my mouth
My epiglottis plays with the "ah" and the long "ee"
Breath by breath I test the "om" and my chest's
    beat

Heartstrings ring in the enchanted expanse of the
    con-sonant
Oh I like it so, lord, I like the Bangla language so
    much
I lick it clean, greedy, as if paradise fruit.
Are you envious? For in this tongue you never

Proclaimed yourself! Yet, all day I keep at it

Hammer and tongs so Queen Bangla in her own

Light and power stays ahead of each and all, my dearest lord.

Some ask today, So, Bangla, are you divine as well?

You too primordial? Allah's alphabet?

I'm glad Bangla's not yours, for if it were –

Her glory'd raise your price, for no reason at all.

Let us look at the last line. *Dānt* is one of those particularly untranslatable idiomatic words: airs and graces, swelled head, hype – you see the choice I've made: "raise your price." What is interesting is that this word has been coupled with *behuda*, another Arabic *tatshamo* word that I have translated "unreasonably." Let me first say that there is a common Sanskrit-origin word – *ajotha* (Sansk. *ayathā*) – that would fit snugly here. *Behuda* points at itself, incomprehensible to "the common reader." I believe now that the word is in general use in Bangladesh. As I have already mentioned, I received a lecture on the Arabic word *huda* from my learned colleague from Kashmir. I could best grasp his meaning by turning it into the English familiar. "Reason" in "for no reason at all" is an ordinary language word. Yet "reason" is also a word of great philosophical weight. *Huda* has a comparable range. What reason is being invoked here to claim a language connected to Revelation by imagination rather than letter? This is a different argument from the right to worship in the vernacular, where, incidentally, content transfer must be taken for granted. I go everywhere in search of the "secular." I will come back to this later. Here is a hint that expanding religion beyond mere reason may bring with it a question of translating rather than recording the transcendental.

HIGHLIGHTING THE "RED" IN DON CAMILLO

Lawrence Venuti is so well known for the political combativeness of some of his writings (see the introduction and chapter 1) that one might forget that he is an accomplished translation historian as well as a dedicated polemicist. Here he is in fine form, examining the American editions of Giovanni Guareschi's best-selling Don Camillo stories. The passage examines how translation choices transformed the books' specifically Italian anti-Communism into a voice that fit American ideology – and marketing strategies – in the 1950s (Venuti 1998):

To highlight the distinctly American nature of this reception, we need only glance at Guareschi's very different impact in Italy. He began publishing the Don Camillo stories in 1946 in the magazine he edited, *Candido,* a mass-audience weekly (circulation: 400,000) devoted to humor and political satire. The ideological standpoint of this magazine was rabidly anti-Communist, but it was also staunchly monarchist, so that Guareschi was addressing a divided readership: in a popular referendum, a narrow margin had chosen a republic over the Savoy monarchy as the form that the Italian government would take in the postwar period. The magazine definitely swayed public opinion, particularly through Guareschi's cartoons: his most bitterly satiric drawings depicted Communists as inhuman, ape-like creatures with three nostrils ("trinariciuti"); his illustrations for the amusing Don Camillo stories defused the ideological conflict by reducing it to a quarrel between two children, making the Christian Democrat a cute angel and the Communist an impish devil. The party that benefited most from Guareschi's popularity was actually not the monarchists, but the Christian Democrats: he contributed to their victory over the Communists in the 1948 elections and was publicly denounced by the Communist party chairman. All the same, Guareschi cannot be described as a propagandist for or even a member of the Christian Democratic Party. In 1954, after a trial that received international attention, he was convicted of libelling a Christian Democrat who had recently served as premier.

Since the opposing political ideologies and parties were woven deeply into Italian social life, supported by a network of very active cultural organizations, Guareschi's writing did not encounter in Italy the same paranoiac fear of Communism that existed in the United States and stigmatized membership in any left-wing group. On the contrary, the local governments in such northern Italian cities as Bologna were controlled by Communists who earned a reputation for improving administrative efficiency and stimulating the regional economy. In Italy's political culture, the humanistic slant of the Don Camillo books ultimately helped the left to gain power in national coalition governments. *Mondo Piccolo: Don Camillo,* first published in 1948, had gone through fifty-two printings by 1975, when the Communist party constructed a "historic compromise" with the Christian Democrats and controlled 34 percent of the vote. Guareschi himself anticipated this development as early as 1952, when he told the interviewer for *Life,* with typical irony, that "I am doing something that no other writer has ever done: I have succeeded in making a Communist sympathetic... "

Whereas in Italy Guareschi was neglected by contemporary intellectuals, omitted from literary histories and curricula, in the United States he was read in schools, reviewed by respected writers and academics, included in a comprehensive anthology and discussed in a scholarly monograph. Here the Don Camillo stories were installed in the canon of Italian literature, juxtaposed to the work of Verga, Pirandello, and Moravia, associated with the neorealist movement in fiction.

Remarkably, American intellectuals also took the popular approach to Guareschi, abandoning the critical appreciation of form that distinguishes the high cultural aesthetic and assimilating his writing to the codes and ideologies that were then dominating American culture at large. For Donald Heiney, professor of English at the University of Utah, "it was a peculiarity of [Guareschi's] talent that he was able to make Peppone, the Communist mayor of the *Don Camillo* sketches, seem both totally human and completely wrong-headed." Eudora Welty, who by the 1950s had been recognized as a leading fiction writer, favorably reviewed *Don Camillo and His Flock* for the *New York Times*, where her remarks displayed the same humanism, ethnic stereotyping, and anti-Communism that generally characterized Guareschi's reception: "The difference between adversaries so evenly matched – who seem really inclined to like each other in their warm, Italian way – is in their backing. Stalin is too far away to do Peppone any good". For a reviewer like William Barrett, professor of philosophy at New York University and editor of the highbrow journal *Partisan Review,* Guareschi's autobiographical book *The House That Nino Built* presented an occasion to affirm the patriarchal family as part of the familiar Italian stereotype:

> only an Italian, certainly no American, could have written it. When comparable stories of family life appear here in magazines like the *New Yorker,* there is always the skeleton of some neurosis in the closet or some attendant irony of sophistication. And when the fiction in our ladies magazines gets around to the family, usually there is breast-thumping self-consciousness. The Italian can escape such awkward self-consciousness because he takes the family for granted in a way that we do not. (Barrett 1953: 49)

Barrett was assuming a Cold War concept of the American family, wherein "the self-contained home held out the promise of security in an insecure world." He also left unstated the ideological reasons why Americans could not take the family for granted: its stability was regarded as an important means of combating Communist infiltration and subversion, a domestic form of the global containment announced in the Truman Doctrine.

The editorial insistence on colloquial English supported the popular demand that artistic representation be indistinguishable from everyday life, and that therefore the Italian text be assimilated to familiar American values. Although Cudahy favored colloquialisms current in both British and American English at the turn of the twentieth century, she included many that were specific to the United States during the postwar period, when the Don Camillo books first appeared. And, most important for Guareschi's bestseller status, these American colloquialisms were comprehensible across different cultural constituencies...

The inscription of the political code in the translation thus invited the American reader to turn the ideological rivalry between Don Camillo and Peppone into an allegory for the Cold War. And since the English terms carried negative connotations of domination and subversion, they inevitably stacked the deck against Peppone and Communism. The English version does in fact display a marked effort to stigmatize the mayor and his political affiliates by characterizing them as criminal or at the least socially undesirable. Where Guareschi referred to Peppone's "banda" ("group") or "squadra" ("squad"), Troubridge and/or Cudahy repeatedly used "gang"; expressions like "gli altri capoccia rossi" ("the other red leaders") and "fedelissimi" ("the most loyal men") were rendered with "henchmen"; and an apparently neutral demonstrative like "quelli" ("those men"), when applied to Peppone's affiliates, became "those ruffians."

At the same time, some translation choices reveal a tendency to whitewash Don Camillo by revising or deleting details that question the morality of his actions. With "Don Camillo rise perfidamente" ("Don Camillo laughed treacherously"), the word "perfidamente" was replaced by the less sinister "unpleasantly"; and Christ's warning that Don Camillo consider himself right "fino a quando non farà qualche soperchia" ("only so long as he doesn't commit some outrage") was mitigated through a more positive rephrasing: "just as long as he plays fair." The translation entirely omitted many sen-

tences in which Don Camillo displays an awareness of his own guilt or performs some unethical act: for example, "Gli dispiaceva di essersi dimostrato
cosi maligno" ("He was sorry to have shown himself to be so evil"); or "di' al
Bigio che se non mi ripulisce, e gratis, il muro, io attacco il vostro partito nel
giornale dei democristani" ("tell Bigio if he doesn't clean up my wall, gratis,
I'll attack your party in the Christian Democratic newspaper").

The remarkable thing about the translation, of course, is that the
inscription of domestic codes and ideologies was invisible to American
readers. This was so partly because the Italian text was edited and translated according to the popular aesthetic: the high degree of fluency, under-
written by the adherence to current American usage and by a rich vein of
colloquialism, resulted in the realist illusion, the effect that the text is a
transparent window onto the world, a true representation and therefore
not a translation, a second-order image. Not surprisingly, then, the translation was rarely mentioned by reviewers; even when the review appeared
in a more highbrow periodical like the *New York Times Book Review* or the
Saturday Review, it included no comments on the quality of the translation
because the popular aesthetic prizes the informative function of any text of
the subtle appreciation of formal elements like translation discourse. One
of the few comments occurred in *Catholic World*, and it confirmed the effect
of transparency: "The translation is such that one never adverts to the fact
that this is one."

FLEXING THE PHANTOM LIMB

Douglas Robinson is a translation theorist who writes with great scholarly authority
yet is also able to riff on ideas that engage his attention – nowhere more so than
in his wide-ranging article "Translation as Phantom Limb," in which he invokes
Oliver Sacks's book *The Man Who Mistook His Wife For a Hat* to explore the relationship
between original author, translator, and reading audience. Robinson likens some
aspects of translation to the physiological concept of "proprioception" – the ability
to sense location and movement of own's own body and its parts – as experienced
by patients who may "feel" the presence of an amputated limb, or lose the sense of
where their limbs actually are (Robinson 1997a):

> I had that experience once myself, briefly: in for a cystoscopy, I was given
> a spinal block and a curtain was rigged at my waist, so I couldn't see what

was being done to me. When the operation was over, I watched over the curtain as a nurse lifted a leg across my field of vision from left to center, then lowered it beneath the top of the curtain. I panicked: whose leg is that? It took me a moment to realize that it was my own – that I couldn't feel it because of the spinal block. Sacks tells many such stories, like the one about the man who awoke horrified to find a strange leg in bed with him, threw it out on the floor, and was even more horrified to find himself flying after it – because it was attached to him!

Where all this begins to connect up with translation, though, is in Sacks' sixth chapter, on prosthetics and the strange proprioceptive phenomenon of the "phantom" – which Sacks defines as "a persistent image of memory of part of the body, usually a limb, for months or years after its loss" – and the striking fact that, as Sacks quotes Michael Kremer as saying, "no amputee with an artificial lower limb can walk on it satisfactorily until the body-image, in other words the phantom, is incorporated into it." If we take this, provisionally, as a metaphor for translation, the translation would be the prosthetic device – an artificial, mechanical contrivance designed to replace a textual limb "lost" through the target-language reader's inability to read a text in the original language – that only comes to feel real, native, strong enough to "walk on" or live through, when a proprioceptive "phantom" is incorporated into it.

This would constitute a tentative explanation of how a foreign text can be appropriated "strangely" into the target language: what makes any text feel "at home" or "one's own" in any language is not the mere fact that it was written (originally or otherwise) in that language, nor the mere fact (or illusion) that it was written in the kind of reductively and unproblematically "fluent" or "transparent" idiom that normative linguists like to reify as "ordinary language" – but the incorporation into it of a proprioceptive phantom, some nexus of felt experience that charges the text, any text, with the feel of reality, of "one's-ownness," of proprioception. A text that is charged with that felt experience – by individual readers, by groups of readers, by whole cultures – will feel real whether it is an original or a translation, whether it is domesticated or foreignized, whether it is easy or difficult to read. A text that is not charged with that felt experience will be like my leg above the curtain: a dead thing, a foreign object...

We have to have textual phantoms when we translate weather reports, business letters, technical documentation, scholarly articles, advertising copy, and the like; and every text we translate, no matter how mundane, has the power to throw us off track, to make us stop and shift or expand phantoms. If this weren't true, machine translation would be a huge unqualified success. The only way machine translation works today is when computers are fed texts carefully pre-edited by humans to facilitate the mechanical replication of stable, abstract calculi – when computers are protected against the kinds of proprioceptive breakdowns to which human beings are susceptible, and for which most of us have developed coping strategies.

And what about the target-language reader who appropriates the translation, makes it her or his "own"? How does this work? Where does the phantom come from then? Think of the King James Bible, which has an almost overpowering proprioceptive sense for English literature. In fact, without the King James Bible modern English literature wouldn't have a leg to stand on. George Steiner has explored this phenomenon at length in *After Babel*, the process by which a translation is so thoroughly assimilated into a culture that it seems that it was always there, that it was originary for the culture – that, say, God was an Elizabethan Englishman. What he didn't explore was the ideological construction of the readerly phantom that keeps the King James Bible alive in and for Anglophone culture: the hegemonic myelination of the proprioceptive fibers in millions of Bible-readers' and church-goers' nervous systems through the sheer force of coerced and normative repetition. You have to go to church, you have to read the Bible, you have to believe what you hear in church and read in the Bible, and what you hear and read is all formulated by the translators for King James, so that what "feels right" in Anglophone Christianity, what feels like the "body" of your religious belief, is an ideological program that runs inside your skull with numbing reliability – "The Lord is my shepherd, I shall not want," "and forgive us our trespasses, as we forgive those who trespass against us" – even when you reject Christianity intellectually, even when you haven't read the Bible for years, even when you dilute the King James with *Today's English Version* or *The New International Bible* or Clarence Jordan's *Cotton Patch Version*.

But then, what does happen when you retranslate the Bible into English? Do the new translations become prosthetics, which only begin to feel real – only become good for walking on – once the King James phantom has been incorporated into them? This is certainly true of the Revised Standard Version and its successors. Can another phantom be incorporated into them instead (or in addition) – a contemporary colloquial English phantom, say? This would be Eugene Nida's explicit ideal for *Today's English Version* – but how does that work? And what does all this have to do with the deadening and revivifying of linguistic sensation, which I discussed at length in the subversion section of *The Translator's Turn*? Is it like the patient Sacks describes, who has to "'wake up' his phantom in the mornings: first he flexes the thigh-stump towards him, and then he slaps it sharply – 'like a baby's bottom' – several times. On the fifth or sixth slap the phantom suddenly shoots forth, rekindled, fulgurated, by the peripheral stimulus. Only then can he put on his prosthesis and walk"?

....

As a lover of literature from all corners of the world I sincerely hope that our translator's pen will not be transformed into a steam roller that irons out different cultural features in a source language. It is always a pleasure to have a choice between T-bone steak and roasted duck, or between French fries and steamed rice on a menu.

— YAU SHUN-CHIU in his essay "The Identification of Gestural Images in Chinese Literary Expressions" (Yau Shun-chiu 1997)

CHAPTER TEN

Language wrangling: A grab bag

When I put occasional Australianisms into academic texts, thus creating expressions that are rarer than a blue-arsed fly, they either just disappear in translations or are turned into something absolutely standard (if indeed the copyeditors do not eliminate them first).

— ANTHONY PYM in "On Toury's Laws of How Translators Translate"
   (Pym 2007)

O ne of the most enjoyable aspects of reading translators on translation is to watch from the sidelines as they pit creativity, experience and tools of their trade against difficult source and target texts (and sometimes difficult authors and publishers). Here, to use Emma Wagner's felicitous expression cited in the previous chapter, are some reports from the "wordface."

FROM HAITIAN CREOLE TO BLACK (AMERICAN) ENGLISH
Sharon M. Bell's essay "In the Shadow of the Father Tongue: On Translating the Masks in J.-S. Alexis" describes the process she calls code-mixing as she moves from one non-standard language to another (Bell 1996).

> The reflections presented here grew out of my translating Haitian writer Jacques-Stephen Alexis's collection of nine short stories, *Romancéro aux étoiles*. The language of these short stories based both on traditional Haitian folklore and on the Western literary tradition includes instances of Creole embedded in an otherwise standard, literary French, embedded so subtly that readers unfamiliar with Haitian language and culture might not be aware that they are reading representations of another language. I came

to believe that these instances of Creolization in Alexis's literary language represent episodes of deliberate code-mixing, a phenomenon which commonly occurs in communities where two or more languages find themselves in contact. As such, they needed to be translated into English in such a way that the code-mixing was preserved. I chose Black English as a target language for the translation of what, following Henry Louis Gates, I shall call Alexis's linguistic masks... In Haiti, the group that is capable of true code-switching between French and Creole is identified by Valdman as the "bilingual urban elite," who number at most between 5 and 10 per cent of the entire population. In the United States, no one is sure exactly how many African Americans are proficient speakers of standard English, and of these how many also are willing or able to function to some degree in Black English vernacular. My guess is that the former group is less than a majority of African-American speakers, and the latter, smaller still. Furthermore, while Haitian Creole is a fully formed language separate from French – neither a "patois" nor "broken French" – Black English is not a separate language, but a dialect of English (of which standard English is a dialect as well). This fact means that some linguists would consider it inappropriate to call alternation between Black English and standard English "code-mixing" or "code-switching"; John Baugh, for one, prefers to call this phenomenon "style-shifting" (58–59). However, the fact that Black English is a dialect and not an autonomous language in the sense that French or Creole is does not diminish the complexity or significance of its functions for African Americans. To those of us who speak it, it *feels* like a language...

In his introduction to the "La romance du petit-viseur," the [story-teller] Old Carib Wind declares his intention of singing the ballad of Little Sharp-Shot to prove that all living things are linked together in a brotherhood that cannot be annihilated. Little Sharp-Shot's adventure begins when he wakes up one day *feeling* particularly contrary. The Old Carib Wind muses,

> Tel jour, on se lève du pied gauche et, bougon, on ne dit pas bonjour au soleil. Tel jour, on se lève du pied droit et, gaillard, on claironne tout le monde.

In my English translation, he says:

> One day you get up on the wrong side of the bed, all *evil*, and don't

even tell the sun good morning. Another day, you get up on the right side, gay as anything, and hail everybody.

Evil is a good Black English word which simply means in a bad mood, ill-humored...

Alliteration is another classic rhetorical device of Black English. The first example here was actually the accidental translation of alliteration where there was very little in the French. But the second was a deliberate recreation of alliteration in the original:

Tudieu! quel oiseau que celui-là! Minuscule arc-en-ciel de couleurs radiantes qui *tintinnabulaient* l'une contre l'autre.

[God, what a bird this was! Miniature *r*ainbow of *r*adiant colors that *j*ust about *j*angled against each other.]

Je m'empressai d'emporter toutes ces *m*agnifiques plumes qu'on *m*'abondonnait, car neveu, me faisant Vieux Vent Caraïbe de *p*lus en *p*lus, je suis frileux en hiver et j'en voulais faire un *bon beau bonnet bien* chaud pour ma tête.

[I rushed to carry off all those magnificent feathers he was throwing my way. You see, son, I get chilly in winter, as I'm becoming the Old Carib Wind more and more, and I wanted to make me a *cozy, comfortable, cushy cap* for my head.]

Alliteration, too, inserts the Old Carib Wind's text in English into a Black rhetorical tradition, continuing to confirm a nonstandard subtext. In one instance, the Old Carib Wind abundantly uses alliteration that I could not duplicate in English. I translated it by using a different Black English rhetorical strategy:

Caramba, quel maestro [speaking of the Bird of God], neveu! Les grands filaos-musiciens de la forêt eux-mêmes en étaient jaloux. Ce *porte-plume coquet, croquenotes et coquecigrue* venait pour les narguer.

[Caramba! What a maestro, son! Even the great filao-musicians of the forest were jealous of him. This *no-singing, jive-talking, dandified turkey* was always coming around to mess with them.]

A term like *no-singing,* creating a negative adjective from a gerund, is a common construction in Black English, as is *dandified,* which creates an adjective from a past participle – in this case, the past participle of a non-standard verb. These two terms, then, use Black English grammar, though the terms themselves are certainly not coined; both already exist in Black English. *Jive-talking*, too, has been well-known for more than fifty years.

NON-STANDARD NON-FICTION

A similar problem, but from a journalistic context, is described in this excerpt from Mona Baker's *In Other Words: A Coursebook on Translation* (Baker 1992). The book to which the excerpt refers, *A Hero From Zero* (1988), was about the acquisition of Harrods department store in London by the businessman Mohamed Al-Fayed; it was published by his business rival Roland "Tiny" Rowland.

Some of the adjustments that a translator may need to make in order to conform to readers' expectations in this area have been discussed and exemplified in previous chapters. However, there are instances in which deviation from normal patterning is a feature of the source text itself. If deviation is motivated and if it is necessary for working out an intended meaning, the translator may well decide to transfer it to the target text. As discussed above, readers' expectations do not necessarily have to be fulfilled. Writers, and translators, often appeal to their readers to modify their expectations if such modifications are required in a given context. We are normally prepared to accept a great deal of unusual and even bizarre linguistic behaviour provided it can be justfied, for instance on the basis of poetic creativity or humour.

The suggestion that deviations from normal patterning have to be motivated implies that they have to occur in a context that is "interpretable" by the hearer/reader. Blakemore suggests that a speaker or writer who wants his/her utterance to be interpreted in a certain way "must expect it to be interpreted in a context that yields that interpretation." The following example illustrates a situation where deviation from normal organization of the language seems justified in translation and where the translator has to enlarge the shared context of writer and reader in order to accommodate this feature in such a way that its relevance is made explicit and coherence is therefore maintained. The extract is from a transcript of conversation which is appended to *A Hero from Zero* and translated from English into French and Arabic. The three people taking part in the conversation

(Mohamed Fayed, Shri Chandra Swamiji, and Kailish Nath Agarwal) are all non-native speakers of English. The conversation is conducted partly in English and partly in Hindi. The speakers, particularly Mohamed Fayed, have a rather poor command of English. Here is an extract from the conversation to illustrate Mohamed Fayed's level of competence in English:

M. Fayed: Sultan, you know, he gets influenced. I can't go sit with him all the time, you know. It's impossible for me, you know. Because he has one terrible, evil man, his aide, Ibnu.

Mamaji: Pardon?

M. Fayed: General Ibnu.

Mamaji: Uh-huh.

M. Fayed: Terrible man. This man takes money from everybody, everybody.

Swamiji: I think girls also.

M. Fayed: Yeah.

Mamaji: Girls?

Swamiji: Girls.

M. Fayed: Girls, everything, everything, everything. He is the big man, but the Sultan don't trust him at all. Bad man. And this Ibnu and Zobel are like that. Build the palace together. Ibnu gives permission to all those people go inside, take pictures of his bedroom, everything, anything. And he's a bad man, you know. But for me, I don't – you know, er, I don't need the Sultan. Sultan doesn't need me. But I made so much good for him, you know, with support him with the British Government, you know.

The problem that the Arab translator faces in rendering this text into Arabic is that Mohamed Fayed is Egyptian; his first language is Arabic. To simply transfer the deviant syntax into Arabic without any comment would leave the Arab reader puzzled as to why a native speaker of Arabic should speak in "broken" Arabic. To adjust Fayed's speech to reflect normal patterns of

Arabic would considerably weaken the carefully structured argument put forward by Tiny Rowland, the "jilted suitor" who wants to show that Fayed is unworthy of the privilege of owning the House of Fraser and incapable of running such a prestigious British concern. After all, Fayed is, among other things, a "foreigner," not very bright, and rather incoherent! The translator decides to compromise by transferring the deviant organization into Arabic in order to convey something of the "stupid foreigner" image of Fayed, while, at the same time, explaining the situation to the reader so that s/he can make sense of it. The following comment is inserted by the Arab translator at the beginning of the transcript of conversation:

ملحوظة. يتضح من قراءة النص الانجليزى للمحادثة المسجلة على الشريط أن الأشخاص الثلاثة الذين اشتركوا فيها ليس لديهم إلمام كاف باللغة الإنجليزية، كما يتبين ذلك بكل وضوح من الجمل الركيكة والمفككة التركيب والتى لا تراعى قواعد اللغة. ولذلك فلابد من أن تنعكس نقاط الضعف هذه فى الترجمة العربية حرصاً على مراعاة الدقة، بقدر الإمكان، فى نقل المعنى.

Back-translation:

> Note: It is clear from reading the English text of the conversation transcribed on the tape that the three people who participated in it do not have sufficient command of the English language. This is also very clear from the use of sub-standard and loosely structured sentences which do not conform to the rules of the language. Therefore, these points of weakness have to be reflected in the Arabic translation in order to maintain accuracy, as far as possible, in the transfer of meaning.

TEENAGER-TALK

One of the features of fiction publishing in recent years has been the proliferation of genres and niche markets. Each of these offers interesting puzzles to literary translators. Cathy Hirano is a Canadian living in Japan who specializes in translating Japanese books for children and young adults into English. Her essay "Eight Ways to Say You: The Challenges of Translation" offers insight into what she calls the "strenuous cultural and mental gymnastics" required not only to translate between Japanese and English, but also to work within the particular genre of children's fiction. Also interesting is the involvement of the American publisher in the process (Hirano 2006).

The objective is to bring the world of Japanese children and adolescents closer to [their English-speaking equivalents], to help them feel what Japanese kids feel, view the world through their eyes, while still appreciating the differences. Ideally, the translation should make them laugh where a Japanese reader would laugh, cry where a Japanese reader would cry, etc. Although I may be underestimating them, I do not expect this audience to have much prior knowledge of the daily life of an ordinary Japanese child or much tolerance for assumptions that are foreign to their culture.

Here's an example. *The Friends* (Japanese title: *Natsu no niwa*) is about three twelve-year-old boys who are afraid of death. They decide to stalk an old man in their neighborhood in order to witness what really happens when a person dies, and the story follows the relationship that develops between the boys and the old man. I knew from the outset that school and *juku*, a kind of school after school, were going to be major obstacles to understanding for American readers. Although most of the story takes place outside of these venues, they set the rhythm of the boys' lives and are an essential part of the backdrop. *Elementary school* conjures up similar images in both cultures, but the school year in Japan begins in April, and summer holidays are much shorter, with fairly heavy homework assignments. Without some knowledge of these aspects, many of the things the boys do just would not make sense to target readers. Similarly, although the word *juku* conjures up a common image for Japanese children, there is no real equivalent in North America. To simply translate it as *cram school* and leave it at that would make it impossible for North American readers to appreciate its implications in Japanese children's lives.

These problems were solved through a three-way communication process. I consulted the author, who was very clear that her priority was to make her work accessible to the North American audience, and asked her to describe in more detail how she envisioned school and *juku* in the boys' lives, including how often they attended, the time of day, etc. I faxed this information to the American editor at Farrar and she suggested a few key places in the text where additional description could be naturally woven in as briefly and unobtrusively as possible. For example, the longest addition reads:

> Every day, Monday to Friday, we have cram school after regular
> school. We're there from six until eight and sometimes even until
> nine o'clock at night, trying to cram in everything we'll need to know

to pass the entrance exams for junior high school next year. By the time we get out, we're exhausted, not to mention starving.

It is short, but it makes a tremendous difference to how readers experience the rest of the book.

You can see from this example the amount of cultural significance that is packed into a single word. Trying to convey those unspoken cultural assumptions without overdoing it is one of the challenges of translation. Similar problems arise because of the different levels of speech in Japanese. Just off the top of my head, I can think of eight ways to say *you*, each with a cultural nuance that reflects the speaker's sex or social status in relationship to the listener: a form only used by male speakers, a polite form for someone of a higher status, a more neutral form for a peer, a more familiar form for someone of lower status, etc. Moreover, the use of you is generally avoided because it is too direct, and therefore when it is used the translator has to consider whether it contains information crucial to understanding a character or a relationship. If it does, then an alternative way to reflect that in the dialogue must be found, because the word *you* will of course convey nothing of the above to a North American reader.

The Spring Time follows the internal journey of Tomomi, a thirteen-year-old girl. She is angry and resentful at having to leave behind her childhood naïveté and sense of security and begin the painful process of growing up. We experience her dawning awareness of herself and others, her letting go of anger and judgment, through her changing perception of the world around her and her relationships with her brother, her grandfather, her parents, and a woman who cares for stray cats. At one point in the story, there is a brief encounter between Tomomi and Kinko, a boy from her school, that reveals an internal shift. Being rather timid and fastidious, Kinko is appalled to see Tomomi petting a stray cat. Parroting his mother, he blames the proliferation of strays on the people who feed them. Tomomi hotly refutes this, demanding to know why he does not blame the people who throw their cats away as if they were garbage. The tone of the encounter is set at the beginning by the following exchange:

"Was that your brother?"
"Yeah, so what? He said 'your.' Why is he putting on airs, that jerk?"

Tomomi's anger seems totally unwarranted in the English. The boy appears to be asking an ordinary question. The word he actually used, however, was *kimi*. When this form is used by a child to his peers, it has a slightly snobbish although not condescending tone. It is an unconscious affectation of someone "well-brought up" and protected from vulgar society, a member of the upper class. To Tomomi he seems to be putting on airs, and she bristles with indignation. In order to give the reader the same impression, I settled for making his speech sound slightly affected and altered Tomomi's response to correspond, as follows:

"That was your brother, I presume?"
"Yeah, so what? You presume indeed. You jerk."

Even without the differences in levels of politeness and familiarity in speech, translating conversations often requires more ingenuity than descriptive passages. Having lived in Japan for 20 years, Japanese as a spoken language is very alive for me. I spend much of my time talking to children – my own children's friends and schoolmates, and the many children who approach me on the street because I look so different. Kazumi Yamoto is adept at capturing the tone and easy-flowing banter of children's conversations, yet the actual words sound stilted or strange in English. In a scene in *The Friends,* one of the boys has been trying to convince his friends to spy on the old man. He finally succeeds, and the resultant altercation directly translated would read:

"All right."
"... say?" Yamashita is nervous.
"To be more precise," I avoid Yamashita's accusing eyes. "It must not cause trouble with the old man."
"Ehh?"
"Did it! Two against one!" Kawabe dances a little jig.

This does not convey any of the humor or rhythm of their give and take.

To maintain a feeling for the way North American children speak and to prevent the Japanese language from dominating, I read American children's books and watch American movies constantly during the translation process. Then, after reading a section like the one above, I close my eyes and visualize English-speaking children and imagine what they would say in the same situation. The result in this case was as follows:

"All right."

"All right what?" Yamashita asks nervously.

I avoid Yamashita's accusing eyes. "But only on condition that it doesn't bother the old man."

"No!" Yamashita explodes.

"Yes! Two against one!" Kawabe shouts gleefully, and he dances a little jig.

The words in English are very different, but they capture the tone of the Japanese more accurately...

There are so many facets to translation, so many problems and so many different ways of solving them, that I could go on forever. Instead, I would like to share with you something that was very meaningful for me as a translator. *The Friends* was published in recorded book form in 1997, and I was sent a copy. It is five hours long, and I started playing it for myself during a car trip with my children. My son, then ten, had never read the book, and I thought that he was too young to understand, especially in English. I was surprised therefore to find him laughing at the funny parts and listening intently to the rest. When we reached our destination, he carried the tapes inside and listened non-stop for two more hours until it was finished. He wept, heartbroken, at the old man's death (I still cry there, even now), and at the end, he said with satisfaction (and in Japanese), "that was a good book, Mom." It is indeed a good book, and it was a gift to be able to share it with my own child, born of both cultures; to see him experiencing Japanese literature through the medium of the English language. And to know that it still came through.

GO ASK ALICE

Bear with me for a paragraph or two: I will get back to niche fiction in a moment...

It is widely agreed that the founding father of machine translation was Warren Weaver, a prodigious polymath with achievements in mathematics, engineering, philosophy and both the administration and popularization of science. His 1949 memorandum "Translation" is probably the single most important text from the early days of machine translation, providing the stimulus for the massive research effort that followed in the 1950s and '60s (Locke and Booth 1955). The memo includes this oft-quoted passage:

Think, by analogy, of individuals living in a series of tall closed towers, all erected over a common foundation. When they try to communicate with one another, they shout back and forth, each from his own closed tower. It is difficult to make the sound penetrate even the nearest towers, and communication proceeds very poorly indeed. But, when an individual goes down his tower, he finds himself in a great open basement, common to all the towers. Here he establishes easy and useful communication with the persons who have also descended from their towers.

Does that resonate somewhat with the famous story of a little girl who fell down a rabbit-hole and found a world of incomprehensible characters beneath the ground? It should: Weaver was fascinated by Lewis Carroll's *Alice's Adventures in Wonderland*. In 1964, having built up a collection of 160 versions in forty-two languages, Weaver wrote a book about the translation history of *Alice* (Weaver 1964). It is a fascinating book, not least for the business correspondence of Lewis Carroll (the Reverend Charles Dodgson) dealing with publishing royalties and permissions, along with Weaver's adventures in acquiring first editions. As a scientist, Weaver had an endearingly geekish interest in measurement, and devised a design to evaluate the quality of the various versions. The exercise included an impressive if eccentric list of collaborators such as Teddy Kollek, the long-time mayor of Jerusalem (for the Hebrew translation), the anthropologist Margaret Mead (Pidgin), and the Nobel prize-winning biochemist Hugo Theorell (Swedish).

I have not attempted, and obviously could not attempt, to answer the really basic questions. What I have done is much more superficial, and indeed is not directed at all to the real question – how good a translation is this? I have asked the much easier and more limited question: How good a translation does this seem to be when examined by an English-speaking person? That is, considering the translation into language X, how successfully *to an English-speaking person* does this translation capture and convey those aspects of the original which seem important to us?

To examine this question – a limited one, but I think an interesting one to English-speaking persons – I have proceeded as follows. I selected a short but familiar and characteristic passage from Chapter vii, "A Mad Tea-Party." I had photostats made of these pages in each of fourteen languages, choosing those which for one reason or another seemed the most interesting, and in almost every case working with the first edition in the language in question. I then sent these packets of pages to friends of mine who are, in each case, completely at home in the "foreign" language in question, and who also have a perfect command of English. For almost all of these people, the "foreign" language was the native language. I asked each person to translate literally back into English without consulting the English original.

As to the particular translations involved, I chose six of the "great seven," namely, the German, French, Swedish, Italian, Danish, and Russian, omitting the Dutch because it was an abridged version. In addition, simply on the criterion that they seemed especially interesting or especially curious instances, I also selected (in order of appearance of the first editions in these languages) Japanese, Chinese, Hebrew, Hungarian, Spanish (Castilian), Polish, Pidgin, and Swahili...

From the adult point of view, the principal problems involved in translating *Alice* relate to:

A) the *verses,* which in almost all of the cases are parodies of English poems, doubtless well known to Dodgson's contemporaries. In the entire book of *Alice's Adventures in Wonderland* there are nine parodied verses, an original prefatory poem by Dodgson, and one familiar nursery rhyme ("The Queen of Hearts, she made some tarts... ") which Dodgson left unmodified.

B) the *puns.*

C) the use of *specially manufactured words* or *nonsense words,* which occasionally occur in the text, and often occur in the verses.

D) the *jokes* which *involve logic.*

E) and finally, the otherwise unclassifiable Carroll *twists of meaning* with underlying humor, always unexpected and disarming, sometimes gentle, and sometimes very abrupt.

The passage selected for study begins, in the 1865 and 1866 editions, on page 103. It is taken from one of the most familiar and certainly one of the most characteristic chapters – "A Mad Tea-Party." The passage closes just before the end of the chapter, on page 110, when the Hatter (interrupting Alice, who begins a sentence, "I don't think –") abruptly remarks, "Then you shouldn't talk."

Since we will be discussing this passage in some detail, it will be conve-nient to run through those parts of it which particularly challenge a transla-tor. And we will insert letters (A), (B), etc., at various points to call attention to the fact that at these points there occur instances of the five categories (puns, etc.) which were described just above.

The passage begins:

> Twinkle, twinkle, little bat!
> How I wonder what you're at!

This verse (A) would, to any English child, sound curiously and disturbingly like the familiar couplet:

> Twinkle, twinkle, little star,
> How I wonder what you are!

except that, as so often happens in dreams, things have gone a little queer and wrong. After the Mad Hatter goes on:

> Up above the world you fly,
> Like a tea-tray in the sky.
> Twinkle, twinkle –

still getting the verse just a little mixed up, the Dormouse half wakes up, and partly asleep, sings "*Twinkle, twinkle, twinkle...* " until they have to "pinch it to make it stop."

The Hatter then reports that the Queen of Hearts, objecting to the meter of the verse, has accused him of "murdering the time! Off with his head!" This is then converted into a pun (B) by the comment that "Time" was so disturbed by this remark that "... ever since that, he won't do a thing I ask." This, you will recall, was why it was always six o'clock, always tea-time; so that there was never a chance to wash up, and the party had to keep moving from place to place to get clean dishes. When Alice asks what they do when they "come to the beginning again," the March Hare inter-rupts (E), "Suppose we change the subject."

The March Hare then demands a story, and after Alice protests that she knows none, they wake up the Dormouse, who tells about the three little sisters, Elsie, Lacie, and Tillie, who lived at the bottom of a well.

> "They lived," says the Dormouse in answer to Alice's question,
> "on treacle" (E).
> "They couldn't have done that, you know," Alice gently remarked.
> "They'd have heen ill."
> "So they were," said the Dormouse; "very ill" (E).

Then the March Hare, apparently disturbed by Alice's query as to why these three little sisters lived in a well, interrupts again:

> "Take some more tea," the March Hare said to Alice, very earnestly.
> "I've had nothing yet," Alice replied in an offended tone: "so I can't take more."
> "You mean, you can't take less," said the Hatter: "it's very easy to take more than nothing."

This point that zero cups of tea plus x cups of tea equals a perfectly real and realizable x cups of tea, whereas zero cups minus x cups leads to a physically unrealizable answer, is a piece of practical algebra that, as we will see, seems to appeal to every person, whatever his language (D).

Alice then comes back to her question as to why the three sisters lived at the bottom of a well. The Dormouse takes "a minute or two to think about it" and then answers, just as though his surprising reply explained everything, "It was a treacle-well" (E).

Alice starts to object but is chided for interrupting the story, and the Dormouse goes on, "And so these three little sisters – they were learning to draw, you know –" (E). Alice forgets her promise not to interrupt any more and asks, "What did they draw?" This time the Dormouse answers at once: "Treacle" (B)...

After his analysis of the translating challenges in the test passage, Weaver describes the translation strategies available to tackle them. He then follows up with his evaluation of the different attempts. (Note that, compared to the work being done today in translation studies, the methodology looks somewhat naïve.)

There are three ways to approach the problem of translating into another language a verse which parodies a poem well known in English. By far the most sensitive and satisfactory procedure is to choose a poem of the same general type which is familiar in the language of translation, and then write a parody of that non-English poem (in the translation language, of course) in a manner which imitates the style of the English author.

A second, and less satisfactory, way is to translate, more or less mechanically, the parodied verse into the second language. This procedure would presumably be followed only by a translator who does not realize that the verse is in fact a parody of a well-known verse, but assumes that it is simply a little, partially nonsensical verse which he is supposed to deal with on a word-forword basis. This second procedure would be automatically necessary, of course, in a language in which there simply do not exist indigenous verses of a suitable character – and we will find such instances.

The third way is for the translator to say, "This is a nonsense verse. I can't translate nonsense into my language; but I can write an entirely different bit of nonsense verse in my own language, and substitute it."

Among our examples, the first and really satisfactory procedure has been used in the Danish, French, German, Hebrew, Hungarian, and Russian translations.

The Danish version, which goes, in retranslation,

> Fly, oh fly, my owl, Fairest of all fowl! Up to the clouds, fly away Like
> tea-things in a bag. Fly, oh fly –

is, so Dr. Holter tells me, "reminiscent of another (Danish) song beginning 'Fly, bird, fly...' but it could in no way be as close and compelling as the 'Twinkle, twinkle, little bat' theme." The Danish version of the verse certainly does not merit a very high mark.

The French version goes:

> Ah, I will tell you, my sister,
> What causes my pain.
> It is that I had some candied almonds,
> And that I ate them.

This is a confused (and it seems to me not very clever) modification of a rhyme apparently well known to French children a century ago:

> Ah! Vous dirai-je, Maman,
> Ce qui cause mon tourment?
> Papa veut que je raisonne

Comme une grande personne.
Moi, je trouve que les bonbons
Valent mieux que la raison.

The German translation does a stunning job with this verse. Working from the poem, familiar to every German child:

O Tannenbaum, O Tannenbaum,
Wie treu sind deine Blätter,

Fräulein Zimmermann produced a verse which reads, in retranslation:

O parrot, O parrot,
How green are your feathers!
You are green not only in peace time,
But even when it snows pots and pans.
O parrot, O parrot –

At this juncture in the German version, the Woodchuck (who, being also a notoriously sleepy animal, replaces the Dormouse) says, as he goes back to sleep:

O Papagei, O Mamagei,
O Papagei, O Mamagei.

This use of the manufactured word *Mamagei* as the feminine of the masculine German word for parrot (*Papagei*) is in the pure spirit of Carroll, and is an improvement over the original.

The Hebrew version of this parody is a delight, showing real imagination and invention. The retranslation goes:

He who divides between holy and profane –
All who are hungry may come and eat –
In everything, with everything, of everything, all:
Celery, to break in half, lettuce, and beans.
"Surely you have heard this song?"
"I have heard, I think, something like it," answered Alice.
"And the end of the song is like this," added the Hatter, and he began to sing again:
"Sins He will forgive, tudum tudum tudum will forgive –"
Suddenly the Dormouse was shocked and began to sing, still

asleep: "With sand, with sand, with sand" and repeated this word countless times until the Hatter pinched her strongly and she became quiet.

What the translator has done here is this: he has taken a number of well-known prayers and sayings, and mixed them up so as to obtain the impression created by misquoting "Twinkle, twinkle, little star." The first line of the quatrain is taken from the Havdalah prayer which is recited by the head of the household at the end of the Sabbath. The only connection with "star" that comes to mind stems perhaps from the custom that Jewish children have of scanning the sky on Saturday night for the appearance of the first three stars. These signify (with certain qualifications) that the end of the Sabbath has come, and preparations for the Havdalah service are then made.

The second line is from the Passover Haggadah, inviting all those who are hungry to come and join the Seder table on Passover night.

The third is a misquotation from grace after meals, in which one prays that the Lord "Bless us as he blessed Abraham, Isaac, and Jacob" with everything. It involves a play on the word "everything." This was explained by the Sages as, "With everything, from everything; therefore, everything."

The last line is a nonsense mixture of part of the Passover Seder, along with the names of the more common vegetables eaten in Israel.

The Hebrew word for "He will forgive" is *Ym-Hol,* and the word *Eem-Hol* means "with sand." This (which is an extra pun) explains the odd refrain the Dormouse picks up from the song of the Hatter.

It must be agreed, I think, that this Hebrew treatment of the parody is excellent. But I am not sure that the Reverend Mr. Dodgson, who was an excessively pious person, would have approved the admixture of family prayers and nonsense...

The Russian version is especially clever and sensitive.

The edition which I had retranslated was published in Berlin, the translator's name being printed as "V. Sirin" or "B. Sirina," depending on how one transliterates the Cyrillic alphabet. It is, however, now known that "Sirin" is the pseudonym used by Vladimir V. Nabokov during his period in Germany (he has recently resumed the occasional use of this nom de plume). An article about Nabokov states that he received five dollars for making this translation.

In retranslation the Russian verse goes:

> Mushroom, mushroom, where hast thou been? On the lawn, drinking the rain.
> I drank one drop,
> And I drank two drops,
> And it became damp in my head.

Following this, the Dormouse sleepily says, "Damp, damp, damp, damp."
Now Russian children of that time knew a rhyme that went:

> Siskin, siskin, where hast thou been?
> I have been at the little fountain, drinking vodka.
> I drank one little glass,
> I drank another little glass,
> And it began to buzz in my head.

Practically all the Russian nouns in the verse are in the specially endearing diminutive forms. The Russian word used for "mushroom" is the name of the saffron milk-cap, a red-topped mushroom; and the same word is applied, rather affectionately, as "you little red-head," to a child or person. Similarly the word *chizhik* for siskin (a small greenish-yellow finch very common in Russia) could be used as a caressing diminutive in addressing a child, as we might say "little chicken" or "honey" or (in the South) "sugar."

The Russian word *vodka* means "water" as well as the alcoholic drink; so that the Russian verse contains a pun which (the Reverend Mr. Dodgson forbid!) was of course not in the original. All in all, the Russian translation of this parodied verse deserves a very high score indeed.

The Chinese, Japanese, Pidgin, Spanish, and Swahili translations follow the second course of simply moving the words of the English version over into the second language. But we must recognize that in Chinese, Japanese, Pidgin, and Swahili there could hardly have been available indigenous verses to parody. In both China and Japan the literature for children was scanty indeed until recently. Thus, of this group, we cannot fairly criticize any of the translators (other than the Spanish, perhaps) for following the course they chose...

There are few efforts more conducive to humility than that of the translator try-
ing to communicate an incommunicable beauty. Yet, unless we do try, something
unique and never surpassed will cease to exist except in the libraries of a few
inquisitive book lovers.

— EDITH HAMILTON, Introduction to *Three Greek Plays* (Hamilton 1937)

CRIME FICTION: UPTOWN, DOWNTOWN OR CHINATOWN?

Even before Raymond Chandler sent his private detective down the mean streets
of Los Angeles, urban geography was an important element in crime fiction. Here,
Umberto Eco takes issue with Schleiermacher's famous dictum about a translation's
direction, underlining his own notion of translation as negotiation (Eco 2003).

> Schleiermacher once said: "The translator either disturbs the writer as little
> as possible and moves the reader in his direction, or disturbs the reader as
> little as possible and moves the writer in his direction. The two approaches
> are so absolutely different that no mixture of the two is to be trusted."
>
> I repeat that such a severe criterion perhaps holds for translation from
> ancient or remote literatures, but that it does not hold for modern texts.
> To choose a target- or source-oriented direction is, once again, a matter of
> negotiation to be decided at every sentence.
>
> In American crime novels the detective frequently asks a driver to take
> him downtown or uptown. By a sort of unspoken agreement, all Italian
> translators have decided to translate these expressions as *portami alla Città
> Alta,* that is, to the high or upper city, or *portami alla Città Bassa,* that is, to
> the low or lower city. Thus Italian readers get the impression that every
> American city is like Budapest or Tbilisi, with a district on the hills beyond
> the river, and a district on the opposite bank.
>
> It is certainly difficult to decide how to translate *downtown* and *uptown,*
> because the sense of these expressions changes according to the city con-
> cerned. Normally uptown is north and downtown is south, but in certain
> cities downtown is the oldest district, in others it is the business area, in
> others the red-light district. In New York, downtown and uptown are rela-
> tive concepts: if you are escaping a black gang in Harlem you ask the driver
> to run downtown in order to reach at least the Plaza; if you are on the verge
> of being killed in Chinatown, you ask the driver to run as fast as possible

uptown, so as to relax at the Plaza. The Plaza is neither uptown nor down-town: which it is depends not on the Plaza's position but on yours.

A good translator should therefore negotiate the translation according to the city, asking the driver to take him to the business district, or to the red-light one, or along the river or elsewhere, according to the situation. But these decisions require vast extra-linguistic knowledge, and translators of detective novels are poorly paid. My suggestion is that one should for-eignise and use *downtown,* in English, to give the tale an exotic connota-tion (and the reader will understand later whether it was wise or not to go there). If you read a criminal story taking place in Barcelona (where you have never been) and you read *Take me to the Barrio Gótico,* do you really understand what it means? Certainly, there is a great difference between going (especially at night) to the Barrio Gótico or to the Barrio Chino, but too bad. Better to get the exotic flavour of Barcelona than to receive ill-translated information. So, if an English translator finds *Take me to the Barrio Chino* in a Spanish novel, it is advisable not to translate this as *Take me to Chinatown.* Exaggerated domestication can bring excessive obscurity.

Besides, translators in every language have their own downtown prob-lems. In his "Pendulum Diary" Bill Weaver reports a similar story.

> Thought for the day. *Periferia.* Outskirts. In most Italian cities, the *periferia* is the slums. In American cities, nowadays, the slums are downtown, the "inner city." So when you say someone lives in *periferia,* you have to watch yourself and not translate it as "in the suburbs," making an Italian slum sound like Larchmont. Casaubon lives and works in an ex-factory *in periferia.* I've eluded the problem, I think, by using "outlying."

As a matter of fact in Italy one can live at the *periferia* of a small non-industrial city and have a comfortable little house with a garden. But Casaubon lived in Milan and Weaver did well in avoiding *suburbs.* Casaubon was not rich enough.

BEAM ME UP, SHLOMO!
Science fiction and fantasy – SF&F to aficionados – are huge niches in the publish-ing world, and have done very well in translation from English to other languages.

(Note, however, that aside from Jules Verne and a few other exceptions, relatively little has come from other languages into English.) In her essay "SF&F in Hebrew – Wake-Up Call? Translating the Past and Future into Recently-Revived Hebrew," Yael Sela-Shapiro describes the special difficulties of translating these genres into Hebrew, a language that was almost entirely reserved for devotional use throughout most of the last two millennia, and only began to be "revived" in the mid-nineteenth century. She also describes the particularly close relationship SF&F translators have with the Israeli reading public (Sela-Shapiro 2007).

The main difficulty in translating fantasy to Hebrew is lexical voids. A typical fantasy novel is set against a medieval background: kings and social classes, knights and horsemanship, medieval agriculture and ships. Hebrew "missed out" on almost all the historical, social, cultural and technological advancements of the last 2 millennia, including the Middle Ages, naturally. And faced with a monumental endeavour of reviving a hibernating language, revivers hardly bothered to fill in some of the blanks: anything that went obsolete before Hebrew's revival was not likely to be addressed when the present concepts were still begging for a Hebrew parallel. Thus, the void was maintained, and the Hebrew translator is left high and dry. Even in the few cases a translation is available, it is most often a purely official translation which is both unacceptable and unfamiliar to the readers; Such are the translations for words such as "bailey," "gorget," "manservant," and "bulwark." Literal translations are therefore quite common. Gorget, for instance, is often translated *shiryon tsavar* – "neck armour."

Fantasy writers often employ rarely-used-yet-not-obsolete synonyms for everyday words, such as "conclave" instead of the more familiar "meeting" or "conference." Current Hebrew has about 120,000 words whereas current English has about 600,000 words, meaning that Hebrew holds few synonyms for almost anything you can think of. In addition, Hebrew revivers have artificially re-allocated many existing words to serve as translations for new terms. These words have therefore changed their meaning. *Miklat*, for instance, was originally a synonym to *machasé*, and they both meant "place of refuge" or "haven." Today it usually means "bomb shelter," and in a country which has had seven wars in its 60 years of existence, the modern meaning naturally gained supremacy and the synonym is therefore unavailable for the fantasy translator.

The bright side of translating fantasy to Hebrew is that Hebrew can easily accommodate fantasy's high register; Hebrew speakers, unlike the speakers of any other language in the world, can easily read 2000-year old Hebrew since modern Hebrew just picked up where ancient Hebrew left off. The high register is still very present in modern Hebrew texts and therefore is an acceptable option. Set against this high register, the otherwise unacceptable "official" translations look a little less out of place. Thus, translators can "get away with them" with the help of explanation.

Since Israel has a booming hi-tech industry and is very open to international markets and cultures, one might think translating science fiction to Hebrew will be quite easy. In fact, Hebrew is resistant to some of the most common naming techniques in hi-tech in general and in science fiction in particular, namely "soldering" and "calques." (Soldering means to create a new word by joining two words together. A calque is a near word-for-word loan from another language, like the Spanish *rascacielos* which comes directly from the English "skyscraper.") Most Hebrew words are 2–3 syllables long, whereas many English words contain only one syllable. Moreover, many prefixes and suffixes ("comp-," "inter-," "tele-," etc.) do not translate well into Hebrew or have awkward parallels which are not in common use. Defying all logic, the Hebrew translation for "pre-" (*trom-*) was very well accepted, whereas the translation to "post-" (*Btar-*) was not. Therefore, a compact expression in English "calqued" to Hebrew may lose all its elegance and with it its acceptability – the reader will find it hard to believe the characters actually use this tongue-tangling word on a day-to-day basis.

So how does one translate science fiction terms? If the source term is of minor importance, then it is all about trade-offs. You need to invent or find a term that both conveys as much as possible of the manifold meaning of the original term, and sounds (and looks) credible and clear in Hebrew. Take, for example, this passage from George Martin's *Tuf Voyaging*, which is about a small-time interstellar trader travelling through space in an antiquated 30-kilometre long starship (Martin 2003).

> It was hard to tell what the cybertech was thinking... The shiny bluesteel fingers of his right hand interlocked with the mocha-colored fleshy digits of his left.

Bluesteel is a type of armour – not a big part of the story, but one of many small details that have to sound right. My translation for it was *Matchelet* (מַתְכֶלֶת), which is a soldering of *tchelet* (sky-blue) and *matechet* (metal). So *matchelet* actually means "Sky-blue Metal" and not *Bluesteel*, but it was clear, acceptable and good-enough, considering its minor role in the text. With "cybertech" I didn't even bother calquing. "Cyber-" is a very common prefix in Hebrew because of "cyberspace," so I just transliterated with minor adjustments: Hebrew speakers pronounce "cyber" like it sounds in Greek: "keeber." So the transliteration was "keebertek" (קיברטק).

If a term's literal translation is too long and cumbersome to be acceptable, the translator may resort to turning it into an acronym. Acronyms are very common in the jargon of some Hebrew circles because of the IDF (Israeli Defense Force). To this day, all Jewish 18 year olds are required to serve 2–3 years in the IDF, and most do. They acquire the military fondness for acronyms and find acronyms a very acceptable translation. In Dan Simmons's *The Fall of Hyperion*, for instance, the term Commlink was translated to KT (ק"ת) – "Kav Tikshoret" (קו תקשורת) which is roughly "communication line."

The Israeli SF&F community, like others around the globe, is very active and out-spoken. The number of active SF&F translators in Israel at any given time is probably two dozen at the most, and since many of them are members of the small but vibrant local SF&F community, the fans know them personally and can contact them directly. This familiarity is definitely a double edged sword – if you are a SF&F translator, fans may criticize your work openly on one of your favourite electronic forums or at a conference you attend. On the other hand, they offer generous praise on the same channels, and also help. You can use them as a sounding board for new words you have invented or for old words you consider using in your translation, and you will get good advice and ideas before the book goes to print.

CARE TO DANCE, MR. STRINDBERG?

Getting a literary translation "right" requires understanding not only of the source language but also of its wider culture. In her article "Translating Scandinavian Drama," Eivor Martinus illustrates this point with the example of August Strindberg's highly nuanced dramatic texts (Martinus 1996). Note that the character she calls "Lady Julie" below is more widely known in English as "Miss Julie" – an appellation

Martinus argues elsewhere in the essay is inaccurate and misleading, given that the character in question's father is a *greve*, the Swedish equivalent of an earl.

Translating Strindberg is a bit like following an expert partner in a tango.

You've got to make sure you know the steps, then feel the music, adopt the correct stance, trust in your partner and let the dance carry you along. There are, of course, a few basic rules without which we could not venture out onto the dance floor. The tango is not an easy dance, nor is Strindberg an easy writer to translate.

He was steeped in a classical tradition which more or less ceased at the end of the sixties, he knows his Bible and frequently alludes to it, he knew about half a dozen languages, he was a practising artist and was no stranger to chemistry, physics or astronomy. All this knowledge is somehow absorbed in his writing and he often sends his translator on a detective hunt for flowers and fruit which are no longer known by the same name. It took me a while, for instance, before I realised that "melon" was a special variety of apple at the turn of the century. I was also bemused by a reference to a tobacco plantation in *The Pelican* but apparently they did grow a certain kind of tobacco in Sweden a hundred years ago. When confronted with a number of mouth-watering varieties of apples in Swedish I realised that many of them had unfamiliar names and it would not do to use well-known English names, so I contacted a 'plant doctor' who runs a large gardening centre in Hampshire, and he managed to find half a dozen varieties which were cultivated at the turn of the century.

While translating Strindberg's plays I have often had to draw on my group of friends for advice: a lawyer who can explain the legal parlance, a clergyman who can place an allusion to the Bible immediately if I am in a hurry, although I have a very useful encyclopedia of Bible quotations both in English and Swedish. I also have two sets of Bibles in both languages: the modern version and the King James (and Swedish equivalent) version. Other essential reference books for translating Strindberg are works on Eastern Mysticism, Botany, Swedish and European History, craftsmen's terminology, Greek and Nordic mythology and technological terms which were extremely modern when Strindberg used them, but which are now out of date. There will undoubtedly come a time, very soon, when audiences need an explanation for a classical or biblical inclusion. For instance, when Lady Julie refers to Jean as Joseph (after he has rejected her advances) she is expressing the fact that she is hurt:

> Lady Julie: ... how incredibly conceited you are. A Don Juan perhaps. Or a chaste Joseph who will not be tempted? Yes, I believe you're a Joseph.

The original Swedish read, literally translated: "... how incredibly conceited you are. A Don Juan perhaps. Or a Joseph? I do believe you're a Joseph!" The reason for including "chaste" and "who will not be tempted" was simply that I don't think that many people today would understand the allusion to Potiphar's wife and her seduction of Joseph in Egypt. An explanation was necessary here. It is no good having a footnote in performance.

Key-terms like "guilt," "blame," "innocence" also abound in Strindberg's plays. Their emotional weight requires careful negotiation at every moment.

In the first scene of *The Father* when the Captain and the Pastor are talking to Nöjd about his relationship with the kitchen maid, the Captain plays around with the words *skuld, skyldig,* and *oskyldig* (guilt, guilty and innocent):

> The boy is probably not entirely blameless... you can't tell of course, but the only thing we can be absolutely sure of is that the girl is not innocent.

The Swedish was funnier because Strindberg could use the same words, only adding a prefix and the meaning became ambiguous. The boy is probably not entirely *oskyldig* meaning two things: blameless and a virgin. Whereas the girl is definitely not a virgin, not innocent, i.e. *skyldig.*

One passage in act one of *The Father* which almost brought me to a standstill was Bertha's affectionate speech addressed to her father. *Literally* she says:

> Oh it is always so gloomy in there, so horrible, as if it were a winter's night, but when you come, father, it is like when you take out the inner windows on a spring morning.

In Sweden, they used to employ a system of secondary glazing which was fixed to the windows on the inside and left there throughout the winter.

The fresh air would come in through the front or back door, but in the spring the inner windows were taken down and stored in the shed or the attic. A very dramatic event and a metaphor for spring, of course. Well, one thing is certain, we can't use the simile about the windows, I decided. Any "double glazing" or "secondary glazing" or American "storm windows" would sound completely alien to an English audience in this context.

So we had to abandon that beautiful period image, but obviously it is important to retain the idea that the father represents all that is fresh, green and healthy whereas the rest of the household has a more suffocating effect on the young girl. This view is given more poignancy as the play progresses, when the father is brought to despair and declared insane. In my translation, therefore, Bertha says:

> Oh it is always so gloomy in there, so horribly dark... like a winter's night, but when you come home daddy, it's like spring's arrived.

Another difficult line was Laura's reference to their sexual relationship:

> Although I enjoyed your embraces they were followed by a guilty conscience as if we were committing an incestuous act. The mother became her son's lover!

The Swedish word for incest is *blodskam* (blood shame). Laura actually says: "as if the blood felt shame," a play on words which unfortunately I had to abandon in English.

In act three, scene seven, Strindberg offers a web of complicated opinions on the institution of marriage based on the image *bolag* meaning "company" or "partnership." I had to find a metaphor which I could use all the way through the long speech. I could have used "partnership," but it wouldn't have been quite so effective, so I opted for "company," which in this instance lent itself to all the extended imagery quite successfully. But that was a rare coincidence.

> Maybe the fault lies with the institution of marriage itself. In the past one married a wife, today one sets up a company with a woman who goes out to work, or one lives with a friend. And then – one either goes to bed with one's working partner or desecrates one's friend. What happened to love – healthy sensual love? It died in the process. And what issue comes from this limited company of love shares?

Who is the main shareholder when the crash comes? Who is the bio-
logical father of the spiritual child?

OPENING LINES

Gregory Rabassa discusses his choice of English words for one of the most famous
opening lines penned during the twentieth century – the beginning of García
Márquez's *One Hundred Years of Solitude* (Rabassa 2005).

> Opening lines are often the most quoted and remembered parts of a story:
> Proust's *Longtemps, je me suis couché de bonne heure;* Cervantes's *En un lugar de
> la Mancha, de cuyo nombre no quiero acordarme;* Kafka's *Als Gregor Samsa eines
> Morgens aus unruhigen Träumen erwachte;* Dickens's *It was the best of times, it was
> the worst of times.* So it has been with this book: *Muchos años después frente al
> pelotón de fusilamiento, el coronel Aureliano Buendía había de recordar aquella tarde
> remota en que su padre le llevó a conocer el hielo.* People go on repeating this all
> the time (in English) and I can only hope that I have got them saying what
> it means. I wrote: "Many years later, as he faced the firing squad, Colonel
> Aureliano Buendia was to remember that distant afternoon when his father
> took him to discover ice." There are variant possibilities. In the British
> army it would have been a "firing party," which I rather like, but I was
> writing for American readers. *Había de* could have been *would* (How much
> wood can a woodchuck chuck?), but I think *was to* has a better feeling to it.
> I chose *remember* over *recall* because I feel that it conveys a deeper memory.
> *Remote* might have aroused thoughts of such inappropriate things as remote
> control and robots. Also, I liked *distant* when used with time. I think Dr.
> Einstein would have approved. The real problem for choice was with *conocer*
> and I have come to know that my selection has set a great many Professors
> Horrendo all aflutter. It got to the point that my wife Clem had to defend
> my choice (hers too) against one such worthy in a seminar in which she
> was participating. The word seen straight means to know a person or thing
> for the first time, to meet someone, to be familiar with something. What
> is happening here is a first-time meeting, or learning. It can also mean to
> know something more deeply than *saber*, to know from experience. García
> Márquez has used the Spanish word here with all its connotations. But *to
> know ice* just won't do in English. It implies, "How do you do, ice?" It could
> be "to experience ice." The first is foolish, the second is silly. When you get

to know something for the first time, you've discovered it. Only after that can you come to know it in the full sense. I could have said "to make the acquaintance of ice," but that, too, sounds nutty, with its implication of tipping one's hat or giving a handshake. I stand by what I put down in this important opening sentence.

LEECHES, MR. SEIDENSTICKER?

The late Edward Seidensticker (he died in August 2007, aged eighty-six) provides more advice on the importance of getting first lines right, before moving on to issues such as critical sniping, post-publishing regrets, and "howlers" – errors that make it into published translations undetected. Seidensticker was best known for his translations of the classic *Tale of Genji* and two novels by the contemporary writer Yasunari Kawabata, which contributed greatly to Kawabata's becoming the first Japanese to win the Nobel Prize for Literature in 1968. The passage is from Seidensticker's memoir *Tokyo Central*, which covers a great deal of Japan's political and cultural history from his privileged point of view as a translator, U.S. government official, teacher in both Japanese and American universities, and high-profile participant in the Tokyo literary scene (Seidensticker 2002).

> The opening lines of the *Snow Country* which I translated are not those of the first magazine installment. Kawabata put them there when he first published the work under the title it now bears. This was very canny of him. They constitute probably the most famous passage in the whole body of modern Japanese literature, and had he left them buried further down in the work it is doubtful that they would have had the same impact. They have been the most thoroughly scrutinized lines in any of my translations. Most of the scrutinizers have been Japanese. Given the esteem in which the passage is held, this is not, perhaps, so very curious. Nowhere else in the world, I suspect, are translations from their literature, given the attention they receive in Japan. Americans, at least, care not at all.
>
> I give as a piece of advice to aspiring translators: "Be careful about opening and closing passages." These are the passages people will notice and find fault with. I think if I had formulated the principle earlier, I would have translated the beginning of *Snow Country* more literally. A train comes out of a long tunnel that passes the border between two provinces, and it is the snow country. Outside the train windows "the bottom of the night"

lies white. My translation, according to unfriendly scrutinizers, is guilty of two serious delinquencies: I did not state that the mountain range through which the long tunnel passes is the provincial boundary; and I failed to include Kawabata's trope.

I do not even now think the matter of the boundary worth worrying about, but I think they are right about the bottom of the night. It is a striking image and the chief reason for the great fame of the passage, and it should be there. My reason for omitting it seems to me now wholly inadequate. I did not like having "night" and "white" in such intimate juxtaposition.

I made amends later, when the translation was published in a limited edition. "Night" and "white" are there side by side. The trouble is that the edition, brought out by the Limited Editions Club in New York, is expensive, and few people have seen it.

Scrutinizers also compile lists of mistakes, sometimes elaborately classified lists: trivial mistakes, considerable mistakes, outright howlers, that sort of thing. None of the mistakes on any of the lists sent to me has included anything that falls unquestionably in the howler category. I have a letter from Tanizaki saying that he is passing my *Some Prefer Nettles* on for the scrutiny of a friend who is an English professor, and another letter arranging a meeting between me and the professor. I thought this just a touch insulting, but did not say so. Tanizaki seemed to think it a natural part of our relationship and my education. The professor did not turn up anything that much bothered me.

I think that we who translate from Japanese into English have on the whole done better by our originals than have those translators who work in the opposite direction. The worst blunder I can think of in translation from Japanese into English is Ivan Morris's, in a sad, lovely story by Hayashi Fumiko called "Tokyo" in the Keene anthology. The story is set immediately after the war. The heroine, a war widow and a peddler of tea, has an affair with a truck driver, who dies in an accident. We are introduced to the driver's lodgings. On the inside of his door he has a card-size pinup, of what Morris calls "the fifty bells of Yamada."

Now this is a celebrated and beautiful actress of film and stage, Yamada Isuzu. Her given name, the second element, is written with the characters for "fifty bells." I was the first person to point out the mistake to Morris.

He looked at the page in silence for a moment, then said: "A howler." In silence I agreed.

It seems very strange that no one along the way, translator to editor and proofreader and reviewer, questioned the fifty bells. Truck drivers the world over tend to be robust, earthy people. Why would a Japanese truck driver have chosen a picture of fifty bells for his pinup (and each of the fifty, given the size of the pinup, so tiny as to be discernible only with the help of a magnifying glass)? In those days the Japanese were looked upon as delicate and ethereal. They were not a few years earlier and they probably are not now. Perhaps everyone along the line, editors and the rest, caught overtones of Zen in the fifty bells. I recently looked at the twentieth printing or so of the anthology. The fifty bells are still there.

But this is more amusing than serious. For the serious howler, one should look at translations into Japanese: at the Japanese title, for instance, of Jean Genet's *Notre dame des fleurs.* It is *Hana no Notre Dame*, which calls to mind a big cathedral in cherry-blossom time…

In the limited edition I made amends in another regard that had come to bother me. In the introduction to the Knopf edition, I likened Kawabata's method of composition to that of a haiku poet. It is true that he habitually started out with a fragment, an account perhaps of something or someone he had seen on a train or a street. If it seemed to work he would add to it, and presently he would have what might be called a novel. So it certainly was with *Snow Country.* The haiku comparison has come to seem so obvious as to approach the trite, however. I now prefer to liken the Kawabata method to *renga* linked verse. This accommodates the fragmentary, episodic quality, and it also accommodates the inconclusiveness of the conclusion – and even after all his attempts, it remains very inconclusive.

Reviewers have objected to the peculiar imagery. "Leeches, Mr. Seidensticker?" said one of them. *"Leeches?"* Yes, it is peculiar, but it is a literal translation, and it is peculiar in the Japanese too. Kawabata more than once likens the smooth, moist lips of his heroine to a pair of leeches. There was, I decided, nothing I could do about the simile. If Kawabata thought leeches beautiful, very well, he thought leeches beautiful, and it was not for me to reform him.

There were other instances in which I chose literal translation as the best way of conveying something subtle and obscure, and perhaps untranslatable. I thought that a moment's thought on the part of the intelligent reader would see him or her past the difficulty...

A WEE CHINESE SWEARIE

Brian Holton's wonderful "Wale a Leid an Wale a Warld [literally "Choose a language and choose a world"]: Shuihu Zhuan into Scots" describes his work on translating a picaresque Chinese text from the thirteenth or fourteenth century (Holton 2004). Of uncertain authorship, *Shuihu Zhuan* (translated into Scots as *Men o the Mossflow*) is a tale of banditry and rebellion which was one of the first classics to be written in the vernacular. Its title has been rendered in previous English translations as *The Water Margin*, *Outlaws of the Marsh*, and *The Marshes of Mount Liang*. Holton's essay discusses a wide range of translation issues as well as the provenance of the original text, and is full of interesting digressions, one of which (on translating the modern poet Yang Lian) is found in chapter 7. Here he deals with the problem of translating profanity, which poses surprisingly subtle challenges:

> Profanity, vulgarity, swearie-words, "mill talk" – what do we do about them? Well, if we're honest, we'll reproduce all of it, no matter how foul we might think it, and we'll reproduce it as closely as we can, because our job is to let the text speak – not to bowdlerise, gut or rewrite it. One word that has raised eyebrows is a great favourite among the braw lads o [brave boys of] the Mossflow: *zhiniang zei*. This would be rendered in English as *motherfucking bandit*, but I didn't like the way this sounded so much like an Americanism, so I took advantage of the fact that *niang* can be used for other female relatives, and came up with *granny-shaggin* for the first part. *Bandit* was another thing: *cateran* or *reiver* were near-hand, but they didn't seem to roll off the tongue the way the original undoubtedly does. So I opted for alliteration – always a good idea with swearie-words, I think – and came up with *granny-shaggin get* [bastard] instead, which is both satisfactorily obscene and satisfyingly rhythmic. Another common term of abuse is *si*, usually in phrases such as *ni zhe si*. Its history is clear as an archaic term for a domestic servant, as is its use as a generalised vaguely offensive appellation. But we don't have an equivalent, so I took instead (with apologies to travellers, Romanies and others to whom it has been misapplied) *tink*, which is a similarly mild though abusive term. And *ni zhe si* (literally, *you this tink*) becomes quite happily *ye tink, ye*.

HUMOUR: A URINATING DINNER OR A DEFECATING DINNER?

Humour is notoriously tough to translate, arguably an even greater challenge than poetry – or profanity. Eugene Eoyang provides some insights into the translatability of humour, using Chinese and English examples (Eoyang 2003).

It is not true that humour cannot be translated: some jokes may, indeed, be untranslatable, but there are others that do survive translingual transport with the wit intact.

As I shall be much occupied with China, let me begin with a panda joke. A panda walks into a bar, orders a sandwich, eats it, takes out a gun, shoots at the ceiling, and leaves. This behaviour puzzles a bystander, who asks someone to explain this bizarre behaviour: he is told that there's nothing unusual – since that's what pandas do. "What do you mean, that's what pandas do?" the bystander asks. "If you don't believe me," he is told, "look up the definition for panda in any reference work, and you'll see what I mean." The bystander looks up an encyclopaedia, and reads the following: "Panda: large black-and-white mammal, resembling a bear, found mostly in the mountains of southwest China. Eats shoots and leaves." [The original version of this paper was presented in Beijing in 1997. Subsequent to that, Lynne Truss published *Eats, Shoots & Leaves* in 2003, which became a bestseller and made this joke even more popular.]

I tell this joke by way of illustrating the difference between translation and cross-cultural communication. This joke cannot be translated, except into a language where counterparts can be found for: a word which can be a verb meaning "to discharge a bullet from a gun," as well as a noun referring to the tender young branches of trees, i.e., "shoots"; and a word which can be both a verb meaning "to depart" and a noun referring to what grows on trees, i.e., "leaves." No other language, to my knowledge, has exact counterparts to these ambivalent meanings.

Translation can transmit information between two cultures, but it cannot convey these subtleties of language and meaning inherent in any culture. For the sake of convenience, let me refer to the first as "definitive sense," and the second as "indefinite nuance." Jokes are a way of playing with definitive sense to create indefinite nuance.

What is "lost in translation" is precisely cross-cultural insight: translation offers the illusion that meaning is universal and that all languages are semantically equivalent to each other, whereas cross-cultural communication focuses on the individual and regional – the particular rather than the general – and shows that each language and culture is clear and distinct, and that each has its unique character.

It's only fair that I share with you as well a story which can only be appreciated in Chinese:

在美国, 有一些学生不仅汉语学的好, 而且对于中国人的礼貌及客气话, 都学的不错. 有一个学生, 他老师请他吃饭, 烧了几个菜, 客气的对他说: [请坐, 请坐. 没有甚么(吗)菜, 就是便饭] 那位学生为了要表示他的汉语 水平, 很得意的回答, 说 [啊, 老师太客气, 这简直不是 "便饭". 假如是便饭, 也不是小便饭, 是大便饭!]

The crux of the humour in this anecdote, which I'm told is a true story, lies in two intersecting semantic propositions: one, that, in Chinese, to refer to something as big (大) rather than small (小) is a form of compliment, raising its importance and value rather than denigrating it; two, that the idiom in Chinese for urinating is (小便) and for defecating is (大便). What the student wanted to say was something like: "What you have cooked me is hardly a small thing, it's a big thing." But the net result of the student's attempt at elegance and politeness was to say to the teacher, "You haven't cooked me a urinating dinner; you've cooked me a defecating dinner."

Let me venture another so-called "joke," which is both un-funny and funny – depending on who the audience is. This joke was especially popular in Eastern Europe before the fall of the Iron Curtain. Americans find this "joke" totally impenetrable, whereas the Rumanians, Czechs, Bulgarians, and Hungarians I have tried it out on find it hilarious. Here is the joke. A man goes to a hotel; the clerk at the reception desk asks: "A double bed or twin beds?" The man is indignant, and shouts: "Comrade, not even if I were alone would I want a double bed!"

East Europeans, with memories still fresh from the rigid moral codes of the former Soviet bloc, are reminded of the sycophants and the lackeys who tried to ingratiate themselves with authorities by insisting on their anti-decadent (read: "anti-capitalist") convictions. In this case, the absurdity is based on the presumption that celibacy under the Soviets was as admired as ideological purity. Hence, the outlandish protest that one would not want a double bed "even if one were alone." The joke doesn't work with

American audiences, because in most American jokes, it is the presumption of preternatural lust that provides the thrust of the humour, whereas in the former Soviet Socialist republics, it was politically correct to proclaim, even to insist on, one's sexual innocence.

Having told two jokes that don't translate from one language to another, or from one culture to another, let me relate a third that does lend itself to translation.

When I visited China in 1979, a driver once asked me if I had ever tasted dog meat. I said no. "It's very tasty," he told me. "Why don't you invite me to America," he asked, "I'll run a dog over for you, we'll cook it, and you'll see how delicious dog meat can be." "No, thank you," I replied. "You don't know how much Americans love their dogs. They hate people who kill dogs more than they hate people who kill people."

Years later, I related this incident to a friend. "Why, yes," she said, "Did you know that Koreans are also fond of dog meat?" Then she added: "I once invited a Korean to visit the U.S. and he wanted to try everything typically American. At a restaurant, we looked at the menu, and he noticed an item called 'Hot Dog.' 'Is that typically American?' he asked. 'There isn't anything more typically American than a Hot Dog,' I told him. 'Well, in that case, I'll order a Hot Dog.' When the food was brought to the table, my Korean friend was aghast: his face turned ashen. 'What's the matter?' I asked. He said: 'That's the only part of the dog we don't eat!'"

Now, this incident, unlike the first two "jokes," can be rendered quite easily into virtually any language. But, aside from its translatability, the story illustrates one of the important lessons of cross-cultural studies: that one is so inured by the conventions in one's native language to the "dead metaphors" that one forgets their literal meanings. Foreigners make mistakes that sometimes remind us of what we've overlooked in our own tongue.

ASTÉRIX AND THE *PETIT-NÈGRE*

Translators are becoming ever more aware of the "sticks and stones" that lurk in the words they deal with. In her essay "Translator's Notebook: Delicate Matters," Anthea Bell discusses how attitudes toward racist language – and even what constitutes racist language – have changed over time, using examples from an internationally successful comic book series (Bell 2006).

Change of attitude, it seems to me, more naturally precedes change in linguistic usage than the other way around: and changes tend to take place at their own rate. Recently I was tracking down the literary roots of Tchaikovsky's ballet *Swan Lake:* they are very tenuous roots, but such as they are, they exist in a complicated pre-Romantic extravaganza by the 18th-century J.K.A. Musäus, featuring a couple of hermits, two swan maidens in successive generations, and a quantity of dreadful remarks uttered by these ladies to the effect that "life, you know, is over for our sex, once Youth and Beauty are fled" (the swan-maiden referred to, or by then ex-swan maiden, as she is the mother of the new-youthful model, must be about 35, poor decrepit soul). Obviously no one would now, a couple of centuries later, write in such terms, the accepted commonplaces of their time as imposed by Musäus on his partly traditional sources, but the process whereby such observations became unacceptable was gradual.

However, I had an example not long since of a much more rapid change of attitude affecting one's choice of language, though this was a matter of style rather than words themselves. A couple of years ago, when one of the London Boroughs aroused some controversy (and a fair amount of ridicule) by accusing Tintin and Astérix of racism, I felt rather indignant on Astérix's behalf, since the only possible basis for the attack was in the character of one of the pirates who put in regular guest appearances: a black man, who, in French, uses the colonial French accent known as *"petit-nègre,"* pidgin French. This accent was judged unacceptable in English; that surprises French people, to whom I have several times had to explain the point. In the Parisian theatre, said one young woman who had never thought of it that way before, there is a comic whose act depends largely on the *petit-nègre* accent. Anyway, much effort, over the years, has gone into making up new and extra jokes to replace that pirate's accent, where the original could get a simple laugh out of his inability to pronounce the letter *r.*

But we began to make that effort after publication of the first four titles, when an American edition of the English translations of the saga was on the cards. At the time American sensitivity was rather greater than that in Britain. Thus, in three of those early Astérix translations the English equivalent of the French accent had been used, and still stood. (The character didn't appear in the first book at all.) I was brought face to face with it when rereading *Astérix in Britain* for [a BBC radio series]. I was absolutely horrified; I reached for the phone to ring our Astérix editor at Hodder and say that the London Borough of Brent was perfectly correct about these particular passages, and I thought we'd better do something about it. So, starting with the radio script itself, and proceeding to new wording of the passages concerned for the next reprints of those three titles, we did do something about it obliterating the accent and providing new allusions in line with subsequent practice. And yet, back at the end of the 1960s, there had seemed nothing wrong, from the translation angle, in just following the French original, though I think we were quite glad to have the excuse of America for abandoning that method and adopting a freer style of translation on this point.

Which I fear goes to show that it is particularly difficult to produce a translation that won't date. At the time of writing or indeed translating, one can't by definition see what will date, or one would avoid it. I suspect, however, that forced change to the language is still no good unless, perhaps, in a work intended to be didactic rather than literary. And of course, if one is translating such a work, one must, as always, find a style to parallel what the original author aimed to do in the original language... but then again, has our Astérix translation gone beyond its brief in abandoning that pirate's accent? The arguments become circular.

But I feel (or think that I feel for this is indeed a delicate and ever-shifting linguistic area) that determinedly saying "humankind" is different from discovering that a *petit-nègre* accent has come to read badly. However, if to eschew the use of such an accent now seems natural and desirable, will the use of "humankind" rather than "mankind" eventually come to seem equally natural and desirable? I believe the difference, in my own mind, resides in the distinction between choice of style and the attempted alteration of words themselves, the actual building blocks of the language. Just look at the trouble the purist French have in trying to banish *franglais*, once accepted, from their own language! But give it another hundred years or so, and such a distinction could seem meaningless.

I began the work in February 2001 and completed it two years later, but it is important for you to know that "final" versions are determined more by a publisher's due date than by any sense on my part that the work is actually finished.

— EDITH GROSSMAN, "Translator's Note to the Reader" in her translation of *Don Quixote* (Cervantes Saavedra and Grossman 2004)

O n April 28, 1971, a translator's translator drowned herself in Ottawa's Rideau Canal. Irène de Buisseret was fifty-three and at the height of her professional powers. People remember her as a solitary and fiercely private person; no one knows why she committed suicide. The daughter of a Russian mother and a Belgian diplomat father, she had qualified as a lawyer in France before emigrating in 1947 to Canada. There she worked her way up to head the Translation Department at Canada's Supreme Court, and also became a respected professor of translation at the University of Ottawa. After her death a group of colleagues took on the task of finding a publisher for the manuscript she had been working on for years, a massive collection of observations, advice, quotations, and analysis. Though sadly out of print, *Deux langues, six idiomes: Manuel pratique de traduction de l'anglais au français* remains an engrossing text for the professional and a delight for anyone who appreciates language (de Buisseret 1975). De Buisseret ends her book with words to stir the heart of translators who might suffer "a certain fatigue on a bad day," or feel oppressed by their own perfectionist standards (English translation by Kevin Cook).

Chaque faute, chaque erreur, chaque faiblesse, nous incite à un progrès. Bon gré, mal gré, au fil des jours, des mois, des années, nous engrangeons des trésors, nous mettons au point cet instrument indispensable dans notre métier et qui s'appelle le doute (douter de ce que nous croyons savoir, premier mot de la sagesse), nous affinons cet outil dont parlait Hemingway avec la verdeur qui le marquait:

Every flaw, every blemish, every frailty is a step forward. As the days, months and years go by, willy-nilly, we squirrel away treasures, we perfect that instrument called doubt which is so essential to our craft (wisdom begins with doubting what we think we already know), and we sharpen that tool described by Hemingway with his characteristic pungency:

The most essential gift for a good writer (*j'ajoute*: for a good translator) is a built-in, shock-proof shit detector. This is our radar, and all great writers (*ajoutons* translators) have had it.

A force de traduire, nous acquérons en effet cet instinct, ce « merdomètre » (pardon, Mesdames et Mesdemoiselles, mais enfin c'est Hemingway qui l'a dit) grâce auquel nous détectons infailliblement ce qui, dans une traduction, ne marche pas et ce qu'il convient de redresser. Et quand nous l'avons détecté, quel plaisir, quelle satisfaction, quelle joie cela procure! Pour moi, j'estime que s'il me fallait attendre trente ou quarante ans pour goûter ces délices intellectuelles et esthétiques, ce ne serait pas trop. Pensons à tous ceux qui attendent ce temps-là pour devenir riches ou célèbres et qui n'y parviennent jamais. Au fond, nous sommes bien mieux placés qu'eux.

Et puis, il y a les *spin-offs*, les retombées favorables. En exerçant avec conscience et avec goût notre métier, nous en arriverons peu à peu à comprendre que ce n'est pas seulement un métier mais aussi une vocation, une aventure, un voyage de découverte, découverte de cultures et de langues variées, et aussi de nous-mêmes, donc une méthode de promotion personnelle. C'est que la discipline volontaire est une tâche faite avec amour, ça paie de forts beaux dividendes. Un jour pourra venir – pour nombre d'entre nous il est déjà venu – où, en regardant dans la glace nos premiers cheveux blancs, nous penserons avec franchise et humilité que non seulement nous sommes en passe de devenir de bons traducteurs, mais que nous avons avancé sur la voie humaine et que nous sommes, ma foi oui, des êtres passables, grâce à Dieu. Alors nous verrons que nos efforts, étalés sur une existence entière, nous ont aidés à atteindre un certain équilibre, une certaine intégrité, une harmonie intérieure grâce auxquels nous pourrons jouir désormais du sentiment de notre propre unité.

The most essential gift for a good writer (I would add: for a good translator) is a built-in, shock-proof shit detector. This is our radar, and all great writers (translators) have had it.

The more we translate, the more we develop this instinct, this "shit detector" (sorry, ladies, but I'm simply quoting Hemingway) which allows us to home in on whatever doesn't work in a translation and fix it. And what a sense of fulfilment, of elation, of rapture when we succeed! As far as I'm concerned, if I had to wait thirty or forty years to taste these intellectual and aesthetic delights, it would not seem too much. Just think of all those who wait that long to become rich or famous and never make it. Aren't we a lot better off than they are?

And then there are the spin-offs. As we conscientiously and discerningly practise our profession, we gradually come to realize that it is not only a profession but also a vocation, an adventure, a voyage of discovery, not only of different cultures and languages but also of ourselves, and hence a method of self-improvement; for self-imposed discipline is a labour of love, and one which pays rich dividends. The day may come – for many of us it may already have done so – when we glimpse our first grey hairs in the mirror and think to ourselves, in all honesty and humility, that we are not only on the way to becoming good translators, but that we have made progress on the path of life and, with God's help, have become – why not? – decent human beings. And then we will see that the efforts of a lifetime have helped us attain the balance, integrity and inner harmony that comes of finally being just who we were meant to be.

We thank the following people for their kind permission to reproduce their work in this volume.

PAUL AUSTER is a poet and the author of novels such as *The New York Trilogy* (1987), *Moon Palace* (1989), and most recently *Man in the Dark* (2008). He was for many years a professional translator from French to English.

MONA BAKER is Professor of Translation Studies at the Centre for Translation and Intercultural Studies, University of Manchester. She is author of many books and articles on translation, editor of the *Routledge Encyclopedia of Translation Studies*, and Editorial Director of St. Jerome Publishing.

LALEH BAKHTIAR is a translator, academic, and mental health counsellor. In addition to her translations from Classical Arabic and Persian, she has written or co-authored many books including the *Encyclopedia of Muhammad's Women Companions and the Traditions They Related* (1998) and *Sufi Women of America: Angels in the Making* (1996).

ANTHEA BELL has translated many works of non-fiction, literary and popular fiction, and books for young people. In 2002 she won the Helen and Kurt Wolff Translator's Prize for her translation of W.G. Sebald's novel *Austerlitz*. She is also well known for her translations of the Astérix comic books.

SHARON M. BELL is a professor at Kent State University and a member of its Institute for Applied Linguistics. Her translation of Jacques-Stephen Alexis's *Romancero aux étoiles* won the American Literary Translators Association's Gregory Rabassa prize for 1989.

ESPERANÇA BIELSA is Lecturer at the Department of Sociology at the University of Leicester. She is the author of *The Latin American Urban Crónica: Between Literature and Mass Culture* (2006), co-author of *Translation in Global News* (2008), and co-editor of *Globalization, Political Violence and Translation* (forthcoming).

ANDREW CHESTERMAN is Professor of Multilingual Communication at the University of Helsinki. His books include *Memes of Translation* (1997) and, with Emma Wagner, *The Map: A Beginner's Guide to Doing Research in Translation Studies* (2002).

KEVIN COOK lives in the Netherlands and can translate from many European languages including modern Greek, Catalan, and Slovene. His first book, *Dubbel Dutch*, a practical guide for students of Dutch, was published in 1995.

MARK DAVIS has been president of the Unicode Consortium since its inception in 1991. He has a long history of managing information technology projects, and is currently working on software internationalization at Google.

JEAN DELISLE was for many years head of the School of Translation and Interpretation at the University of Ottawa, where he is now Professor Emeritus. He has written many scholarly articles and books, including *Translators through History* (1996) and *Portraits de traductrices* (2002).

PER N. DOHLER is a professional translator working in English and German. He specializes in dentistry, medicine, medical technology, IT, and pharmacology.

CAY DOLLERUP is an academic and the editor of language-international.net. He was editor-in-chief of the journal *Perspectives: Studies in Translatology* from 1993 to 2006, and has organized several conferences on the theme of Teaching Translation and Interpreting.

UMBERTO ECO is a novelist, semiotician, and philosopher most widely known for his bestselling novel *The Name of the Rose* (*Il nome della rosa*). Much translated himself, Eco has also translated works such as Gérard de Nerval's *Sylvie* and Raymond Queneau's *Exercices de style* into Italian.

EUGENE EOYANG is Professor Emeritus of Comparative Literature and of East Asian Languages and Cultures at Indiana University. From 1996 to 2008, he was Chair Professor of English and Chair Professor of Humanities at Lingnan University, Hong Kong.

ANDREW FENNER has been a freelance translator since 1984. He is a member of the U.K.-based Institute of Translation and Interpreting (ITI), which he has represented at European translation standards meetings.

PETER FRANCE is Professor Emeritus of French at the University of Edinburgh. He is the author of *Rhetoric and Truth in France: Descartes to Diderot* (1972) and other books, and the editor of both the *Oxford Guide to Literature in English Translation*

(2000) and the *New Oxford Companion to Literature in French* (1995).

ESTELLE GILSON, who introduced the fiction of the late Italian magic realist Massimo Bontempelli to readers of English, is a writer and translator in New York. She translates from Italian, Hebrew, and French.

HOWARD GOLDBLATT is Research Professor of Chinese at the University of Notre Dame. He has published English translations of more than forty novels and story collections by writers from China, Taiwan, and Hong Kong. He is the founding editor of the scholarly journal *Modern Chinese Literature*.

JOHN D. GRAHAM was Head of Central Foreign Language Services at Mannesmann Demag for many years and is currently vice-president of the International Association of Language and Business.

EDITH GROSSMAN is a major figure in the translation of Latin American and Spanish fiction into English. The authors she has translated include Ariel Dorfman, Gabriel García Márquez, Álvaro Mutis, Mario Vargas Llosa, and the late Carmen Laforet.

JENS HARE HANSEN is a writer specializing in educational topics. After taking a doctorate in textual linguistics, he was an Associate Professor at the University of Aalborg and Part-time Lecturer at Copenhagen Business School.

CATHY HIRANO has translated many Japanese children's books, including *The Friends* by Kazumi Yumoto, which won the 1997 Boston Globe-Horn Book Award for children's fiction. She also freelances as a translator in such fields as anthropology, sociology, architecture, and medicine.

DOUGLAS HOFSTADTER is College of Arts and Sciences Distinguished Professor of Cognitive Science at Indiana University. Among his numerous books is the Pulitzer Prize-winning *Gödel, Escher, Bach: An Eternal Golden Braid*. He has translated many poems and several novels, including Alexander Pushkin's classic novel-in-verse *Eugene Onegin*.

BRIAN HOLTON teaches in the Department of Chinese and Bilingual Studies at Hong Kong Polytechnic University. He has translated many works of classical and modern Chinese literature into both Scots and English, most recently Yang Lian's collection *Notes of a Blissful Ghost: Selected Poems*.

JOHN HUTCHINS retired from a career in university librarianship in 1999. He is currently the compiler of the Compendium of Translation Software and the Compendium of Machine Translation Archive.

DENYS JOHNSON-DAVIES has championed modern Arabic literature as both translator and anthologist for more than sixty years. He has also been a businessman, lawyer, broadcaster, and lecturer at Cairo University. His *Memories in Translation: A Life Between the Lines of Arabic Literature* was published in 2006.

ANNE CATESBY JONES is a professional translator who specializes in translating legal and manufacturing texts into Spanish, notably for the pharmaceuticals industry.

GEOFFREY KINGSCOTT is a longtime technical translator and consultant with a particular interest in translator education and assessment of translation quality. He has also published several books on railways.

HERBERT KRETZMER is a songwriter, journalist, and long-time theatre and television critic for British newspapers. He is most famous for the English lyrics of *Les Misérables* and for his longtime songwriting collaboration with the French singer Charles Aznavour.

ARNAUD LAYGUES teaches at the University of Girona in Spain. A translation studies scholar, he recently received his PhD from the University of Helsinki.

CONSUELO LÓPEZ-MORILLAS is Professor of Literatures in Spanish at Indiana University, and a specialist in Hispano-Arabic language and literature.

SHANE MALONEY is the creator of Australia's bestselling crime novel series featuring Murray Whelan, a ministerial aide. His website states that he is also "co-author of *The Happy Phrase: Everyday Conversation Made Easily*, a self-help book for people wanting to enhance their unintelligibility."

EIVOR MARTINUS translates from and to English, Norwegian, and Swedish, and has won many awards for her work. She is also a novelist and playwright whose plays have been performed in London, New York, and Stockholm.

IGOR A. MEL'CUK has been a professor at the University of Montreal's Department of Linguistics and Translation since 1976, when he left the former Soviet Union. He is the author of many books and articles and a leading exponent of Meaning-Text Theory.

SCOTT L. MONTGOMERY is a geologist, independent scholar, and adjunct faculty member in the Jackson School of International Studies, University of Washington. He has written widely on scientific communication, the history of science, translation, science and art, and contemporary culture. His *Powers Rich and Afflicted: Energy in the 21st Century—Resources,*

Issues, Geopolitics will be published by the University of Chicago Press in 2009.

WALTER MURCH is an Oscar-winning film editor and sound designer. He was recently the subject of Michael Ondaatje's book *The Conversations: Walter Murch and the Art of Editing Film.*

PETER NEWMARK is Professor of Translation at the University of Surrey. He has published many books and articles on translation, and currently writes the bimonthly column "Translation Now" for *The Linguist*, the journal of the Chartered Institute of Linguists.

EUGENE NIDA is one of the great figures of modern bible translation and of translation theory. He began working as a linguist with the American Bible Society in 1943, and retired in the early 1980s as its Executive Secretary for Translations. His memoir *Fascinated by Languages* was published in 2003.

ROBERT PAQUIN has taught literature and translation in several Quebec universities and is a past president of the Literary Translators' Association of Canada. As well as novels and poetry, he has translated dozens of feature films and TV programs into French.

MARGARET SAYERS PEDEN is Professor of Spanish in the Department of Romance Languages at the University of Missouri. Her translations include works by Isabel Allende, Octavio Paz, Juan Rulfo, Ernesto Sabato, and Carlos Fuentes.

EUGENE H. PETERSON is a writer, poet, and retired pastor. He is Professor Emeritus of Spiritual Theology at Regent College in Vancouver, British Columbia.

ANTHONY PYM is a translator and academic. He heads the Intercultural Studies Group at the Universitat Rovira i Virgili in Tarragona, Spain. His most recent book is *The Moving Text. Localization, Translation, and Distribution* (2004).

GREGORY RABASSA is a literary translator working from Spanish and Portuguese, and a professor at Queens College, New York. He is particularly known for his translations of major Latin American novelists such as Jorge Amado, Julio Cortázar, Gabriel García Márquez, and Mario Vargas Llosa.

BURTON RAFFEL is a translator, poet, and teacher of classics and comparative literature. He is currently Professor Emeritus, University of Lousiana at Lafayette. He has translated classics from several European languages (most recently his 2006 *Das Nibelungenlied: Song of the Nibelungs*, from High Middle German), as well as the work of several contemporary Indonesian poets.

ALASTAIR REID is a poet, translator, essayist, children's book author, and, since 1959, a staff writer at *The New Yorker*. He has taught Latin American studies and literature in both the United States and the U.K., and has published more than forty books.

BARBARA REYNOLDS is a translator, academic, and lexicographer, and was for many years General Editor of the *Cambridge Italian Dictionary*. She was awarded the Premio Monselice in 1976 for her translation of Ariosto's epic poem *Orlando Furioso*.

PAULA RICHMAN is Professor of South Asian Religions at Oberlin College, where she teaches courses on Hinduism, South Asian epic literature, and modern India.

DOUGLAS ROBINSON teaches critical theory at the University of Mississippi. Editor of the monumental *Western Translation Theory: From Herodotus to Nietzsche* (1997) and author of numerous books and articles, he translates from Finnish, German, Russian, Serbian, and Spanish.

RICCARDO SCHIAFFINO is a translator and translation project manager. He teaches the Theory and Practice of Translation and Interpreting course at the University of Denver. He writes the blog About Translation, and has published several articles with the ATA *Chronicle*.

YAEL SELA-SHAPIRO is a translator and editor, and also teaches at Tel Aviv University and Beit Berl College. Recent translations from English to Hebrew include *The Golden Compass* by Philip Pullman, George R.R. Martin's series *A Song of Fire and Ice*, and the *Hyperion* series by Dan Simmons.

MARY SNELL-HORNBY is Professor of Translation Studies at the University of Vienna. Her most recent book in English is *The Turns of Translation Studies: New Paradigms or Shifting Viewpoints?* (2006).

GAYATRI CHAKRAVORTY SPIVAK is a literary critic, translator, and academic who teaches at both Columbia University and the Centre for Studies in Social Sciences, Calcutta. She is probably best known for her groundbreaking post-colonialist essay "Can the Subaltern Speak?" and her translation of Jacques Derrida's *Of Grammatology*.

MARGHERITA ULRYCH is Professor of English Linguistics and Translation at the University of Trieste's School of Modern Languages for Interpreters and Translators.

TIBOR VÁRADY is a professor of law at the Central European University in Budapest, and at Emory University, Atlanta. He has taught, written articles, and acted as an arbitrator in five languages (English, French, German, Serbian, and Hungarian). In 2006 he published *Language and*

Translation in International Commercial Arbitration.

LAWRENCE VENUTI is Professor of English at Temple University, Philadelphia. He is the author of books such as *The Translator's Invisibility* (1994) and *Scandals of Translation* (1997), and editor of *The Translation Studies Reader* (2nd ed., 2004). He has translated a number of Italian authors, including Dino Buzzati, I.U. Tarchetti, and Antonia Pozzi.

STEVE VLASTA VITEK has run a freelance translation business in San Francisco since 1987. He specializes in technical translation, mostly from Japanese but also from German, Czech, and Slovak, and occasionally also from Russian, Polish, and French.

EMMA WAGNER is a translator and translation manager at the European Commission in Luxembourg. She is the initiator of the Fight the FOG campaign to encourage clear writing at the European Commission.

WILLIAM WEAVER has translated many of Italy's most prominent authors, including Italo Calvino, Umberto Eco, and Ignazio Silone. As well as novels he has translated poetry and opera, and is on the faculty of Bard College, New York.

CAROLINNE WHITE is an Oxford academic and a specialist in patristics and medieval Latin. Her books include *Christian Friendship in the Fourth Century* (1992), *Early Christian Lives* (1998), *The Confessions of St. Augustine* (2001), and *The Rule of Benedict* (2008).

VICTOR H. YNGVE is Professor Emeritus of Linguistics at the University of Chicago. His long career included some of the earliest research in computational linguistics and natural language processing, as well as machine translation.

American Bible Society. *Holy Bible: Contemporary English Version.* New York: American Bible Society, 1995.

Arberry, A. *The Koran Interpreted.* New York: Macmillan, 1955, 7–28.

Atlani-Duault, L. *Humanitarian Aid in Post-Soviet Countries: An Anthropological Perspective,* translated by Andrew Wilson. London: Routledge, 2007.

Auden, W.H. *The Dyer's Hand and Other Essays.* New York: Random House, 1962, 23–24.

Baker, M. *In Other Words: A Coursebook on Translation.* London: Routledge, 1992, 251–53.

Bakhtiar, L. *The Sublime Quran: Based on the Hanafi, Maliki and Shafii Schools of Law.* Chicago: Kazi Publications, 2007. See preface at http://www.sublimequran.org.

Bell, A. "Translation as Illusion." Talk delivered at Shelving Translation Conference, April 17, 2004, Oxford University. www.brunel.ac.uk/4042/entertext4.3sup/ET43SBellEd.doc.

———. "Translator's Notebook: Delicate Matters." *The Translation of Children's Literature: A Reader,* edited by G. Lathey. London: Clevedon, 2006, 238–40. Originally published in *Signal* 49 (1986): 17–26.

Bell, S.M. "In the Shadow of the Father Tongue: On Translating the Masks in J.-S. Alexis." *Between Languages and Cultures: Translation and Cross-Cultural Texts,* edited by A. Dingwaney and C. Maier. Pittsburgh: University of Pittsburgh Press, 1996, 51–74.

Berriatúa, Z. *El perro existencialista y otros cuentos de perro / The Existentialist Dog and Other Tales.* Madrid: Panta Rhei, 2004.

———. *Monstruos del subconsciente colectivo / Monsters from the Collective Subconscious.* Madrid: Sinsentido, 2006, 22, 50.

Bielsa, E. "Globalisation as Translation: An Approximation to the Key But Invisible Role of Translation in Globalisation." csgr Working Paper No. 163/05. Coventry: University of Warwick, Centre for the Study of Globalisation and Regionalisation, 11–12, 2005. http://warwick.ac.uk/fac/soc/csgr/research/workingpapers/2005/wp16305.pdf

Borges, J.L. "The translators of the Thousand and One Nights." *Selected Non-Fictions*, edited by Eliot Weinberger, translated by Esther Allen. New York: Viking, 1999.

Budberg, M. "On Translating from Russian." *The World of Translation*. New York: PEN American Center, 1971, 151.

Burroughs, K. "Metropolitan metamorphosis." *Financial Times*, November 17, 2006.

Burton, R.F. *A Plain and Literal Translation of the Arabian Nights' Entertainments, Now Entitled the Book of the Thousand Nights and a Night, with Introduction, Explanatory Notes on the Manners and Customs of Moslem Men, and a Terminal Essay upon the History of the Nights*. London: Burton Club, 1885, xiv. The complete translation is at http://en.wikisource.org.

Cervantes Saavedra, M. *Don Quixote*, translated by Edith Grossman. London: Secker & Warburg, 2004, xx.

———. *The First (Second) Part of the History of the Valorous and Wittie Knight-Errant Don-Quixote of the Mancha*, translated by Robert Shelton, 1620. Republished by the Ashendene Press, 1927.

———. *The Ingenious Hidalgo Don Quixote de la Mancha*, translated by J. Rutherford. London: Penguin, 2003, xiv.

———. *Segunda parte del ingenioso hidalgo don Quijote de la Mancha*, Instituto Cervantes, 255–56. Quoted text from 1780 edition, published by the Academia Real.

Chesterman, A. *Memes of Translation: The Spread of Ideas in Translation Theory*. Amsterdam: John Benjamins, 1997. Quoted text is from the preface, www.helsinki.fi/~chesterm/1997cMemes.html.

Chesterman, A., and E. Wagner. *Can Theory Help Translators? A Dialogue Between the Ivory Tower and the Wordface*. Manchester: St. Jerome Publishing, 2002, 7, 8–11, 98–101, 107.

Cheung, M.P.Y., ed. *An Anthology of Chinese Discourse on Translation*, vol. 1. Manchester: St. Jerome Publishing, 2006.

Clastres, P., and P. Auster. *Chronicle of the Guayaki Indians*. London: Faber & Faber, 1998, 7–13.

Cook, K. Personal communication to the author, 2008.

Craig, A. "Traduttore traditore? The work of Michel Tremblay translated into Scots." *Performing Arts & Entertainment in Canada*, spring 1993.

Cronin, M. *Translation and Globalization*. London/New York: Routledge, 2003. Cited in Bielsa 2005, above.

da Fonseca, J.D., and P. Carolino. *English As She Is Spoke: Selections from O novo guia da conversação em Portuguez e Inglez em duas partes, The New Guide of the Conversation in Portuguese and English in Two Parts*, edited by Paul Collins. New York: McSweeney's Books, 2001.

Davis, M. "Globalization: Resistance is Futile." LISA Global Strategies Summit, March 4, 2003, San Francisco, California, Localization Industries Standards Association, 2003. http://www.lisa.org/utils/getfile.html?id=3829020.

de Buisseret, I. *Deux langues, six idiomes: manuel pratique de traduction de l'anglais au français.* Ottawa: Carlton-Green Publishing Co., 1975, 426–27. Originally published in 1972 as *Guide du traducteur* by her colleagues at the Association des traducteurs et interprètes de l'Ontario (ATIO).

Delisle, J. *La terminologie au Canada: Histoire d'une profession.* Montréal: Linguatech éditeur, 2008.

Delisle, J., and G. Lafond. *The History of Translation.* CD-ROM (educational edition). Gatineau, QC, 2008. Distribution: jdelisle@uOttawa.ca.

Delisle, J., and J. Woodsworth. *Translators through History.* Amsterdam: John Benjamins, 1995, 131–32. Note that the cited passage has been amended slightly based on the book's recent second edition in French (*Les traducteurs dans l'histoire*, 2e éd. Ottawa: Les Presses de l'Université d'Ottawa, 2007, 139); the English version has not been updated.

D'hulst, L. *Cent ans de théorie française de la traduction. De Batteux à Littré (1748–1847).* Lille: Presses Universitaires de Lille, 1990.

Dillon, W. *An Essay on Translated Verse. In verse. With laudatory verses by John Dryden and others. The second edition, corrected and enlarg'd.* London: Jacob Tonson, 1685, 5, 7.

Dinh, L. "On translation." *Tinfish* 3 (2007). http://tinfishpress.com/tinfishnet3/linh.html.

Dohler, P. N. "How Not to Become a Translator." *Translation Journal* 7(1) (2003). http://www.accurapid.com/journal/23prof.htm.

Dollerup, C., and V. Appel. *Teaching Translation and Interpreting 3: New Horizons: Papers from the Third Language International Conference, Elsinore, Denmark, 9–11 June 1995.* Amsterdam/Philadelphia: John Benjamins, 1996, 20–22.

Duff, A. *The Third Language: Recurrent Problems of Translation into English.* Oxford: Pergamon, 1981, 3.

Eco, U. *Mouse or Rat? Translation as Negotiation.* London: Weidenfeld & Nicolson, 2003, 100–1.

Eoyang, E.C. *"Borrowed Plumage": Polemical Essays on Translation.* Amsterdam: Rodopi, 2003, 27–29, 151–53, 157–58.

Fenner, A. "Techniques, Presentation and Specifications." *The Translator's Handbook,* edited by C. Picken. London: Aslib, 1989, 43–58.

France, P. "Peter France on the Art of the Translator," 2000. http://www.oup.co.uk/academic/humanities/

literature/viewpoint/peter_france.

Gilson, E. "Some Further Thoughts About the Translator's Craft." *CurtainUp: The Internet Theater Magazine of Reviews, Features, Annotated Listing* (1998). http://www .curtainup.com/translat.html

Goldblatt, H. "The Writing Life," *Washington Post* (April 28, 2002): BW10.

Graham, J.D. "Checking, Revision and Editing." *The Translator's Handbook,* edited by C. Picken. London: Aslib, 1989, 99–105.

Grey, G. *Polynesian Mythology and Ancient Traditional History of the New Zealand Race, as furnished by their priests and chiefs,* 2nd ed. Auckland: H. Brett, 1855, x–xiii.

Hamilton, E. *Three Greek Plays.* New York: W.W. Norton, 1937.

Hansen, J.H. "Translation of Technical Brochures." *Text Typology and Translation,* edited by A. Trosborg. Amsterdam: Benjamins Translation Library, 1997, 185–202.

Hirano, C. "Eight Ways to Say You: the Challenges of Translation." *The Translation of Children's Literature: A Reader,* edited by G. Lathey. Clevedon: Multilingual Matters, 2006, 228–31. Reprinted from *The Horn Book Magazine* (January/February 1999) by permission of the Horn Book, Inc., http://www.hbook.com.

Hofstadter, D.R. *Le Ton beau de Marot: In Praise of the Music of Language.* Lon-don: Bloomsbury, 1997, 388 (originally published by Basic Books, New York).

Holton, B. "Wale a Leid an Wale a Warld: Shuihu Zhuan into Scots." *Frae Ither Tongues: Essays on Modern Translations into Scots* (Topics in Translation 24), edited by B. Findlay. Clevedon: Multilingual Matters, 2004, 15–16, 18–20.

Horguelin, Paul A. *Anthologie de la manière de traduire – Domaine français,* 2nd ed. Montréal: Linguatech éditeur, 1981. On CD-ROM *The History of Translation* by J. Delisle and G. Lafond.

Hutchins, W.J. *Early Years in Machine Translation: Memoirs and Biographies of Pioneers.* Amsterdam: John Benjamins, 2000.

International Federation of Translators. "The Translator's Charter." 1994. http://www.fit-ift.org/en/charter .php#oblig.

Johnson, S. *A Dictionary of the English Language, in which the words are deduced from their originals, and illustrated in their different significations by examples from the best writers. To which are prefixed a history of the language, and an English grammar.* London: Knapton, 1755, xii.

Johnson-Davies, D. *Memories in Translation: A Life Between the Lines of Arabic Literature.* Cairo / New York: The American University in Cairo Press, 2006, 17–21, 36, 57–59.

Jones, A. "Ever-Changing English: A Translator's Headache." 2006. http://www.translationdirectory.com/article1060.htm.

Keeley, E. "Collaboration, Revision, and Other Less Forgivable Sins in Translation." *The Craft of Translation,* edited by J. Biguenet and R. Schulte. Chicago: University of Chicago Press, 1989, 54.

Kelly, L.G. *The True Interpreter: A History of Translation Theory and Practice in the West.* Oxford: Blackwell, 1979.

Kittel, Harald, ed. *International Anthologies of Literature in Translation.* Berlin: Erich Schmidt, 1995.

Kingscott, G. "The Impact of Technology and the Implications for Teaching." *Teaching Translation and Interpreting 3: New Horizons: Papers from the Third Language International Conference, Elsinore, Denmark, 9–11 June 1995,* edited by C. Dollerup and V. Appel. Amsterdam: John Benjamins, 1996, 295–300.

Laygues, A. "Death of a Ghost: A Case Study of Ethics in Cross-Generation Relations between Translators." *The Translator* 7(2) (Manchester: St. Jerome Publishing, 2001): 169–83.

Lea, R. "Lost: Translation." *The Guardian,* November 16, 2007. http://books.guardian.co.uk/departments/generalfiction/story/0,,2212304,00.html.

Lefevere, A. *Translation, Rewriting, and the Manipulation of Literary Fame.* London: Routledge, 1992, 41–42.

Levi, P. *Other People's Trades,* translated by Raymond Rosenthal. London: Abacus Sphere Books, 1991.

Locke, W.N., and A.D. Booth. *Machine Translation of Languages: Fourteen Essays.* London: Chapman and Hall, 1955, 15–21.

López, Garcia D. *Teorías de la traducción. Antología de textos.* Cuenca: Ediciones de la Universidad de Castilla-La Mancha, 1996.

López-Morillas, C. "'Trilingual' Marginal Notes (Arabic, Aljamiado and Spanish) in a Morisco Manuscript from Toledo." *Journal of the American Oriental Society* 103(3) (1983): 500.

Maloney, S. "When Language Gets on Your Unicorn's Goat." *Australian Author* 36(3) (2004). http://www.csse.monash.edu.au/~jwb/maloneytrans.html.

Marlowe, M.D. "An Open Letter on Translating" (revised from translation by Dr. Gary Mann for project Wittenberg). *Bible Research: Internet Resources for Students of Scripture.* 2003. http://www.bible-researcher.com/luther01.html.

Martin, G.R.R. *Tuf Voyaging.* Atlanta: Meisha Merlin Publishing, 2003.

Martinus, E. "Translating Scandinavian Drama." *Stages of Translation,* edited by D. Johnston. Bath: Absolute Classics, 1996, 110, 117–19.

Mel'cuk, I.A. "Machine Translation and Formal Linguistics in the USSR." *Early Years in Machine Translation: Memoirs and Biographies of Pioneers,* edited by W.J. Hutchins. Amsterdam: John Benjamins, 2000, 205–6, 216, 219–220.

Mendel, D. "Primo Levi and Translation." (1998). http://www.leeds.ac.uk/bsis/98/98pltrn.htm.

Metzger, B. "Important Early Translations of the Bible." *Bibliotheca Sacra* 150 (January 1993). The cited passage is discussed at http://www.bible-researcher.com/aramaic4.html.

Montaigne, M.D. *The Essayes of Michael Lord of Montaigne Translated by John Florio,* vol. 1. London: Dent & Son, 1910, 7, 11.

Montgomery, S.L. *Science in Translation: Movements of Knowledge through Cultures and Time.* Chicago: University of Chicago Press, 2000, 232–35.

Murch, W. "Malaparte's 'Partisans, 1944.'" *Zoetrope: All-Story* 2(3) (1998). http://www.all-story.com/issues.cgi?action=show_story&story_id=26.

Nabokov, V.V. "On Translating *Eugene Onegin.*" *The New Yorker* (January 8, 1955): 34. http://www.tetrameter.com/nabokov.htm

Nerval, Gérard. "Préface de la quatrième édition" (1853). *Faust,* by Johann Wolfgang Goethe. Paris: Joseph Gibert, 1947, 25–27.

Newmark, P. *Paragraphs on Translation.* Clevedon: Multilingual Matters, 1993.

———. *A Textbook of Translation.* Hemel Hempstead: Prentice-Hall International, 1987, 4–5, 8.

Nida, E.A. *Fascinated by Languages.* Amsterdam: John Benjamins, 2003.

Nothomb, A. *Loving Sabotage.* New York: New Directions, 2000, 47–49, 96–97.

———. *Loving Sabotage.* London: Faber & Faber, 2005.

Paquin, R. "In the Footsteps of Giants: Translating Shakespeare for Dubbing." *Translation Journal* 5(3) (2001). http://accurapid.com/journal/17dubb.htm

Paz, O. "On Translation." *UNESCO Courier* (May–June 1986).

Peden, M.S. "Building a Translation, the Reconstruction Business: Poem 145 of Sor Juana Ines De La Cruz." *The Craft of Translation,* edited by J. Biguenet and R. Schulte. Chicago/London: University of Chicago Press, 1989, 13.

Peterson, E.H. *The Message: The Old Testament Books of Moses.* Colorado Springs: NavPress, 2001.

Pound, E. "How to Read." *Literary Essays of Ezra Pound.* Norfolk CT: James Laughlin, 1954, 25.

Pym, A. "Localization, Training, and the Threat of Fragmentation." May 2006. http://www.tinet.org/~apym/welcome.html.

———. "On Toury's Laws of How Translators Translate." 2007. http://www.tinet.org/~apym/on-line/translation/2007_toury_laws.pdf.

Rabassa, G. *If This Be Treason: Translation and Its Dyscontents, A Memoir.* New York: New Directions, 2005, 4, 77–78, 97–98.

Radosh, D. "The Good Book Business." *The New Yorker* (December 18, 2006): 54.

Raffel, B. *The Forked Tongue. A Study of the Translation Process.* The Hague, Paris: Mouton, 1971, 111–12.

Reid, A. *Whereabouts: Notes on Being a Foreigner.* San Francisco: North Point Press, 1987, 98–102.

Reynolds, B. "The Pleasure Craft." *The Translator's Art: Essays in Honour of Betty Radice,* edited by B. Radice, W. Radice and B. Reynolds. Harmondsworth: Penguin, 1987, 136–37.

Richman, P., and N. Cutler. "Gift of Tamil: On Compiling an Anthology of Translations from Tamil Literature." *Between Languages and Cultures: Translation and Cross-Cultural Texts,* edited by A. Dingwaney and C. Maier. Pittsburgh, London: University of Pittsburgh Press, 1995, 245–66.

Robinson, D. "Translation as Phantom Limb." *What Is Translation? Centrifugal Theories, Critical Interventions.* Kent, OH, and London: Kent State University Press, 1997. http://home.olemiss.edu/~djr/pages/writer/articles/html/phantom.html.

———. *Western Translation Theory: From Herodotus to Nietzsche.* Manchester: St. Jerome Publishing, 1997, 85.

Rossetti, D.G. *Poems and Translations 1850–1870.* London: Oxford University Press, 1919, 176.

Santoyo, Julio-César. *Teoría y Crítica de la traducción. Antología.* Barcelona: Universitat Autònoma de Barcelona, 1987.

Sarcevic, S. "Legal Translation and Translation Theory: A Receiver-Oriented Approach." Proceedings of the International Colloquium Legal Translation: History, Theory/ies and Practice, University of Geneva, February 2000. http://www.tradulex.org/Actes2000/sarcevic.pdf.

Schiaffino, Riccardo. "Advice to Beginning Translators (4) – Translation Tests." About Translation. 2006. Accessed November 5, 2007. http://aboutranslation.blogspot.com/2006/05/advice-to-beginning-translators-4_08.html.

Seidensticker, E.G. *Tokyo Central: A Memoir.* Seattle: University of Washington Press, 2002, 124–26.

Sela-Shapiro, Y. "SF&F in Hebrew – Wake-Up Call? Translating the Past and Future into Recently-Revived Hebrew." Conference paper. 2007.

Sheahen, A. "The Barricade Interview."
The Barricade. 1998. http://www
.herbertkretzmer.com/pdf/
alsheahen.pdf.

Smith, M. "The Translators to the
Reader," introduction to *The Holy
Bible, King James version: containing
the Old and New Testaments translated
out of the original tongues and with the
former translations diligently compared
and revised by His Majesty's special
command*. London: Robert Barker,
Printer to the Kings Most Excellent
Majesty, 1611.

Snell-Hornby, M. *The Turns of Translation
Studies: New Paradigms or Shifting
Viewpoints?* Philadelphia: John
Benjamins, 2006, 133.

Spivak, G.C. "Translating into English."
*Nation, Language, and the Ethics of
Translation*, edited by S. Bermann
and M. Wood. Princeton: Princeton
University Press, 2005, 93–110.

Steiner, G. *After Babel: Aspects of Language
and Translation*. London: Oxford
University Press, 1976, 59, 378.

Steiner, T.R. *English Translation Theory
1650–1800*. No. 2, Approaches to
Translation Studies series. Assen/
Amsterdam: Van Gorcum, 1975.

Tesio, G. "L'enigma del tradurre."
Cited by David Mendel in
"Primo Levi and Translation."
Nuova Società (1983). http://
www.leeds.ac.uk/bsis/98/
98pltrn.htm).

Ulrych, M. "Real-World Criteria in
Translation Pedagogy." *Teaching
Translation and Interpreting 3. New
Horizons: Papers from the Third
Language International Conference,
Elsinore, Denmark, 9–11 June 1995*,
edited by C. Dollerup and V. Appel.
Amsterdam/Philadelphia: John
Benjamins, 1996, 137–44.

Várady, T. *Language and Translation in
International Commercial Arbitration:
From the Constitution of the Arbitral
Tribunal through Recognition and
Enforcement Proceedings*. The Hague:
TMC Asser Press, 2006.

Vega Cernuda, M.A. *Textos clásicos de
la teoría de la traducción*. Madrid:
Cátedra, 1994.

Venuti, L. *The Scandals of Translation:
Towards an Ethics of Difference*.
London/New York: Routledge, 1998,
1–2.

———. *The Translation Studies Reader*.
London/New York: Routledge, 2000.

———. *The Translator's Invisibility: A
History of Translation*. London/New
York: Routledge, 1995, 1.

Vitek, S.V. "The Changing World
of Japanese Patent Translators."
Translation Journal 5(2) (2001). http://
accurapid.com/journal/16japan.htm

Voltaire. *Letters on the English*, vol. XXXIV,
part 2. New York: P.F. Collier & Son,
1919. http://www.bartleby.com/34/2/.

Weaver, W. *Alice in Many Tongues. The
Translations of Alice in Wonderland*.

Madison: University of Wisconsin
Press, 1964. © 1964 by the Regents
of the University of Wisconsin
system. Reprinted by permission of
the University of Wisconsin Press,
77–78, 80–83, 85–89.
———. "The Process of Translation."
The Craft of Translation, edited by J.
Biguenet and R. Schulte. Chicago/
London: University of Chicago
Press, 1989, 117–24.
White, C. *The Correspondence (394–419)*
between Jerome and Augustine of Hippo.
Lewiston: Edwin Mellen, 1990,
133–37.
Wilson, A. "'Sabotage, eh?' Translating
Le sabotage amoureux from the
French into the Canadian and
the American." *Amélie Nothomb:*
Authorship, Identity, and Narrative
Practice, edited by S. Bainbrigge
and J. den Toonder. Belgian
Francophone Library, vol. 16. New
York: Peter Lang, 2003, 167–68,
170–71.
Wilson, E. "The Strange Case of
Pushkin and Nabokov." *New York*
Review of Books (July 15, 1965). http://
www.nybooks.com/articles/12829.

Yang Lian. *Where the Sea Stands Still: New*
Poems, translated by Brian Holton.
Newcastle-upon-Tyne: Bloodaxe
Books, 1999, 138–39, 164.
Yates, F.A. *John Florio: The Life of an*
Italian in Shakespeare's England,
Cambridge: Cambridge University
Press, 1934, 227.
Yau Shun-chiu. "The Identification
of Gestural Images in Chinese
Literary Expressions." *Nonverbal*
Communication and Translation: New
Perspectives and Challenges in Literature,
Interpretation and the Media, edited
by F. Poyatos. Benjamins Translation
Library 17. Amsterdam/Philadelphia:
Benjamins, 1997, 69–82.
Yngve, V.H. "Early Research at MIT in
Search of Adequate Theory." *Early*
Years in Machine Translation: Memoirs
and Biographies of Pioneers, edited by
W.J. Hutchins. Amsterdam: John
Benjamins, 2000, 39–40, 44–45.
Zimmer, B. "Ma Ferguson, the
Apocryphal Know-Nothing (April
26, 2006)." *Language Log.* http://itre
.cis.upenn.edu/~myl/languagelog/
archives/003084.html.

PERMISSIONS

Every reasonable attempt has been made to identify owners of copyright.
Errors or omissions will be corrected in subsequent editions.

Is My Invisibility Showing:
A Personal Introduction

xx: Berritúa 2006. Reproduced
by permission of Sinsentido,
copyright 2006.

1. Open windows and reversed
tapestries: The work

3: Scripture quotations marked (CEV) are
from the Contemporary English Version
Copyright © 1991, 1992, 1995 by American
Bible Society. Used by permission.

3 ("The Message"): Peterson 2001. Scripture
taken from *The Message.* Copyright © 1993,
1994, 1995, 1996, 2000, 2001, 2002. Used by
permission of NavPress Publishing Group.

4 ("The tongue of Eden"): Steiner 1976.
Reproduced by permission of Oxford
University Press.

4 ("This was God's punishment"): Budberg
1971. Reproduced by permission of PEN
American Center.

5: Nabokov 1955. Reproduced by permission
of *The New Yorker.*

6: Wilson 1965. Reproduced by permission
of *New York Review of Books.*

9: Cervantes Saavedra and Rutherford
2003. Reproduced by permission of John
Rutherford.

11: Snell-Hornby 2006. Reproduced by
permission of John Benjamins.

13: Venuti 1998. From: Lawrence Venuti,
The Scandals of Translation: Towards an
Ethics of Difference, London/New York:
Routledge, Copyright 1998. Reproduced
by permission of Taylor & Francis
Books U.K.

14: France 2000. Reproduced by permission
of Oxford University Press.

15: Eoyang 2003. Reproduced by permission
of Rodopi.

18: Peden 1989. Reproduced by permission
of University of Chicago Press.

19: Montgomery 2000. Reproduced by
permission of Scott Montgomery.

2. Art, profession, or vocation? The trade

23: *Epigraph.* Steiner 1976. Reproduced by
permission of Oxford University Press.

24: Johnson-Davies 2006. Reproduced by
permission of the American University
in Cairo Press.

27: Dohler 2003. Reproduced by permission
of Accurapid the Language Service.

30: Murch 1998. Reproduced by permission
of *Zoetrope: All-Story.*

36: Goldblatt 2002. Reproduced by
permission of *Washington Post.*

38: Reynolds 1987. "The Pleasure Craft," *The Translator's Art: Essays in Honour of Betty Radice*, edited by B. Radice, W. Radice and B. Reynolds, Harmondsworth: Penguin, Copyright 1987: 136-37. Reproduced by permission of Penguin Books Ltd.

39: Newmark 1987. Reproduced by permission of Prentice-Hall International.

40: Newmark 1993. Reproduced by permission of Multilingual Matters.

41: Clastres and Auster 1998. Reproduced by permission of Faber & Faber.

47: Richman and Cutler 1995. Excerpts from "A Gift of Taml: On Compiling an Anthology of Translations from Tamil Literature" by Paula Richman and Norman Butler from *Between Languagues and Cultures: Translation and Cross-Cultural Texts*, edited by Anuradha Dingwaney and Carol Maier, © 1996. Reprinted by permission of the University of Pittsburgh Press.

3. Betray, domesticate, or negotiate? The process

52: Fenner 1989. Reproduced by permission of Aslib.

53: Newmark 1987. Reproduced by permission of Prentice-Hall International.

55: Weaver 1989. Reproduced by permission of University of Chicago Press.

63: Paquin 2001. Reproduced by permission of Accurapid the Language Service.

69: Eco 2003. Umberto Eco, *Mouse or Rat? Translation as Negotiation*, London: Weidenfeld and Nicolson, Copyright 2003. Reproduced by permission of Weidenfeld and Nicolson, a division of Orion Publishing Group.

70 ("For those with slightly"): Burroughs 2006. Reproduced by permission of *Financial Times*.

70 ("At the end of"): Lefevere 1992. From: André Lefevère, *Translation, Rewriting, and the Manipulation of Literary Fame*, London: Routledge, Copyright 1992. Reproduced by permission of Taylor & Francis Books U.K.

72: Gilson 1998. Reproduced by permission of *CurtainUp: The Internet Theater Magazine of Reviews, Features, Annotated Listing*.

73: Fonseca and Carolino 2001. Reproduced by permission of McSweeney's Books.

74: Hofstadter 1997. Reproduced by permission of the U.S. publisher, Basic Books, a member of the Perseus Books Group, and the U.K. publisher, Bloomsbury Publishing Plc.

75: Snell-Hornby 2006. Reproduced by permission of John Benjamins.

76: Sheahen 1998. Reproduced by permission of *The Barricade*.

79: Cook 2008. Reproduced by permission of Kevin Cook.

81: Cervantes Saavedra and Rutherford 2003. Reproduced by permission of John Rutherford.

4. "If Swahili was good enough for Jesus Christ...": Translating religion

83: Zimmer 2006. Reproduced by permission of *Language Log*.

84: White 1990. Reproduced by permission of Edwin Mellen.

87: Robinson 1997b. Reproduced by permission of St. Jerome Publishing.

89: Marlowe 2003. Reproduced by permission of *Bible Research: Internet Resources for Students of Scripture*. Revised from translation by Dr. Gary Mann for project Wittenberg.

90: Nida 2003. Reproduced by permission of John Benjamins.

94: López-Morillas 1983. Reproduced by permission of *Journal of the American Oriental Society*.

95: Arberry 1955. Reproduced by permission of Macmillan.

97: Bakhtiar 2007. Reproduced by permission of Kazi Publications.

5. Govspeak: Translating the official version

105: Delisle and Woodsworth 1995. Reproduced by permission of John Benjamins. Note that the cited passage has been amended slightly based on the book's recent second edition in French (*Les traducteurs dans l'histoire*, 2e éd. Ottawa: Les Presses de l'Université d'Ottawa, 2007); the English version has not been updated.

106: Yngve 2000. Reproduced by permission of John Benjamins.

108: Mel'cuk 2000. Reproduced by permission of John Benjamins.

111: Chesterman and Wagner 2002. Reproduced by permission of St. Jerome Publishing.

6. L1on to G1on and back again: Business and technical translation

118 ("Globalisation has caused an"): Bielsa 2005. Reproduced by permission of University of Warwick, Centre for the Study of Globalisation and Regionalisation.

118 ("In Denmark, the first"): Dollerup and Appel 1996. Reproduced by permission of John Benjamins.

119: Graham 1989. Reproduced by permission of Aslib.

121: Ulrych 1996. Reproduced by permission of John Benjamins.

122: Kingscott 1996. Reproduced by permission of John Benjamins.

123: Laygues 2001. Reproduced by permission of St. Jerome Publishing.

129: Schiaffino 2006. Reproduced by permission of About Translation.

131: Jones 2006. Reproduced by permission of Anne Catesby Jones.

134: Hansen 1997. Reproduced by permission of Benjamins Translation Library.

137: Pym 2006. Reproduced by permission of Anthony Pym.

140: Vitek 2001. Reproduced by permission of Accurapid the Language Service.

144: Várady 2006. Reproduced by permission of Tibor Várady.

7. Lost and found: Translating poetry

149: Auden 1962. From *The Dyer's Hand and Other Essays* by W.H. Auden, copyright 1948, 1950, 1952, 1953, 1954, 1956, 1957, 1958, 1960, 1962 by W.H. Auden. Used by permission of Random House, Inc.

150: Pound 1954. Reproduced by permission of James Laughlin.

151: Reid 1987. Reproduced by permission of North Point Press.

153: Holton 2004. Reproduced by permission of Multilingual Matters.

155: Yang Lian 1999. Reproduced by permission of Bloodaxe Books.

158: Raffel 1971. Reproduced by permission of Mouton.

8. Collusion, collision, conversation: The author/translator relationship

164: Maloney 2004. Reproduced by permission of Monash University.

166 ("I am very well"): Craig 1993. Reproduced by permission of *Performing Arts & Entertainment in Canada*.

166 ("It is worth saying"): Mendel 1998. Reproduced by permission of University of Leeds.

167: Mendel 1998. Reproduced by permission of University of Leeds.

169: Johnson-Davies 2006. Reproduced by permission of the American University in Cairo Press.

171: Rabassa 2005. By Gregory Rabassa, from *If This Be Treason*, copyright © 2005 by Gregory Rabassa. Reprinted by permission of New Directions Publishing Corp.

173: Wilson 2003. Reproduced by permission of Peter Lang.

9. When I hear the words "Translation Theory...": Translation studies

177: *Epigraph.* Rabassa 2005. By Gregory Rabassa, from *If This Be Treason*, copyright © 2005 by Gregory Rabassa. Reprinted by permission of New Directions Publishing Corp.

178 ("Many practising professional translators"): Chesterman 1997. Reproduced by permission of John Benjamins. Quoted text is from the preface, helsinki.fi/~chesterm/1997cMemes.html.

178 ("'Translation theory? Spare us...'"): Chesterman and Wagner 2002. Reproduced by permission of St. Jerome Publishing.

183: Spivak 2005. Bermannn, Sandra, Wood, Michael: *Nation, Language, and the Ethics of Translation*. © 2005 by Princeton University Press. Reprinted by permission of Princeton University Press.

190: Venuti 1998. From: Lawrence Venuti, *The Scandals of Translation: Towards an Ethics of Difference*, London/New York: Routledge, Copyright 1998. Reproduced by permission of Taylor & Francis Books U.K.

193: Robinson 1997a. Reproduced by permission of Kent State University Press.

196: Yau Shun-chiu 1997. Reproduced by permission of John Benjamins.

10. Language wrangling: A grab bag

197 ("When I put occasional"): Pym 2007. Reproduced by permission of Anthony Pym.

197 ("The reflections presented here"): Bell 1996. Excerpts from "In the Shadow of the Father Tongue: On Translating the Masks in J.-S. Alexis" by Sharon Masingale Bell from *Between Languagues and Cultures: Translation and Cross-Cultural Texts*, edited by Anuradha Dingwaney and Carol Maier, © 1996. Reprinted by permission of the University of Pittsburgh Press.

200: Baker 1992. Reproduced by permission of Routledge.

203: Hirano 2006. Reprinted from the January/February 1999 issue of *The Horn Book Magazine* by permission of the Horn Book, Inc., www.hbook.com.

207: Weaver 1964. Weaver, Warren. *Alice in Many Tongues: The Translations of Alice in Wonderland*. © 1964 by the Regents of the University of Wisconsin System. Reprinted by permission of The University of Wisconsin Press.

215: Eco 2003. Umberto Eco, *Mouse or Rat? Translation as Negotiation*, London: Weidenfeld and Nicolson, Copyright 2003. Reproduced by permission of

Weidenfeld and Nicolson, a division of
Orion Publishing Group.

217: Sela-Shapiro 2007. Reproduced by
permission of Yael Sela-Shapiro.

220: Martinus 1996. Reproduced by
permission of Absolute Classics.

223: Rabassa 2005. By Gregory Rabassa,
from *If This Be Treason*, copyright ©
2005 by Gregory Rabassa. Reprinted
by permission of New Directions
Publishing Corp.

224: Seidensticker 2002. Reproduced
by permission of University of
Washington Press.

227: Holton 2004. Reproduced by
permission of Multilingual Matters.

228: Eoyang 2003. Reproduced by
permission of Rodopi.

231: Bell 2006. Reproduced by permission of
Clevedon.

233: Cervantes Saavedra and Grossman
2004. From *Don Quixote* translated by
Edith Grossman, published by Secker
& Warburg. Reprinted by permission of
The Random House Group Ltd.